This is a collection by a lovely group of Europeans who choose to wear flowers rather than armour, as Nils Christie expresses it. The book takes us to Vienna's Womens Café where Muslim and non-Muslim women sit in the restorative circle, to action research on the politics of Roma exclusion in Hungary, to intercultural borderlands of Serbia, Northern Ireland and Belgium. It shows that justice and security can be transformed in the face of intercultural challenges. This is accomplished by rethinking restorative justice in terms of a politics of participation, hope and conviviality. Restorative justice must meet the challenges of redistribution (the 'what' of justice), recognition (the 'who' of justice), and (political) representation, as Nancy Fraser and Iris Marion Young put it. The result of this reframing is a fresh, challenging contribution to the restorative justice literature. A vital book for reflective scholars of restorative thought.

John Braithwaite, *Distinguished Professor at the School of Regulation and Global Governance (RegNet), Australian National University, Australia*

Intercultural and superdiverse urban environments have created the need for scholars to explore new tools and vocabularies in which attention shifts from the classic themes of 'power and order' to a more comprehensive approach of security. By focussing on the possibilities created by restorative approaches to justice and security, this book serves the generally interested reader as well as the scientific reader and provides an important source of discussion to draw inspiration and motivation from.

Marc Schuilenburg, *Assistant Professor in the Department of Criminal Law and Criminology, VU University Amsterdam, Netherlands*

Restoring Justice and Security in Intercultural Europe

The intercultural contexts and new configurations in Europe offer fertile ground for social conflict, tensions and threat. This book challenges predominant and fear inducing approaches of justice and security as they appear in intercultural contexts, and develops alternative understandings by exploring both theoretically and empirically the potential of dialogic and restorative justice oriented actions in sensitive areas of living together. The book offers unique opportunities for rethinking frames of (in)justice, (in)security, and their intersections, and for reshaping European practices and policies in a more sustainable way.

This book is based on an innovative and exploratory action research project in four European countries, which challenges the obsessive focus on security concerns, the merging of the security discourse with intercultural contexts, and the emphasis on technology and surveillance as a way to conceive the doing of security. Both the project and the book offer another vision on what security means and how it can be done, by multiplying participatory encounters between different groups in society, promoting opportunities for deliberations and dialogue about alternative forms of conviviality.

The book is one of two volumes resulting from the work by a group of researchers in six European countries having cooperated intensively during four years in ALTERNATIVE, an action research project funded under the EU Seventh Framework Programme.

Brunilda Pali is a postdoctoral researcher at the KU Leuven Institute of Criminology. She has worked as a researcher on several EU-funded projects, besides the FP7 project ALTERNATIVE. She publishes on multiple themes, including restorative justice, critical criminology, security, social movements, gender, and arts. She is co-editor of the book *Critical Restorative Justice*.

Ivo Aertsen is Full Professor of Criminology at the University of Leuven and leads the Leuven Institute of Criminology Research Line on 'Restorative Justice and Victimology'. His main fields of research and teaching are victimology, penology and restorative justice. He is Editor-in-Chief of *Restorative Justice: An International Journal*. He was the academic coordinator of the European FP7 project ALTERNATIVE.

Routledge Frontiers of Criminal Justice

www.routledge.com/Routledge-Frontiers-of-Criminal-Justice/book-series/RFCJ

39 Restorative Policing
Concepts, Theory and Practice
Kerry Clamp and Craig Paterson

40 The Penal Voluntary Sector
Philippa Tomczak

41 Transforming Summary Justice
Modernisation in the Lower Criminal Courts
Jennifer Ward

42 Stop and Search and Police Legitimacy
Ben Bradford

43 Young Offenders and Open Custody
Tove Pettersson

44 Restorative Responses to Sexual Violence
Legal, Social and Therapeutic Dimensions
Edited by Estelle Zinsstag and Marie Keenan

45 Policing Hate Crime
Understanding Communities and Prejudice
Gail Mason, JaneMaree Maher, Jude McCulloch, Sharon Pickering, Rebecca Wickes and Carolyn McKay

46 The Special Constabulary
Historical Context, International Comparisons and Contemporary Themes
Edited by Karen Bullock and Andrew Millie

47 Action Research in Criminal Justice
Restorative justice approaches in intercultural settings
Edited by Inge Vanfraechem and Ivo Aertsen

48 Restoring Justice and Security in Intercultural Europe
Edited by Brunilda Pali and Ivo Aertsen

49 Monitoring Penal Policy in Europe
Edited by Gaëtan Cliquennois and Hugues de Suremain

50 Big Data, Crime and Social Control
Edited by Aleš Završnik

Restoring Justice and Security in Intercultural Europe

Edited by Brunilda Pali and Ivo Aertsen

LONDON AND NEW YORK

First published 2018
by Routledge
2 Park Square, Milton Park, Abingdon, Oxon OX14 4RN

and by Routledge
711 Third Avenue, New York, NY 10017

Routledge is an imprint of the Taylor & Francis Group, an informa business

British Library Cataloguing in Publication Data
A catalogue record for this book is available from the British Library

Library of Congress Cataloging in Publication Data
Names: Pali, Brunilda, editor. | Aertsen, Ivo, editor.
Title: Restoring justice and security in intercultural Europe / edited by Brunilda Pali and Ivo Aertsen.
Description: Abingdon, Oxon ; New York, NY : Routledge, 2018. | Series: Routledge frontiers of criminal justice ; 48 | Includes bibliographical references and index.
Identifiers: LCCN 2017017396| ISBN 9781138120938 (hardback) | ISBN 9781315651439 (ebook)
Subjects: LCSH: Restorative justice–Europe. | Criminal justice, Administration of–Europe. | Social conflict–Europe. | Ethnic conflict–Europe. | Security, International–Europe.
Classification: LCC HV9960.E85 R47 2018 | DDC 364.6/8–dc23
LC record available at https://lccn.loc.gov/2017017396

ISBN: 978-1-138-12093-8 (hbk)
ISBN: 978-1-315-65143-9 (ebk)

Typeset in Times New Roman
by Wearset Ltd, Boldon, Tyne and Wear

Printed and bound in Great Britain by
TJ International Ltd, Padstow, Cornwall

To Nils Christie

**'A warrior wears armour, a lover flowers.
They are equipped according to expectations of what is to happen, and their equipment increases chances that their expectations will prove right.
So also with the institution of penal law'.**

Contents

Illustrations

Figure

Table

Contributors

Ivo Aertsen is Full Professor of Criminology at the University of Leuven (Belgium). He holds degrees in psychology, law and criminology from the same university. At the Leuven Institute of Criminology (LINC), he is leading the research line on 'Restorative Justice and Victimology'. His main fields of research and teaching are victimology, penology and restorative justice. Ivo Aertsen was chair of the European Forum for Restorative Justice (EFRJ) from 2000 to 2004, and coordinated COST Action A21 on restorative justice research in Europe from 2002 to 2006. He has been expert for the UN, the Council of Europe, the Organization for Security and Co-operation in Europe (OSCE) and the EU. Furthermore, he was appointed as expert to the Belgian Parliamentary Commission on sexual abuse in the church (2010–2011), followed by membership of the Permanent Arbitration Chamber on sexual abuse (2012–2016). He is editor-in-chief of *Restorative Justice: An International Journal.* In ALTERNATIVE, he acted as the European academic coordinator.

Hugh Campbell is a senior lecturer in the School of Sociology and Applied Social Studies at Ulster University. From 2003, he has led the Restorative Practice developments in the University. This has meant co-authoring the Northern Ireland Youth Conference Service Practice Manual; the establishment of postgraduate diploma and Master's programmes in Restorative Practices and an undergraduate certificate; management and delivery of the above programmes; and engagement with the practice field in Northern Ireland, including community groups, current and former prisoners, the Police Service NI, the Youth Justice Agency, the Prison Service NI and the Criminal Justice Inspectorate. Prior to 2003, Hugh was the course director for the BSc Hons in Community Youth Work at the University. Hugh also has a long background in sports coaching in rugby, soccer, Gaelic football and athletics.

Tim Chapman is a visiting lecturer at Ulster University in Northern Ireland, UK, teaching on the Master's in Restorative Practices. He has contributed to the development of restorative conferencing in both the voluntary and statutory sectors in Northern Ireland. He spent 25 years working in the Probation Service in Northern Ireland. He played an active part in developing effective practice in the UK, particularly through the publication of *Evidence Based*

Practice, written jointly with Michael Hough and published by the Home Office. His 'Time to Grow' model for the supervision of young people has influenced youth justice practices, especially in Scotland. He has published widely on restorative justice and effective practice and has conducted significant research into restorative justice in Northern Ireland, including the ALTERNATIVE project. In 2015, he wrote with Maija Gellin and Monique Anderson 'A European Model of Restorative Justice with Children and Young People'. He is chair of the Board of the European Forum for Restorative Justice. In ALTERNATIVE, he was leader of Work Package 7 – 'Activating community through a multi-agency approach'.

Erik Claes is a lecturer and senior researcher in social work at Odisee University College in Brussels. He is the author of *Legality and Adjudication in the Criminal Law* (Leuven University Press, 2001, awarded the Fernand Collin Prize) and co-editor of *Facing the Limits of the Law* (Springer, 2009). He has published many articles on criminal law theory and restorative justice. His current (action) research focuses on restorative justice and citizenship in urban settings. He is the co-founder of Insjalet, an urban restorative practice on storytelling in public spaces.

Sanja Ćopić is a senior research fellow at the Institute of Criminological and Sociological Research in Belgrade and a researcher and president of the Executive Board of the Victimology Society of Serbia. She has participated in numerous research and action-oriented projects on victims of crime, domestic violence, human trafficking, discrimination, reconciliation, victim support and restorative justice, and has published extensively on these topics. The main focus of her recent work has been on the use of restorative justice in criminal matters and the victim's position in restorative justice programmes, and applying restorative approaches in intercultural settings. She is deputy editor of *Temida* – an academic journal on victimisation, human rights and gender, published by the Victimology Society of Serbia. In the past years, she was also engaged with research conducted by the Victimology Society of Serbia and other European research institutions within the EU-funded FP7 research project ALTERNATIVE, in which she acted as leader of Work Package 6 – 'Fostering victim-oriented dialogue'.

Espen Marius Foss defended his PhD in social anthropology at the University of Oslo in June 2016 on the topic of restorative justice. He did fieldwork in four comparative fields in Norway: the Norwegian Mediation Service, Minhaj Ul Quran's Mediation Service, the Red Cross's Street Mediation and Hywa – a youth organisation formed after a murder of a 17-year-old boy, understood as a spontaneous bottom-up form of restorative justice. As part of the fieldwork, Foss worked as a mediator and conference facilitator in the Norwegian Mediation Service, and as a volunteer instructor for Street Mediation. During that period, he also produced four ethnographic films together with his informants as part of both the research and the dissemination strategy. During

2007–2011, he was a university lecturer and scholarship-holder at the University of Agder, Department of Psychosocial Health. In parallel with finishing his PhD, Foss during 2011–2016 worked as a senior adviser in the Norwegian Red Cross, promoting Street Mediation as a national activity. During that period, there was also international interest in Street Mediation, and Foss assisted with training of trainers in various contexts such as Denmark, Belize, Lebanon and Zimbabwe. Today, he works as an associate professor at the Department for Psychosocial Health Work at Østfold University College, Norway.

Gábor Héra is a postdoctoral researcher and sociologist. He has researched extensively the manifestation of racist violence, extremism and negative attitudes towards the Roma minority in Europe and in Hungary during the last 20 years; therefore, he has gained not only theoretical but also practical insights into the nature of social exclusion and discrimination. Currently, he works at the Foresee Research Group in Budapest and supports several national and international programmes as a researcher. He was a lecturer in methodology courses at four universities in the last 15 years. He graduated at the Sociology of Science Doctoral School at the Budapest University of Technology and Economics (BME) in Budapest.

Ida Hydle is a Norwegian research professor at NOVA, the Welfare Research Institute, University College of Applied Sciences in Oslo and Akershus, and adjunct professor at the University of Tromsø, Department of Social Work and Child Protection. She holds PhD degrees in medicine and social anthropology. She has experience from practical work as a medical doctor within social medicine and rehabilitation, geriatrics and mental health work, as well as teaching and training at all academic levels, research planning and implementation within social medicine, mental health work, medical and legal anthropology, visual cultural studies and peace studies, restorative justice and restorative practice studies. In ALTERNATIVE, she took the lead for Work Package 2 – 'Conflict transformation analysis'.

Katrin Kremmel is a PhD candidate at the Social and Cultural Anthropology Department of the University of Vienna, where she works on asylum practices, statehood and citizenship in a rural Austrian town. Prior to her PhD studies, she worked as a researcher at the Institute for the Sociology of Law and Criminology (IRKS) in Vienna, where she pursued her research interests in migration and legal sociology within the ALTERNATIVE project, in which she was the leader of Work Package 4 – 'Activating civil society'.

Katrien Lauwaert is a senior researcher at the Leuven Institute of Criminology, KU Leuven and holder of the Bianchi Chair on Restorative Justice at the Vrije Universiteit Amsterdam. Her recent work has focused on the link between restorative justice and community building, on victims of corporate violence, on EU policies on victims and restorative justice, and on the link between desistance and restorative Justice. Katrien studied law and criminology at KU Leuven, l'Université Catholique de Louvain (Louvain-la-Neuve), the

Rijksuniversiteit Leiden and the American University (Washington DC). She obtained a PhD from the University of Maastricht for her dissertation on 'Procedural Safeguards in Restorative Justice'. She worked as an assistant professor at the criminal law and criminology departments of Maastricht University in The Netherlands and the University of Liège in Belgium, where she conducted research and taught courses on restorative justice, victimology, youth delinquency, criminology and criminal procedure. Katrien Lauwaert is involved in the non-profit organisation Moderator. Forum voor herstelrecht en bemiddeling, which organises victim–offender mediation for adult offenders and their victims and which acts as a forum on restorative justice developments in Belgium. She is a founding member of the European Forum for Restorative Justice.

Vesna Nikolić-Ristanović is Full Professor of Criminology, Victimology, Juvenile Delinquency and Child Abuse at Belgrade University/Faculty for Special Education and Rehabilitation, director of the Victimology Society of Serbia, an active member of the European Academy of Sciences and Arts, and former president of the European Society of Criminology. Her research work is focused on war victimisation, violence against women, truth and reconciliation, restorative justice, yoga, victim support and trafficking in people. She is the initiator and coordinator of the 'Association Joint Action for Truth and Reconciliation' in Serbia. In past years, she was also engaged with research conducted by the Victimology Society of Serbia and other European research institutions within the EU-funded FP7 research project ALTERNATIVE. She is a founder and editor-in-chief of *Temida*, the journal on victimisation, human rights and gender. Dr Nikolić-Ristanović is an author and co-author of a large number of books, book chapters and articles published in Serbia and abroad.

Brunilda Pali is currently a postdoctoral researcher in the Leuven Institute of Criminology. She obtained her PhD in 2016 at the KU Leuven Institute of Criminology on 'Doing restorative justice in intercultural contexts: An alternative discourse of justice and security'. In the Leuven Institute of Criminology, Brunilda has also worked as a researcher on several EU-funded projects, besides the FP7 project ALTERNATIVE. She is also co-editor of *Critical Restorative Justice*. Besides criminology, Brunilda has a background in psychology (Bosphorus University, Istanbul), gender studies (Central European University, Budapest) and cultural studies (Bilgi University, Istanbul). She is currently the secretary of the European Forum Restorative Justice Board. She publishes on multiple themes, such as restorative justice, critical criminology, security, social movements, gender and arts. In ALTERNATIVE, she was leading Work Package 1 – 'Alternative epistemologies of justice and security'.

Christa Pelikan is a researcher at the Institute for the Sociology of Law and Criminology in Vienna. She has worked in the field of criminal law, especially juvenile justice, and in the field of family law. Starting in 1985, she has done accompanying research on the large Austrian pilot project on 'Victim-offender mediation in juvenile justice' and later on a pilot project

'Victim-offender mediation in general criminal law'. She has chaired the 'Committee of experts on mediation in penal matters' within the European Committee on Crime Problems (CDPC) and has been a member of the Criminological Scientific Council to the CDPC of the Council of Europe. She is a founding member of the European Forum for Restorative Justice and has been the chair of its 'Communication Committee', participating in various GROTIUS, AGIS and COST projects at EU level. She was involved in research within the project ALTERNATIVE.

Nikola Petrović is an assistant professor in the Department of Psychology, Faculty of Philosophy, University of Belgrade and a research fellow in the Victimology Society of Serbia. He is also the secretary general of the Association for Cognitive and Behavioral Therapies of Serbia and a member of the Ethics Board of the Association of Psychologists of Serbia. His research was primarily focused on psychotherapeutic practice and ethics, victimisation and juvenile delinquency, but he also participated in action-oriented projects on topics such as domestic violence and reconciliation. Dr Petrović is a rational emotive behavioural psychotherapist and works in the field of individual and couples therapy. In past years, he was also engaged with research conducted by the Victimology Society of Serbia and other European research institutions within the EU-funded FP7 research project ALTERNATIVE.

Mario Ragazzi is a consultant on international development cooperation. He has worked for the Catholic Church, international non-governmental organisations and the EU in post/during-conflict countries such as El Salvador, Colombia, Pakistan and Afghanistan for a dozen years. His research interests are on issues of state formation, institution-building and security in development.

Bejan Šaćiri is a PhD student at the Department of Psychology, Faculty of Philosophy, University of Belgrade, and a researcher in the Victimology Society of Serbia. He is involved in supporting victims in the victim support service 'VDS info and victim support', which works within the Victimology Society of Serbia. His research work has been mainly focused on discrimination, peacebuilding, reconciliation and restorative justice, professional ethics in psychology, domestic violence and the position of female prisoners. Bejan is a transactional psychotherapist in training and actively works in the field of individual and marital counselling. In past years, he was also engaged with research conducted by the Victimology Society of Serbia and other European research institutions within the EU-funded FP7 research project ALTERNATIVE.

Marie Louise Seeberg is a social anthropologist, research professor, coordinator of migration research at NOVA-HiOA, and leader of the Norwegian Network for Migration Research and of the international research group Contested Childhoods (IMISCOE). Seeberg has conducted research on ethnicity and migration for 25 years. Her wide array of research includes relations of diversity and ethnicity in Norwegian schools and workplaces, nurse immigration to Norway, the onward migration of asylum seekers within Europe, the many meanings of home and homeland among Vietnamese refugees in Norway, relations between Swedish welfare institutions and refugees from Vietnam, and conditions for asylum-seeking children in Norway. Among her publications are *Contested Childhoods: Growing up in Migrancy* (Springer 2016, IMISCOE academic book series, co-edited with Elzbieta M. Gozdziak), *The Holocaust as Active Memory: The Past in the Present* (Ashgate Academic 2013, co-edited with Irene Levin and Claudia Lenz), 'Immigrant careworkers and Norwegian gender equality: institutions, identities, intersections' in the *European Journal of Women's Studies* (2012), and 'No Place: small children in Norwegian asylum-seeker reception centres' in *Childhood – a Global Journal of Child Research* (with Cecilie Bagge and Truls Enger, 2009).

Edit Törzs studied law at the ELTE University Budapest in Hungary, where she later followed the PhD programme in the field of criminology. She also has a degree in European and French Law from Université Panthéon-Assas, Paris. From 2004 she worked for the Hungarian Office of Justice, Probation Service, and from 2006 she was responsible for coordinating the implementation of victim–offender mediation in Hungary. In 2012 she moved to Belgium to start working at the European Forum for Restorative Justice (EFRJ) as project officer in the four-year-long ALTERNATIVE project. Since November 2016 she has been the executive director of the EFRJ. She is a trained mediator and facilitator of restorative conferences and circles, and she also followed a course on Integral Dance and Movement Therapy for four years. In ALTERNATIVE, she was the leader for Work Package 3 – 'Restorative justice models application' and for Work Package 9 – 'Dissemination'.

Derick Wilson has been involved in the Corrymeela Reconciliation Community since 1965. He is Reader Emeritus in Education at Ulster University, specialising in Community Relations and Restorative Practices. He chaired the Youth Council for Northern Ireland (1987–1989) and was a founder of Mill Strand Integrated School (1987–1992), a member of the Broadcasting Council for NI, a founding trustee of the Spirit of Enniskillen Awards, a commissioner with the Equality Commission for Northern Ireland (2003–2008) and a member of the Victims and Survivors Forum. A qualified youth worker and teacher, he was a detached youth worker (NI Community Relations Commission 1970–1973); established professional courses for indigenous youth workers (1973–1978); directed the Corrymeela Centre (1978–1985); was a research fellow at the Centre for the Study of Conflict (1985–1989); established and co-directed Future Ways, a University team supportive of reconciliation, organisational change and public policy development (1990–2006); and was an assistant director of the UNESCO Centre (2006–2009) and a reader in Education. His doctorate was on facilitating contentious issues in mixed-tradition groups. He was awarded the MBE for Community Relations in 1994, a Distinguished Community Fellowship by the University in 2003, and a Lifetime Award for Services to Community Relations from the Northern Ireland Community Relations Council in 2007.

Acknowledgements

This book – together with a second book publication and a series of research papers – is the result of lengthy and collective efforts spent in the ALTERNATIVE project during more than four years. We are grateful to the EU, which funded the project through its Seventh Framework Programme for research and innovation, and to Carla Rocha Gomes from the Research Executive Agency, who accompanied us as project adviser. In addition to these, many people and organisations are to be thanked.

We would like to thank first of all everyone who believed in the project, everyone who supported it, but also people who questioned or challenged some of our premises and actions, as without them we would not have been able to move forward in the true spirit of participatory action research.

First of all, our deepest gratitude goes to the core teams of the ALTERNATIVE project based in our partner organisations in six European countries, who worked together as one big committed, engaged and creative team. The research participants were, more specifically: from the Leuven Institute of Criminology (LINC), KU Leuven – Ivo Aertsen, Inge Vanfraechem, Brunilda Pali and Mario Ragazzi; from the European Forum for Restorative Justice (EFRJ) – Edit Törzs, Katrien Lauwaert, Emilie van Limbergen and Emanuela Biffi; from Ulster University – Tim Chapman, Derick Wilson, Hugh Campbell and Philip McCready; from the Institute for the Sociology of Law and Criminology in Vienna (IRKS) – Christa Pelikan, Katrin Kremmel and Evelyn Klein; from the Norwegian Social Research Institute (NOVA) – Ida Hydle, Espen Marius Foss and Marie Louise Seeberg; from the Victimology Society of Serbia (VDS) – Vesna Nikolić-Ristanović, Sanja Ćopić, Nikola Petrović, Bejan Šaćiri and Jelena Srna; and from the Foresee Research Group in Budapest – Borbala Fellegi, Gabriella Benedek, Gábor Héra, László Balla, Gyula Galyas, Éva Győrfi, Erika Magyar, Szilvia Süki-Szíjjártó, Dóra Szegő, Balázs Berkovits and Eszter Balogh.

Second, we would like to extend our gratitude to the local actors that were central to the work of all the project partners. Sometimes they felt supported by us, but at other times they made themselves willingly vulnerable to our research, and without that openness and trust there would have been no project. This gratitude is extended more specifically to the following persons and organisations.

On behalf of our coordinating team in Belgium, we would like to thank, for efficient administrative, budgetary and legal support, KU Leuven Research and Development, in particular Tine Heylen, Karolien Mariën and Laurent Vandevelde; for support with films, the KU Leuven Institute for Media and Learning, in particular Christoph Cammans, Erwin Heylen, Anke Pesch and Stef Stes; for the exchange of ideas with our colleagues from Brussels, Odisee University College, namely Erik Claes, Iman Lechkar and Nele Gulinck; Monique Anderson and Kris Vanspauwen for support by the European Forum for Restorative Justice Secretariat; and Nadia Fadil, Lode Walgrave and Stephan Parmentier for support for the doctoral project of Brunilda Pali. Additionally, the members of the project's Advisory Board are to be thanked for their advice and valuable input during the project: Marieke Arnou, Martina Fischer, Joachim Kersten, Tove H. Malloy, Raul Carstocea, Ilina Taneva and Bas van Stokkom.

On behalf of our team in Norway, we would like to thank employees, volunteers and participants in the Norwegian Mediation Service and Red Cross Street Mediation for willingly sharing their experiences, which have given us valuable insights as comparative ground in the project.

On behalf of our team in Austria, we deeply thank the women of the Women's Café, who so warmly welcomed us into their group, and all residents, who supported our work with their patience, openness and participation. Further, we thank the team of the community centre Bassena, who embarked on reflective journeys with us and all *wohnpartner* staff members, who provided us with insightful depictions of their work and courageously dared to explore the potential of restorative justice for neighbourhood disputes in social housing estates.

On behalf of our team in Hungary, we would like to thank all the local residents, organisations and institutions and the City and Roma Minority Council of Kisváros for supporting our action research with their ongoing contribution, participation, openness and trust and by sharing their opinion, feedback and even critical reflections with us.

On behalf of the team of the Victimology Society of Serbia, we deeply thank our local partners in three multi-ethnic communities in Serbia – Prijepolje, Bačka Palanka and Medvedja – for their support, dedicated fieldwork and commitment to exploring the potential of restorative approaches in preventing and solving problems and conflicts in their communities. Further, we thank citizens of these three local communities who participated in the survey for their trust and sharing personal stories and victimisation experiences with us as researchers: this offered valuable knowledge that helped us to better understand the context and to implement the action research. Last, but not least, we are grateful to seminar participants for their active participation and showing readiness to network and further work on promoting restorative approaches in the intercultural field. Thanks to all of them, this research was a valuable journey in exploring the potential role restorative approaches have to play in a much wider context of people's everyday life and in various relationships.

On behalf of our team in Northern Ireland, we would like to acknowledge the contribution of Mark Black and Deborah Guy from the CARE project; Harry

Maguire and Jim McCarthy from CRJI; Sam White from the Resolve Project; David Kennedy from John Jay College, New York; John McCord from Ulster University; Old Library Trust Derry City; Restorative Justice for Oakland Youth; California Intervention Network Approach, Antioch, California; The Northlands Centre, Derry City; and The Creggan Healthy Living Centre, Derry City.

Finally, we thank all those who cannot be mentioned by name, the participants and speakers in regional workshops and at our final conference, but also – at the more personal level – our families, our colleagues, the strong network of caring hands that is behind anyone and anything.

Editors,
Brunilda Pali and Ivo Aertsen

Introduction

Doing restorative justice in intercultural contexts

Ivo Aertsen

The context

From its early beginning, the development of restorative justice theory and practice has found its gravitational centre in its response to criminal justice, as an alternative way of dealing with crime and the aftermath of crime (see Bosnjak, 2007; Pelikan, 2007). Less understood and developed is the potential of restorative justice philosophy and practices in complex, urban and intercultural settings that reflect issues of poverty, social exclusion and intercultural tensions. An engagement with such complex contexts and intersections of *problematique* challenges and enriches restorative justice enormously, both in terms of its theoretical grounds and in terms of its practices, revitalising a field that risks losing its creative potential.

This book therefore explores the potential and the limits of restorative justice in restoring justice and security in Europe by focusing on *conflicts in intercultural contexts*. Intercultural settings offer fertile ground for rethinking frames of (in)justice, (in)security and their intersection, and, what is most important, the role of restorative justice in tackling similar challenges. The book is based on an *action research project* (ALTERNATIVE) funded by the European Commission under the Seventh Framework Programme, which lasted from 2012 to 2016.[1] The project designed a solid form of action research, which in itself proposed an alternative to traditional forms of research, and thus contributed further to the epistemology of justice and security. The main findings of the action research methodology are published simultaneously in a separate book (Vanfraechem and Aertsen, 2018).

The project was innovative and exploratory, withdrawing in a certain sense from restorative justice's main agenda in order to create time and space for independent and critical reflections. The project challenged first of all the tendency – both in research and in practice – to an excessive focus on technology and surveillance as a way to conceive the doing of security. Efforts to do security by means of preventative and surveillance technology and control tend to produce feelings of insecurity, while security prevails when actors have a sense of being able to control their environment, belong to it, and feel connected to others. With this insight, the project has attempted to offer another vision of what security means and how it can be done, by enacting the ideas of participation, encounter and dialogue.

Second, the project challenged the heightened and obsessive concern with security, which has put at risk other principles and concerns, of which justice is the most important. This risk is reflected in the widespread implementation of surveillance devices violating the right to privacy, 'war on terror' practices violating human rights, restrictions on asylum seekers, and racist practices in the detention and deportation of immigrants. Security, we argued, while an important concern, is just one of the societal values and concerns that must be balanced against others, and therefore the project proposed to investigate justice and security together.

Third, the project challenged the merging of the security discourse with migration in particular and intercultural settings in general. Discourses of (in)security often attribute inevitable social conflicts to intercultural societies, or when these conflicts arise, the same discourses produce exclusionary and immunitary mechanisms for social groups to coexist, mechanisms which have endangered ideas of both justice and community. Such discourses, imbued with moral credibility and political authority, have been built upon the concept that *cultural difference* is foundational of social identity and leads to inevitable social breakdown. As a result, increasingly in social conflicts, tensions and perceptions of insecurity, culture has become a refracting lens through which conflict perceptions are formed. Both the produced and the emerging cultural diversity introduce challenges related to security and justice, calling for better communicative and participatory approaches that would support the handling of conflicts, and this is what the project has proposed to do.

In light of the *problematique* identified above, the idea for the project arose based on the awareness of restorative justice's potential application in the field of security. The repressive and controlling response is to a large degree the obvious, and increasingly reified as the natural, response, based on the affect of fear and ideologies of 'clashes of civilisations'. On the contrary, we argue that resorting to concrete experiences of wrongdoing, harm, conflict or injustice can counteract the tendency to react to conflicts repressively and can provide an antidote to ideology-driven images, politics feeding on these images, and the fears evoked. Dialogical and restorative approaches aim at bringing together different groups in society, promoting opportunities for deliberations about conviviality. We believe that such an approach stands a better chance of producing security rooted in the lifeworld of the individuals and groups participating in such a process and therefore is apt to become sustainable.

The action research sites

The project had at its core *four case studies*, which were located at four sites with different levels of intercultural conflicts. The action research in *Vienna* dealt with everyday conflicts at the micro-level between local residents and residents with migrant backgrounds in public/social housing estates. Researchers explored the potential of active participation of citizens and of civil society organisations, aiming at enhancing perceptions of justice and safety. The action research in *Kisváros*, a small town in Hungary, dealt with different – if mostly undercurrent – sources of tension between the inhabitants (e.g. between old residents and newcomers, Roma and non-Roma, etc.). The action research focused on finding out how and at what points restorative theory and practice can be integrated into the existing institutional structure, with special attention to the justice and law enforcement system. The action research in *Serbia* focused on the perceptions and involvement of citizens from multi-ethnic communities in three border towns – Bačka Palanka, Prijepolje and Medvedja – with ethnically diverse populations (Serbs, Albanians, Croats and Muslims). The researchers paid special attention to victims of past abuses and observed their roles in democratic processes for peace-building and conflict resolution. The action research in *Northern Ireland* focused on the relationship between the state system and local communities in three research sites (south Belfast, east Belfast and Derry/Londonderry) in the context of the violent conflict and the restorative potential of promoting active citizenship and community development. Local capacity to resolve intra- and inter-communal conflict is being evaluated in projects dealing with problems between local communities and gangs of youths, and between long-term residents and recent immigrants, and inter-community sectarian conflict.

Main questions

The theoretical, critical and normative thought that is the basis of this book and the application of this focused thought in real lifeworld contexts is invaluable and should offer an original contribution to conflict regulation and security fields, mainly restorative justice. The main questions this book aims to answer are: What do justice and security mean in plural societies with various degrees and types of social differences? What are some of the existing discourses regarding both justice and security, and what are their dangers? Can restorative approaches offer an alternative to the existing discourse? And if yes, then under what critical conditions?

Overview of the book

The first four chapters in the book set the context by describing the societal changes and developments that tackle the triangle of (inter)culturalism–justice–security, both in terms of discursive developments and in terms of changes of social structures and social practices. They reflect on the problems that are created when plurality and social difference are framed exclusively in terms of culture, when such differences become securitised, and especially when justice as a principle or a practice stops being the 'guiding star' for plural societies. Further, the chapters make the link to restorative justice's potential in intercultural settings.

In Chapter 1, Ida Hydle and Marie Louise Seeberg trace the change in the framing of social difference as a cultural difference, and the rise of the discourses of interculturalism, multiculturalism and diversity throughout Europe, arguing that this rise has important implications for the ways in which we live together through peace and conflict. Their concern is that discourses based on cultural difference potentially lead to a tightening definition of 'otherness' and a corresponding dehumanisation of immigrants and other groups of people who are defined as 'cultural others'. In order to address these concerns, they take a look at how European scholars have attempted to grasp and conceptualise aspects of difference over the past decades, and how these academic trends have fluctuated along with related political discursive trends.

In Chapter 2, Brunilda Pali, following on from the first chapter, which contextualised the cultural turn in both social sciences and policies, addresses in particular the merging of the cultural turn with the (in)security discourses. The chapter argues that both the produced and the emerging cultural diversity introduce challenges related to security and justice, calling for better communication and participatory approaches that would support the handling of social conflicts, while aiming at reducing uncertainty, restoring trust and promoting cooperative actions. As restorative justice is being promoted (see Chapter 4) as an approach that aims to counteract the (in)security discourses in intercultural contexts, the author sketches here some critical perspectives on security which offer useful insights that can support the agenda of restorative justice, both strategically and normatively.

Tim Chapman (in Chapter 3) reflects on how discourses of (in)security can produce, and have produced, exclusionary mechanisms which have damaged both the ideals and practices of (social) justice and the social fabric through the enforcement of sentiments of fear rather than solidarity and hospitality. This chapter inquires into whether this security response has become too dominant and whether it weakens or excludes responses to conflicts in intercultural contexts based upon the values of justice and inclusion. Northern Ireland is used as an example to ask whether the underlying drivers of a conflict are sustained by managing it through a politics based upon the fear of the other and through security measures. This leads to a discussion of what justice and inclusion might mean and of what might be a supplementary restorative response (given that there must always be some degree of coercive security) based upon these values, using case studies from the ALTERNATIVE research project in Northern Ireland.

In Chapter 4, Christa Pelikan and Ivo Aertsen analyse, through the action research that took place in the ALTERNATIVE project, the role of restorative justice in becoming a counter-security discourse, and what is most important in being counter in the sense of doing both justice and security. They propose 'participatory justice' as the counter-justice, the other justice sought in ALTERNATIVE, as well as 'participatory security/safety' as a counter-security. The radicalisation of the participatory element towards community ownership, on the one hand, and the extension of the reparative element towards transformation, on the other, have oriented the interventions of the action researchers. They are grounded in the lifeworld. This implies resorting to concrete experiences of wrongdoing, harm, conflict or injustice, and they can therefore counteract the tendency to react to conflicts repressively. The descriptions of the societal ecology of the research sites have laid open the dynamics of existing fears as produced by social and political upheavals, which vary at the four sites. In any case, the latter result in experiences of insecurity/uncertainty and injustice, oftentimes coming together. Restorative justice and restorative practices offer ways to tackle these fears – to find a new societal balance and a new togetherness, no longer based on people being in the same 'secure' situation, the same secure place with neatly separated compartments or social strata, but on people being together within their being different. This approach, espousing active participation and dialogue, is highly demanding, though, as the readiness of people to enter these participatory processes is not self-evident but has to be fostered and tended with care and caution. If 'participatory justice' and 'participatory security/safety' appear as hallmarks of an alternative governmentality, its intricacies and its ramifications have to be traced carefully, and this is what the authors have attempted through the presentation of case stories from ALTERNATIVE.

The following five chapters centre on specific conceptual and concrete problems that arise within the area of conflict handling between justice and security, and how these problems were addressed through a restorative approach in four action research sites. The idea is that these chapters, through concrete illustration of what a restorative approach can mean in various intercultural settings, expand conceptually beyond the intercultural–justice–security triangle and show instead both that these concepts are context bound and that they relate to, or create, or depend on other societal developments.

In Chapter 5, Erik Claes and Katrin Kremmel explore the potentials (and limits) of restorative justice in urban settings. The research findings are drawn from two specific urban research sites in Europe: the social housing estates in Vienna ('*Gemeindebau*'), and the specific context of an urban quarter in the heart of Brussels, where alternative restorative practices inspired by an innovative restorative framework have been tried out. These practices are designed in response to urban challenges as well as urban opportunities. Applying restorative justice principles and values to these urban settings requires an exploration of the field far beyond criminal justice and raises a whole set of conceptual, as well as practical, challenges. Both research projects are driven by the same general aim: to stretch restorative theory and practice beyond its classic ideas, assumptions and tensions, and to make it sensitive to pressing urban issues, as well as promising opportunities. Since urban contexts are so specific, so differentiated and often unpredictable, one of the main questions is how to refine and even reinvent the conceptual building blocks of restorative justice in order to guide key actors in these specific settings. Another important, more practical, issue revolves around the question of whether firmly established restorative practices like mediation or peacemaking circles can be simply replicated in urban settings.

Gábor Héra (Chapter 6) introduces some of the academic debates on the concept of social exclusion, identifying its core elements and highlighting the main points by concretely referring to the situation of the Roma minority in Hungary. The chapter presents the findings of action research that was conducted in a small Hungarian town and analyses the mechanism of exclusion, which affected the local Roma, by putting emphasis on the coexistence of exclusion and the lack of open communication between the Roma and non-Roma groups of the community under investigation. The author argues that the approach of restorative justice is an adequate answer not only for addressing the lack of open communication between different groups but also for supporting vulnerable groups and thereby counteracting social exclusion.

In Chapter 7, Vesna Nikolić-Ristanović, Sanja Ćopić, Nikola Petrović and Bejan Šaćiri explore and reimagine the concepts of security and justice in post-conflict societies through restorative lenses. They reflect on the concept of 'post-conflict society' or societies in transition and on the peculiarities of these contexts in relation to justice and security when compared with other European contexts. They particularly focus on challenges in developing justice in the post-conflict society in terms of developing the rule of law and other democratic values, and its move towards democratic society. Particular attention is paid to analysing the use of retributive and restorative justice approaches in the post-conflict societies for dealing with conflicts, and the position and treatment of victims. All these issues are analysed and discussed using the example of Serbia as a post-conflict society.

Derick Wilson and Hugh Campbell (in Chapter 8) explore the possibilities, and limitations, of those wishing to promote restorative justice practices that underpin security and justice using the example of the 'ethnic frontier society' of Northern Ireland. The authors examine the opportunities made possible in Northern Ireland since the Good Friday Agreement in 1998 to promote restorative practice approaches within what Braithwaite and Rashed (2014) identify as a 'politics of hope' approach. Against the background of addressing historical asymmetries of access to the state and the law and order systems before the conflict, this chapter examines the importance of restorative practices being embedded in wider societal institutions and societal transformation and not restricted, or confined, to the criminal justice system alone.

Tim Chapman and Katrin Kremmel (in Chapter 9) focus on the concept of community, a concept that is relevant both to understanding conflict in intercultural settings and to the practice of restorative justice beyond the remit of the criminal justice system. Drawing on the work of broader disciplines, sociology and social and political theory, and grounding their analysis in two research fields in which the ALTERNATIVE project has undertaken action research, working-class areas of south and east Belfast in Northern Ireland and social housing estates of Vienna, Austria, the authors offer a comparative analysis of the different and new understandings of community in these settings, and apply these new understandings to actual restorative responses with a view to identifying how the positive aspects of community can be activated to transform conflict.

In the remaining three chapters, an attempt is made at both conducting a critical analysis of some of the main tenets of restorative justice, such as 'participation' and 'informality', and offering constructive proposals for policy developments at the intersection of the themes discussed in the book.

In Chapter 10, Christa Pelikan and Mario Ragazzi engage in a comparative discussion of the meaning of 'active participation' in restorative practices, mainly as it relates to the specific settings in our project, illustrating its ambivalence. The chapter reflects on the ambivalence of participation and mobilisation, especially as it interplays with stakeholders in the four action research sites achieved mainly through comparative research. This research points to the potential role of restorative justice in societies with diverse degrees of leadership, public institutions and socio-economic redistributive policies towards the de-securitisation of conflicts, the strengthening of social solidarity between stakeholders, and improving the perceptions of safety.

Espen Marius Foss and Brunilda Pali (in Chapter 11) offer a critical analysis of the implications of informal justice mechanisms, such as restorative justice, for the amplification of social control. Here, security and social control are both looked at critically as different sides of the same coin. This chapter reflects on the transition in modern states from being disciplinary societies to societies of control, a transition that has led to the emergence of a new organisation of state power in processes that decentralise and outsource state functions to civil and private actors under mottos of liberalisation and democratisation, developments which can intensify state control over citizens. Restorative justice principles and objectives emerge as a critique of *disciplinary* punishment, bureaucratic forms of state control and criminal justice, and the alienation of citizens from their own conflicts. Although not directly deriving from it, they are embedded in and fed by the neoliberal discourse and its techniques of responsibilisation, autonomy and empowerment, active citizenship and democracy, thus representing an approach that is not only acceptable but even attractive to its subjects, and whose goals become closely aligned with those of the corporate state power. In the perspective of the emergence of societies of control, it remains crucial to understand the relation between corporate state power and decentralised restorative justice processes. In this chapter, the authors focus on the complex dynamics of this relationship, hoping to shed light on their tight coexistence and co-dependence, on the consequences of the new organisation of state power for the participants of such processes, and on the implications for restorative justice.

Edit Törzs, Katrien Lauwaert and Ivo Aertsen (Chapter 12) follow up on the European policy and practice implications of the ALTERNATIVE project. Their chapter explores whether these policies support a restorative justice approach for dealing with conflicts in intercultural settings. In light of that question, the most relevant EU and Council of Europe policy developments are screened in the fields of security, migration and integration, restorative justice, intercultural dialogue and intercultural cities. The chapter concludes with the observation that European policies are ambivalent, supporting at the same time repressive security-based approaches and initiatives that support more inclusive and tolerant societies. The authors argue that more sustainable support to local, bottom-up initiatives based on restorative justice approaches could contribute to achieving policy aims set at the European level for creating and maintaining safe and democratic societies.

The book concludes with some thought-provoking ideas and suggestions by Brunilda Pali to reframe predominating justice and security discourses in intercultural Europe and to design new spaces for contradiction and conviviality.

Note

1 This project has received funding from the European Union's Seventh Framework Programme for research, technological development and demonstration under grant agreement no. 285368. The project's full name is *Developing alternative understandings of security and justice through restorative justice approaches in intercultural settings within democratic societies.* The project was coordinated by the Leuven Institute of Criminology, Katholieke Universiteit Leuven (LINC-KU Leuven) in Belgium, in partnership with the Norwegian Social Research Institute (NOVA) in Norway, the European Forum for Restorative Justice (EFRJ) in Belgium, the Institute for the Sociology of Law and Criminology (IRKS) in Austria, the Foresee Research Group (Foresee) in Hungary, the Victimology Society of Serbia (VDS) and the University of Ulster (UU) in Northern Ireland. The results of the research are available on the website (www.alternativeproject.eu) and Film online platform (http://alternativefilms.euforumrj.org). The opinions expressed throughout the book are those of the authors.

References

Bosnjak, M., 2007. Some thoughts on the relationship between restorative justice and the criminal law. In: R. Mackay, Bosnjak, M., Deklerck, J., Pelikan, C., van Stokkom, B., and Wright, M., eds, 2007. *Images of Restorative Justice Theory*. Frankfurt am Main: Verlag für Polizeiwissenschaften, pp. 93–112.

Pelikan, C., 2007. The place of restorative justice in society: making sense of developments in time and space. In: R. Mackay, Bosnjak, M., Deklerck, J., Pelikan, C., van Stokkom, B., and Wright, M., eds, 2007. *Images of Restorative Justice Theory*. Frankfurt am Main: Verlag für Polizeiwissenschaften, pp. 35–55.

Vanfraechem, I. and Aertsen, I., eds, 2018. *Action Research in Criminal Justice: Restorative Justice Approaches in Intercultural Settings*. London: Routledge.

1 Difference as culture

Roots and implications of a mode of framing

Ida Hydle and Marie Louise Seeberg

Introduction

Increasingly, questions of conflict, security and risk as posed by individuals, groups, states and the European Union are framed in terms of 'culture'. Has culture become a vehicle for talking about social difference? Are terms like culture and identity used too much, and may this lead to thinking about conflict in terms of 'the other' of ethnicity, religion and nationalism? What are the consequences – and, paradoxically, possible risks – implicated in such discourses? This chapter addresses the framing of social difference as cultural difference, and therefore the rise of discourses on interculturalism, multiculturalism and cultural diversity throughout Europe. As part of this endeavour, we also critique a social scientific epistemology of 'society', 'community' and 'culture' as ideally and normally ordered and free of conflict.

We posit that there has been a rise in the discourse and policies of culture and multi- or interculturalism in Europe, and argue that this rise has important implications for the ways in which we live together in peace and conflict. Tracing some theoretical premises and implications of discourses on multiculturalism, interculturalism and cultural diversity, we investigate some of the assumptions of culture underlying these discourses. Our concern is that discourses based on cultural difference potentially lead to a tightening definition of otherness and a corresponding dehumanisation of immigrants and other groups of people who may be defined as 'cultural others'.

In order to address the questions raised above, we take a look at how European scholars have attempted to grasp and conceptualise aspects of difference over the past decades, and how these academic trends have fluctuated along with related political discursive trends.

Difference: inequality or diversity?

Societal differences are often analytically distinguished through concepts such as gender, class or ethnicity. Explicit definitions of such concepts tend to emphasise what sets them apart from other types of differences, such as gender as primarily referring to biology, class to economy, and ethnicity to history.

However, these and other societal dimensions of difference also include significant cultural characteristics associated with groups of people. The recognition and identification of some cultural differences as significant (e.g. those of ethnicity) and of other cultural differences as being less important (e.g. those of class) takes place through political processes or other processes of power. Such processes increasingly span several fields of interaction, especially through the use of social and mass media, where policy makers, civil society and scholars mutually influence one another. Through such mutual interactions, some differences are linked with inequality, thus forming the life chances of individuals.

Two main types of multi- or intercultural settings are often represented in these culture-related discourses. First are settings that have been perceived as historically multi- or intercultural, such as in the central European countries stemming from the Austrian-Hungarian Empire and the tumultuous past of the countries that more or less belonged or belong to Germany, or to the former Ottoman Empire. Second, we find settings that are regarded as having become multi- or intercultural through past immigration from earlier colonies or other, often more recent immigration, such as immigrants taking up residence in the Nordic countries, which are widely regarded as 'otherwise' culturally homogeneous.

However, historical evidence shows that not one single European country has ever been 'mono-cultural' or 'mono-ethnic' in the past. For example, all the Nordic countries, conventionally described as culturally 'homogeneous' societies, have always been inhabited by groups who defined and define themselves as culturally, ethnically, religiously or linguistically different from the politically and numerically dominant majority population. In Norway, social scientists and historians repeatedly err in presenting Norwegians as having been 'one people' in cultural terms until the mid-twentieth century (Brochmann and Kjeldstadli, 2008).

There was an increase in immigration to Europe and North America from the 1970s onwards, due to several reasons, such as wars, economic disparity, globalisation and labour market changes. Behind many such reasons are changes in world financial regulations, like the Bretton Wood Agreement in 1947, the separation of the US dollar from the gold standard in 1971 and the development of the US 'surplus regulations',[1] allowing the USA to benefit from the 'controlled disintegration' and 'unbalanced equilibrium' of the world's markets and national investments (Varoufakis, 2011), where the euro-zone is one of the 'disintegrated and unbalanced' regions.

Most, if not all, urban areas in today's Europe are characterised by culturally diverse communities. People from different backgrounds, with different religious and cultural affiliations, world views and values are living together in the same neighbourhoods – not necessarily in peace with one another. Demographic changes have led to a number of challenges for individuals, local communities and states in adapting to new constellations of diversity. In many areas, however, cultural – or ethnic – diversity is old news. More than four decades ago, social anthropologist Fredrik Barth wrote:

> In most political regimes, however where there is less security and people live under a greater threat of arbitrariness and violence outside their primary community, the insecurity itself acts as a constraint on interethnic contacts. In this situation, many forms of interaction between members of different ethnic groups may fail to develop, even though a potential complementarity of interests obtains. Forms of interaction may be blocked because of a lack of trust or a lack of opportunities to consummate transactions. What is more, there are also internal sanctions in such communities, which tend to enhance overt conformity within and cultural differences between communities. If a person is dependent for his security on the voluntary and spontaneous support of his own community, self-identification as a member of this community needs to be explicitly expressed and confirmed; and any behaviour which is deviant from the standard may be interpreted as a weakening of the identity, and thereby of the bases of security. In such situations, fortuitous historical differences in culture between different communities will tend to perpetuate themselves without any positive organisational basis; many of the observable cultural differentiae may thus be of very limited relevance to the ethnic organisation. The processes whereby ethnic units maintain themselves are thus clearly affected, but not fundamentally changed, by the variable of regional security.
>
> (1969, pp. 36–37)

Barth here puts into words several of the concerns of present-day European politics: insecurity and a mutual lack of trust as major obstacles to everyday interethnic contacts; the question of political leadership, which only too often feeds on interethnic conflicts; and the closely related framing of all sorts of conflicts of interest as issues of ethnicity and culture. When, for example, perceived increasing 'uncontrollable' immigration from Africa and the Middle East is discursively combined with terrorist attacks throughout Europe and the Middle East, Barth's comments are strikingly pertinent. This is also true when it comes to the effects of populist discursive framing of social problems on the increasing number of citizens without work, and thus also potentially without food and housing where welfare systems prove inadequate.

In the following, we will present some theoretical and descriptive research relevant to such realities. Concepts of conflict, culture and intercultural contexts or settings and ethnicity are building blocks in European security discourses. We shall briefly review the current state of the art within the research fields framed by these concepts, and then suggest definitions for the purposes of analysing security and peace.

We base our review on two levels of knowledge. On the epistemic level (theory of knowledge), our approach derives from the French theorist Michel Foucault and his view on knowledge as always dependent on the discourse within which it was created. This notion of discourse does not only refer to knowledge as ideas and to discourse as the written or spoken word, but includes both the socio-historical context in which the ideas and verbalisation came into existence, and their practices.

The relations between a certain body of knowledge, for example the disciplines of law, theology or medicine, and their institutions, such as court rooms, churches or hospitals, as well as the leading persons and practices related to these disciplines, will always entail relationships of power, social control and social possibilities. Thus, the second level is the paradigmatic level, as we refer to certain patterns of empirical and theoretical investigations relevant to our focus in this chapter.

This two-level approach is in accord with the analytical viewpoints of several of the central authors we will refer to in the following text (Avruch, 1998; Bakhtin *et al.*, 1981; Sen, 2009; Sommers, 2012). To our understanding, they all agree with the premise of this approach, that notions of truth and reality will always depend on the socio-historical context of the person(s) or groups who proclaim the truth, the reality and so on. This does not imply that there is no objective reality, but that human conceptions of this reality will always be situated and vary according to specific contexts and paradigms.

Understanding culture, understanding conflicts?

The word 'culture' originates from the Latin verb *colere*, which means to cultivate in a wide sense, including the cultivation and inhabitation of the land as well as worship or cult and the nurture of children and animals, and the noun *cultūra*, which means cultivation in a correspondingly wide sense. Hence, the scientific study of 'culture' means acquiring knowledge about what humans cultivate. Throughout the past century, 'culture' has been one of the most contested words in the social sciences, as it has been described as one of the two most complicated words in the English language (Williams, 1981 as quoted in Eriksen, 2001, p. 3). In 1952, Alfred Kroeber, Wayne Untereiner and Clyde Kluckhohn (1952) presented 161 different definitions of culture. Today, there are more than 300 definitions. It is well beyond the scope of this chapter to provide an overview of all these definitions. We will try to clarify some of the most relevant uses of the concept and propose an understanding of culture in line with the state of the art in the social sciences. This may be fruitful for a possible redefinition of present anxieties and quests for justice.

Four main types of definitions and uses of the word 'culture' have been identified (Eriksen, 2001; Norvoll and Thorbjørnsrud, 2009; Riches, 1986; Sert, 2010):

- as a sector in society (ministry of culture, youth culture, fine culture, etc.)
- as a life form (American culture, farmer culture, child culture, etc.)
- as in various subcultures (immigrant culture, women's culture, student culture, etc.)
- as ideas and values that enable human agency and communication.

The last category of culture definitions includes the ways in which the concept of culture is used in the social sciences. Eriksen (2001) points out that 'culture' carries with it a basic ambiguity of sameness and difference: on the one hand, every human is equally cultural; on the other hand, people are different because of culture. Consequently, 'culture' refers to both basic similarities and to systematic differences between humans (Eriksen, 2001, p. 3).

In the 1970s, Clifford Geertz (1973, 1974) had great influence on the understanding of culture in social anthropology as an integrated whole with distinct borders, as a puzzle where all the pieces were at hand, and as a system of meanings that was largely shared by a population. However, this influential understanding was criticised throughout the 1970s and 1980s because, in many cases, it could be said that national or local culture is neither shared by all or most of the inhabitants, nor sharply bounded, nor an integrated 'puzzle' where all the pieces fit together (Eriksen, 2001). Alternative conceptualisations of culture were proposed as 'unbounded cultural flows' or as 'fields of discourse' or as 'traditions of knowledge', whereas others even wanted to get rid of the culture concept altogether.

Today, one may organise scholarly uses of the concept of 'culture' into two main types of definitions: one that emphasises historical continuity (e.g. Klausen, 1999; Sen, 2009) and another that emphasises 'that which enables communication' (Eriksen, 2010; Riches, 1986). The first kind of definition implies cultural inheritance and is more bounded and exclusive than the second, which claims that if two persons are able to have a mutually meaningful communication, they share certain aspects of culture, no matter their origins or backgrounds. These two ways of defining 'culture' should be regarded as complementary, since historical continuity (for instance through primary socialisation) will always be an important dimension of culture, while at the same time communication across cultures of origin is always a possibility.

Gerd Baumann, in a slightly different take, also identifies two ways of talking about culture: on the one hand, 'culture is comprehended as a thing one has', and on the other 'as a process one shapes' (1996, p. 83). The former version entails a reification of culture, an understanding, which may be misleading, since understanding of culture as a 'thing' is in itself the product of a cultural process of which the individual actor need not be aware. Nevertheless, Baumann underlines that both ways of talking about culture capture some of the complexities to which the term refers: both are necessary, and choosing one at the expense of the other is a fallacy.

Similarly, Margaret Archer argues from a critical realist perspective that the culture–agency problem needs to be examined in its empirical manifestations, because individual agency and cultural constraints interplay in different ways in different contexts (1996). While scholars differ in their emphases on how culture may constrain or facilitate individual agency, there is general agreement that it is a fallacy to regard culture as a social agent or as a 'thing'. The task of scholars is, however, not to condemn lay discourse that may, and often does, imbue culture with agency, but to analyse such reifications of the concept of culture in terms of wider contexts of power and inequalities.

The social anthropologist Kevin Avruch is one of the few scholars who have published widely on the issues of culture in contexts of conflict, violence and war. His work is therefore especially pertinent to discussions about fear and security. He discusses and conceives culture in a socio-historical perspective as something which is derived from individual experience, learned or created by individuals themselves, or passed on to them socially by contemporaries or ancestors (Avruch, 1998). This way of understanding culture differs from the one that dominated colonial anthropology and which has later, through a 'time lag' (Stewart, 1997), dominated most of the other social sciences, especially in security discourse and conflict resolution studies. Avruch's book on conflict resolution was, as viewed from within social anthropology, part of a paradigm shift carried forth by the better-known works of, for example, James Clifford and George Marcus (1986).

In line with the paradigm shift, Avruch moves away from the previously dominating view of culture as a stable or homogeneous entity. He focuses less on patterns and structures, and more on social and cognitive processes, than had until the mid-1980s been the case in social anthropology. This more fluid understanding of culture is now part of the theoretical mainstream in the social sciences, and encompasses the diversity of social and experiential settings that individuals encounter. Although Avruch may be positioned within mainstream and general contemporary anthropology, he is one of the few who have made explicit the issues of culture and conflict. Thus, his outline may act as an example of the kind of cultural understanding that we are aiming at.

Avruch is one of the many scholars active in the 1980s and 1990s who expand the scope of reference of culture to include not just quasi- or pseudo-kinship groupings (tribe, ethnic group and nation) but also groupings that derive from profession, occupation, class, religion or region. He highlights the fact that culture is always psychologically and socially unevenly distributed in a group: not all members of a group see the world in the same way. This also brings into view the dimension of power often missing in more conventional or everyday usage of 'culture': if the members of a group have different understandings of the world, how do the world views of some members achieve status as representative of the world views of the group as a whole?

Avruch's aim is to fashion a working definition of culture for both theory and practice in conflict resolution, and he emphasises the need to focus on the implications and dynamics of the local – that is, on variability and diversity – rather than searching for the universal and homogeneous characteristics of any culture. In line with most contemporary anthropologists, (Avruch, 1998, pp. 14–15) points to six pitfalls when it comes to understanding culture:

- Culture is not homogeneous (it is not free from internal paradoxes and contradictions).
- Culture is not a thing (it cannot act independently of human actors; 'clash of civilisations' is a good example of this sort of perception. It is easy to overlook intracultural diversity and the fact that culture changes over time).
- Culture is not uniformly distributed among members of a group (this idea imputes cognitive, affective and behavioural uniformity to all members of the group).

- For any individual, culture always comes in the plural. Rather than possessing and controlling one distinct culture, every individual combines and belongs to several, often overlapping, cultures.
- Culture is not just customs (to see culture as merely custom or tradition again downplays individual agency).
- Culture is not timeless (related to 'culture is custom' and all of the above views).

As noted above, culture is not an actor, but is often spoken about as such for various, often political reasons, for example in nationalistic, ethnic or racialising discourses. Hence, the word 'culture' may not mean the same in everyday language as it does in academic analyses. In lay usage of the term 'culture', scholars argue, cultural phenomena and practices are often 'reified' and endowed with a mystical agency of their own in ways that hinder constructive dialogue and promote orientalism (Anthias, 2001; Børtnes, 2001; Covey, 2010; Csordas, 1990).

Reality is not necessarily ordered in a manner perceptible to human beings. Researchers within the social sciences and the humanities have, during the last century, been concerned with why and how people create order from social and other phenomena, and several ordering principles have emerged, especially within the religious, literary and philosophical fields of science. The emphases in analyses of ordering systems vary from cosmological (Derrida, 2001) to genealogical (Keesing, 1990) to bodily systems (Csordas, 1990; Douglas, 1984; Keesing, 1990; Lakoff and Johnson, 1999; Merleau-Ponty, 1996). Roger Keesing (1990) points to new approaches within cognitive science concerning the cross-cultural knowledge of categorisation. The linguist George Lakoff described his theory of natural categorisation as

> a logic of mind [...] in which categories are defined not in terms of necessary and sufficient conditions for class membership, but in terms of central and prototypic cores of meaning, extended outward on the basis of shared features and relationships or metaphor and metonymy.
>
> (As cited in Eriksen, 2010, p. 162)

The above examples of theoretical approaches to the ordering of experience[2] are likely to be useful to most social scientific researchers and projects. All of us – researchers, lawyers, social workers, mediators, doctors, nurses, engineers, other professionals and non-professionals of different kinds, groups and regions – belong to different 'ordering groups' (language, ethnicity, religion, class, gender, age, education ...). Ordering implies valuation, that is, moral knowledge. There is thus a need for great care in the selection of terms in policy and polity, in order to find a constructive common language to express and create understanding. Furthermore, terms should be chosen as a result of critical and explicit discussions in order to prevent misunderstanding and to ensure that policies and polities proceed on a common ground.

Multicultural or intercultural?

Terms like 'ethnicity', 'culture' and 'religion' are often used to refer to socio-cultural differences and 'otherness' in the population. However, in conflict situations the uses of these terms may result not only in confusion, but also in the maintenance and escalation of conflicts. 'Conflicts in intercultural settings' are often confused with 'intercultural conflicts', yet they mean quite different things and have very different implications for research, policy and practice. Looking into the different conflict contexts in Europe, the contexts or settings are defined or described as intercultural, but the conflicts may comprise as their central aspects such things as gender, age, class, income, or injustice from the outside or the aftermaths of war, which is transferred to new generations. 'Intercultural settings' is the broader concept – it includes conflicts around issues other than those pertaining to 'culture' and does not presuppose that difference in 'culture' is a primary problem in itself. In an intercultural setting, such as many inner-city housing areas, conflicts about, for example, noise, smell or littering may be framed as an intercultural conflict, a conflict of 'native Viennese' versus 'Turkish immigrants', 'ethnic Norwegians' versus 'Pakistani immigrants' or 'local Pakistanis' versus 'Roma migrants', just to name a few examples. Other interpretations or framings of such particular conflicts are possible and could well be more accurate, such as intergenerational, social or class conflicts, but such alternative framings rarely appear. Hence, conceptions of 'culture' related to conflict and polarisation are often in use and thus disguise what is at stake for people, rather than becoming an analytical point of departure for the clearing of misunderstandings and for mitigating harm. Our task as culture analysts and social researchers is to ask: How could this conflict be alternatively interpreted in terms of other social variables and power dimensions such as generation, gender, politics, class and so on? This is not to say that conflicts cannot be of an intercultural character, but rather, that other frames of interpretation are usually at least as relevant and almost always more constructive.

Intercultural settings are the loci of our interest. The conflicts that we approach in our studies have to be analysed in order to find out about the societal structure and especially the power relations that are 'behind' the conflicts and might go beyond differences of 'culture'. Ideas about 'culture' are often mobilised during the escalation of a conflict between people from different backgrounds and perceived as representative of 'cultural differences', whereas the root of the conflicts may not have anything to do with differences in culture in itself. This is an empirical question, and that makes it important to pay attention to the ways in which the people involved frame these conflicts. This is where 'intercultural conflicts' will come into focus as the view from 'inside' the conflict. Thus, in order to study whether a conflict is culturally based, there is a need for close and careful investigations of how and why the people involved see, act and explain what their engagement is about.

Careful comparison from the researchers' point of view will give additional insight into the context of a conflict – the comparison will give information on why and how such surface-framing has eventually been overcome (Howell, 2010; Lien, 2015; Scheffer and Niewöhner, 2010).

For social scientists working on conflicts in 'intercultural settings' (the view from 'outside', e.g. from the analyst's point of view) – it is crucial to work with insider concepts of 'intercultural conflicts' as a critical focus of interest. This interest makes it especially important to look at societal and political forces that lie beneath the surface of conceptions of the so-called 'intercultural conflicts'.

The term 'intercultural' also appears in a less descriptive and more ideological and academic form: 'interculturalism'. In the following, we will take a closer look at this concept and its epistemic or political surroundings, as it is likely to be encountered as part of empirical contexts of studies on contemporary conflict lines in Europe, whether openly described as 'cultural' or not.

Interculturalism and multiculturalism

Multiculturalism and interculturalism are contested and competing terms in scholarly debates. Whereas both terms refer to policies aimed at dealing with, or organising, differences or diversity in plural societies, the definition of each concept varies a good deal, from country to country, from politician to politician and from scholar to scholar. Multiculturalism may be seen as a term referring to state policies of plural societies with, for example, indigenous peoples and migrants (e.g. one is allowed or not allowed to keep two citizenships and thus two passports; or minorities are accepted as having their own political rights within the nation-state, e.g. their own parliament). As part of a current wave of critique of the multiculturalism concept, Robert Wilson has even suggested that it is little more than a continuation of the colonial concept of 'indirect rule': it presupposes that the 'others' of Western nations constitute distinct 'cultural groups' with a leadership that may be useful for Western governments in controlling and ruling their 'others' (Wilson, 2012).

The concept of interculturalism has been more strongly linked to the idea of 'intercultural dialogue' and communication, and thus contrasted with multiculturalism by the assumption that it stands for something more mutually enriching than mere peaceful coexistence. Interculturalism is also, by extension, assumed to be more synthesising, that is, more committed to a stronger sense of the whole, to social cohesion, and also to open and constructive criticism of illiberal cultural practices (Modood and Meer, 2012). Within the European polity of inclusion and integration, these connotations of interculturalism find more resonance than the more structural or organisational versions of multiculturalism, and several good and explicit intentions of integration and inclusion are also defined through an emphasis on 'intercultural' dialogue. However, it should be noted that proponents of multiculturalism argue that this concept encompasses the aspect of dialogue (Modood and Meer, 2012).

The term 'multiculturalism' generally refers to an applied ideology of racial, cultural and ethnic diversity within the demographics of a specified territory or organisation. The term is variously used; for instance, many prefer the terms cultural or ethnic or religious difference, plurality or diversity. One of the leading scholars on multiculturalism, Will Kymlicka, points out that the political reason behind the current multiculturalism versus interculturalism discussion is that there is a need to find an 'alternative strategy for addressing popular discontent with diversity' (2012, p. 215). In other words, there is a widespread perception especially among European politicians that their electorates are not happy with immigration, and in an attempt to 'tell a story that can revive the flagging political commitment to diversity' (Kymlicka, 2012, p. 214), the rhetorical solution is to find a new word for policies to deal with 'multicultural populations', interculturalism being the answer.

As a response to this critique, but timewise in advance, Marie Louise Seeberg (2004) in her article 'Anthropologists and multiculturalism in Norway and beyond' explored the potential of critical realism as an approach to debates about multiculturalism. She claims:

> There is a need to renew the closely interrelated academic and political discussions about multiculturalism. Constitutive of national versions of multiculturalism are images of a national self, as transmitted by each nation-state to its citizens. Multiculturalisms as social phenomena, thus formed by nationalisms, are intertwined with anthropological concepts of multiculturalism, which depend on concepts of culture that are often contradictory or essentialising.
>
> (Seeberg, 2004, p. 215)

Critical realism is a term within the field of science theory developed by the British philosopher Roy Bhaskar, emphasising the social developments and constructions of science, both social and natural sciences (1997 [1975]). This is in line with the French science theorist/anthropologist Bruno Latour. Both emphasise the importance of the social in the different scientific practices. Thus, Seeberg suggests that a manifold concept of culture may provide a more fruitful point of departure: 'Such a concept also reflects empirical complexities more adequately and at the same time enables us to think in new ways about organising society' (2004, p. 215). This is compatible with the economist philosopher Sen's notion of a justice with many dimensions (2009). Such multidimensional perspectives and views invite us to a careful and close look at what is empirically at stake for people and in a comparative perspective in order not to jump to easy conclusions that are likely to cause harm.

Culture and other differences: gender, class, ethnicity

'Ethnicity' has long been a contested term, not least because it has been and is associated with the problematic term 'race'. However, 'ethnicity' is one of the key analytical terms within the field of social anthropology. A common anthropological understanding of the term is 'ethnic identity', consisting of ideas of common ancestry, language, history, belief system and world view (religion) shared by a group of people. According to Barth, cited above, as well as to contemporary scholarship informed by Barth's work (Eriksen, 2010; Guild, 2009; Takle, 2012) ethnicity is a relational term; that is, it emerges as relevant only in the encounter with another group of people who are conceived to be 'different' concerning such cultural characteristics. 'Ethnicity' in this perspective refers to dynamic relations – such as communication, conflict, cooperation or adaptive coexistence – between ethnic groups. Thus, 'interethnic' refers to communication in one way or another between, among or involving people perceived as belonging to, and often as representative of, different ethnic groups.

Often, the use of terms such as 'ethnic' conflict may refer to conflicts that do not spring from ethnic differences as such. Other circumstances, such as differences in access to material or political resources, may have a large part in such conflicts. In these cases, conflict lines often follow ethnic lines, often through manipulative political discourse, but the differences between the groups are not the only or original sources of conflict. When discussing conflict, we may refer, for example, to inner-city social housing, where not only 'generational conflict', as we suggested above, but also 'gender' or 'class conflict' seems to be just as relevant as 'ethnic conflict'. Cultural as well as material aspects of conflicts may relate to ethnic differences, but this is not necessarily so. In many cases, other dimensions of difference are at least as relevant to understanding and hence to transforming conflicts. Class is one such dimension that should not be underestimated. The cultural dimension of class relates closely to education and what Bourdieu (1986) called 'cultural capital', while the material dimension is rooted in differences in income and economic capital. In our times, appealing to voters on the basis of class solidarity appears to be less politically opportune than using ethnic or national belonging as a common platform, which may be the explanation for the growth in (ethnic or racist extremist) right-wing parties in several European countries.

Another example of the need to examine carefully any underlying causes of violent conflict was displayed in an anthropological youth study from Oslo (Sundnes, 2004). The focus was on young male ideals of how to address each other, in particular profane name-calling and offending and insulting verbal practices, which sometimes cause aggressive reactions. These reactions were locally interpreted as pertaining to cultural differences. However, the study shows that reactions were 'shaped by subtle processes of interpretation, and that conceptions of honour may be more related to marginalised positions than to cultural differences' (Sundnes, 2004, p. 3, our translation). In this case, the root conflict was neither culture (honour based) nor ethnicity (a group with honour-based culture), but rather, negotiations of marginalised identities.

Consequently, there is a great need for caution when applying terms such as 'interethnic conflict' or 'intercultural conflict', and the close empirical investigation of the assumed role and status of ethnicity and culture in any conflict line must be considered in light of other differences. In addition to class, one may also have differences of generation, of gender and of access to labour, food and housing – not all of which are necessarily causally related to differences in history, religion, ancestry or language. In addition, the problem may not be difference in itself but the hierarchisation of difference, which is implicit in the conflict: someone or something is valued above or below the other. It is in the task of redefining and reframing conflicts that the participation and engagement of civil society are especially important.

Living together safely

In anthropological studies, a common approach is studying at the borders or the limits of phenomena, in order to describe general features and patterns of peoples' interaction and organisation. Thus, the margins or extremes disclose the general; it is at the limits of phenomena that one may catch a glimpse of what is otherwise taken for granted and remains unseen. Bourdieu called this the 'doxic' part of experience: for instance, one does not explain one's grammar when talking because grammar is taken for granted among speech partners – although linguistic research shows the unrecognised space for misunderstanding that exists.

'Intercultural' and 'context' are two terms representing phenomena that are often taken for granted and not explicitly described. How is that to be interpreted? We would suggest that it relates to the current framing of intercultural and interethnic contexts as central to security matters and threats in Europe. Globalisation of the economy and the financial market has dramatically increased the number and intensity of encounters between people defined as being of different origin and with different cultural identities. This emphasis on cultural and ethnic difference when resources are, or appear to be, scarce has often increased mutual prejudices, hostilities and hatred. In some cases, it has triggered 'othering', the asymmetric process of dehumanisation between dominant and minority groups. In other cases, it has generated new hybrid groups, which tend to overcome traditional or previous 'otherness', for example exclusion.

This also resonates with the interpretation and use of the term 'conviviality' as a useful concept when analysing ongoing antagonisms in multicultural contexts. Community life is a day-to-day reality, in spite of – or perhaps because of – contradictory tendencies and practices of both inclusion and exclusion, solidarity and antagonism, sameness and otherness simultaneously. Based on three years of intensive fieldwork, Parker and Karner (2010, p. 16) describe such conviviality in an inner-city area of Birmingham: 'It is not shared values but involvement in the material practices of daily life and struggle for resources that generate a stake in a locality.' We are back where we started: far from building on the widespread assumption that conflict is a threat to social life, conviviality means living together constructively, in peace *and* conflict.

Notes

1 Regulated by the US military-industrial complex.
2 Douglas' ordering of experience (Douglas, 1984) may be seen in accord with Foucault's notion of discourse (Foucault, 1997): people's ordering of experience will always rely upon and reflect the socio-historical conditions for their ordering.

References

Anthias, F., 2001. The material and the symbolic in theorising social stratification: issues of gender, ethnicity and class. *British Journal of Sociology, 52*(3), pp. 367–390.

Archer, M. S., 1996. *Culture and agency: the place of culture in social theory*. Rev. edn. Cambridge: Cambridge University Press.

Avruch, K., 1998. *Culture and conflict resolution*. Washington, DC: United States Institute of Peace Press.

Bakhtin, M. M., Emerson, C., and Holquist, M., 1981. *The dialogic imagination: four essays*. Austin: University of Texas Press.

Barth, F. ed., 1969. *Ethnic groups and boundaries: the social organisation of culture difference*. Bergen: Universitetsforlaget.

Baumann, G., 1996. *Contesting culture: discourses of identity in multi-ethnic London*. London: Cambridge University Press.

Bhaskar, R., 1997 [1975]. *A realist theory of science*. 2nd edn. London: Verso.

Børtnes, J., 2001. Bakhtin, dialogen og den andre. In: O. Dysthe, ed, *Dialog, Samspel og læring*. Oslo: Abstrakt Forlag, pp. 91–105.

Bourdieu, P., 1986. The forms of capital. In: T. Kaposy and I. Szeman, eds 1986. *Cultural theory: an anthology*. Malden, MA: Wiley-Blackwell, pp. 81–93.

Brochmann, G. and Kjeldstadli, K., 2008. *A history of immigration: the case of Norway 900–2000*. Oslo: Universitetsforlaget.

Clifford, J. and Marcus, G. E., 1986. *Writing culture: the poetics and politics of ethnography*. Berkeley, CA: University of California Press.

Covey, H. C., 2010. *Street gangs throughout the world*. Springfield, IL: Charles C Thomas.

Csordas, T. J., 1990. Embodiment as a paradigm for anthropology. *Ethos, 18*(1), pp. 5–47.

Derrida, J., 2001. *On cosmopolitanism and forgiveness*. London: Routledge.

Douglas, M., 1984. *Purity and danger: an analysis of concepts of pollution and taboo*. London: Ark Paperbacks.

Eriksen, T. H., 2001. *Small places, large issues: an introduction to social and cultural anthropology*. London: Pluto.

Eriksen, T. H., 2010. *Ethnicity and nationalism: anthropological perspectives*. 3rd edn. London: Pluto.

Foucault, M., 1997. Ethics: subjectivity and truth. In: M. Foucault and P. Rabinow, eds, *The essential works of Michel Foucault, 1954–1984*. London: Allen Lane.

Geertz, C., 1973. *The interpretation of cultures/selected essays*. New York: Basic Books.

Geertz, C., 1974. From the native's point of view: on the nature of anthropological understanding. *Bulletin of the American Academy of Arts and Sciences*, pp. 26–45.

Guild, E., 2009. *Security and migration in the 21st century*. Cambridge: Polity.

Howell, S., 2010. Whatever happened to the spirit of adventure? In: H. Jebens and K.-H. Kohl, eds, *The end of anthropology?* Wantage: Sean Kingston, pp. 139–155.

Keesing, R. M., 1990. Theories of culture revisited. *Canberra Anthropology, 13*(2), pp. 46–60.

Klausen, A. M., 1999. *Olympic Games as performance and public event: the case of the XVII Winter Olympic Games in Norway*. New York: Berghahn Books.

Kroeber, A., Untereiner, W., and Kluckhohn, C., 1952. *Culture: a critical review of concepts and definitions*, Vol. 47:1. Cambridge, MA: The Museum.

Kymlicka, W., 2012. Comment on Meer and Modood. *Journal of Intercultural Studies, 33*(2), pp. 211–216.

Lakoff, G. and Johnson, M., 1999. *Philosophy in the flesh: the embodied mind and its challenge to Western thought*. New York: Basic Books.

Lien, M., 2015. Terrapolva-effekten – om postkolonial antropologi og prekære relasjoner. *Norsk Antropologisk Tidsskrift, 26*(2), pp. 185–194.

Merleau-Ponty, M., 1996. *Phenomenology of perception*. Delhi: Motilal Banarsidass.

Modood, T. and Meer, N., 2012. Rejoinder: assessing the divergences on our readings of interculturalism and multiculturalism. *Journal of Intercultural Studies, 33*(2), pp. 233–244.

Norvoll, R. and Thorbjørnsrud, B., 2009. *Mellom mennesker og samfunn: sosiologi og sosialantropologi for helse- og sosialprofesjonene*. Oslo: Gyldendal akademisk.

Parker, D. and Karner, C., 2010. Reputational geographies and urban social cohesion. *Ethnic and Racial Studies, 33*(8), pp. 1451–1470.

Riches, D., 1986. *The anthropology of violence. Selected papers from a conference on violence as a social institution, St. Andrews, Scotland, January 1985*. Oxford, New York: Basil Blackwell.

Scheffer, T. and Niewöhner, J., 2010. *Thick comparison: reviving the ethnographic aspiration*, Vol. 114. Leiden: Brill.

Seeberg, M. L., 2004. Antropologer og multikulturalisme i Norge og andre steder. *Norsk antropologisk tidsskrift, 4*, pp. 215–226.

Sen, A., 2009. *The idea of justice*. Cambridge, MA: Belknap Press of Harvard University Press.

Sert, D. S., 2010. Cyprus: peace, return and property. *Journal of Refugee Studies, 23*(2), pp. 238–259.

Sommers, T., 2012. *Relative justice: cultural diversity, free will, and moral responsibility*. Princeton: Princeton University Press.

Stewart, M., 1997. *The time of the gypsies*. Boulder, CO: Westview.

Sundnes, A., 2004. Sparrer kontra fighter. *Tidsskrift for ungdomsforskning, 4*(2), pp. 3–19.

Takle, M., 2012. The Treaty of Lisbon and the European Border Control Regime. *Journal of Contemporary European Research, 8*(3), pp. 280–299.

Varoufakis, Y., 2011. *The global minotaur: America, Europe and the future of the global economy*. 2nd edn. Chicago: University of Chicago Press Economics Books.

Williams, R., 1981. *The sociology of culture*. Chicago: University of Chicago Press.

Wilson, R., 2012. *The urgency of intercultural dialogue in a Europe of insecurity*. Paper presented at the CRONEM 8th Annual Conference. The future of multiculturalism: Structures, Integration Policies and Practices. 26–27 June, 2012. University of Surrey, Guildford.

2 Mapping the cultural turn in (in)security discourses

Highlighting the path for restorative justice

Brunilda Pali

Introduction

Following on from the first chapter, which contextualised the cultural turn in both social sciences and policies, this chapter addresses in particular the merging of the cultural turn with the (in)security discourses. A product of researchers, practitioners, policy makers, media and governments in different places and periods, security will be conceived here as a particular assemblage of discourses and practices.

The chapter argues that both the produced and the emerging cultural diversity introduce challenges related to security and justice, calling for better communication and participatory approaches that would support the handling of social conflicts while aiming at reducing uncertainty, restoring trust and promoting cooperative actions. As restorative justice is being promoted (see Chapter 4) as an approach that aims to counteract the (in)security discourses in intercultural contexts, I sketch here some critical perspectives on security which offer useful insights that can support the agenda of restorative justice, both strategically and normatively. I approach the perspectives as complementary to each other, in the sense that they all contribute towards understanding, and I think that the differences between them have usually been presented as more conflicting than they need to be.

In the first section, I focus briefly on security as a threat to collective identity, perceived as a sort of exceptional politics. In the second section, I elaborate further the merging of security with notions of 'cultural difference' by turning to the work of Michel Foucault, looking at security as a routinised biopolitical apparatus. In the third section, I move on towards ways of thinking about security that might be more fruitful for conceiving the contribution of restorative justice, by linking the framework of 'immunisation' with the notion of conviviality. In the fourth section, I discuss further normative approaches needed when thinking about security, and finally I conclude the chapter by highlighting a possible path for restorative justice.

Security as a threat to collective identity: exceptional politics

The end of the Cold War challenged the traditional assumption that security could be understood and practised only within an interstate framework. The widening of the security agenda has led to a convergence between internal security and external security, which in Western Europe has become more evident in the securitisation of migration, the process in which migration is constructed as a security threat (a threat to employment, welfare, housing, borders, bodily safety, law and order, moral values, collective identities, and cultural homogeneity) (Huysmans, 1995; Bigo, 2000; Ceyhan and Tsoukala, 2002; Faist, 2004). This merging relies upon the fear that cultural difference threatens societal identity, leading to social breakdown. It is thus seen as rational and legitimate to preserve one's culture through the exclusion of other cultural groups. In this process, societies become reified and treated as constant and unchanging.

Developed as a conceptual approach by a group of scholars affiliated with the Copenhagen Peace Research Institute (COPRI), 'societal security' was primarily related to the ability of a society to survive and persist in its essential character (identity) under changing conditions and possible or actual threats (Buzan *et al.*, 1998). This notion has been criticised on the grounds that clashes over identity might not be the cause, but the outcome, of a process through which economic and political conflicts are reframed as conflicts of identity (McSweeney, 1999, p. 73).

Despite this critique, the Copenhagen School with its approach of securitisation was very successful in moving beyond the objectivist accounts of security towards a discursive account. The most important argument derived from the approach of securitisation is that by securitising an issue or putting it on the security agenda through a socially and politically successful speech act, the public authorities present it to audiences as an existential threat and persuade them that it requires emergency and high-priority measures by justifying exceptional actions outside the normal bounds of political procedure, leaving the realm of political deliberation and law for the realm of securitisation (Buzan *et al.*, 1998, p. 24). The securitisation approach offers, therefore, important tools and resources for understanding how policy makers legitimise practices of exceptionalism and for contesting them (C.A.S.E. Collective, 2006, p. 466).

Giorgio Agamben (2005) has argued that the state of exception today has become a paradigm of government or, in other words, a 'permanent state of exception'. While originally the features of the 'state of exception' were its absolute necessity and its temporary character, today both these features have been reversed. In other words, if its origins lie in an exception, the apparatus of security becomes the new norm, functioning like other bureaucratic organisations, by reproducing itself (Ragazzi, 2015). The Paris School of critical security studies has contributed to the securitisation analysis by moving the focus towards a material understanding of security as a 'technique of government' that can take multiple forms, emphasising the routinised and diffuse processes and practices of security instead of its exceptional aspects (C.A.S.E. Collective, 2006). This perspective has accentuated risk as a routine instrument of governance rather than the articulation of existential threat as leading to a 'state of emergency'. In the following section I will elaborate further on the merging of security with notions of 'cultural difference' by turning to the work of Michel Foucault, the main source of inspiration for the Paris School of security studies.

Security as a biopolitical apparatus: routinised politics

As noted in the previous section, one of the most striking things about the security discourse in the post-Cold War era has been the prominence and pervasiveness of the notions of culture and identity. The cultural turn has not been exclusive to the security discourse, but this merging is particularly worrying for obvious reasons. We need, therefore, to understand more profoundly the implications of both the inflation and the reification of the notion of cultural difference today. Despite our living under a differential ideology which celebrates rather than denies differences, this proliferation of differences of identity (culture, ethnicity, religion, etc.) is defined in a heavily deterministic and hierarchical manner, and as such, introduces patterns of exclusion at all levels. According to Slavoj Žižek (2008), politics become culturalised when differences conditioned by political inequality or economic exploitation are neutralised into cultural differences and naturalised into different 'ways of life', which are given and therefore cannot be overcome.

This culturalised politics relies on the presupposition of cultural difference as the foundational basis of identity and belonging, a presupposition that entails an understanding of culture that is essentialised, reified, bounded, biologised, inherited, static, consensual and uniformly shared by all members of a group (Gilroy, 1987; Strathern, 1995; Banton, 1996; Hannerz, 1999; Wikan, 1999; Grillo, 2003; Gullestad, 2004). A large number of scholars have interpreted this discursive shift towards a culturalised politics as a symptom of a 'new racism' through which notions of racial difference are increasingly concealed inside language about culture, whereby cultural fitness contours the new lines of political struggle (see Barker, 1981; Seidel, 1986; Policar, 1990; Taguieff, 1990; Balibar, 1991; Todorov, 1993; Stolcke, 1995; Lentin, 2005). The defining features of the new racism are incommensurability (the idea of differences as unbridgeable and incommunicable), that relations between cultures are by nature hostile and mutually destructive, and that cultural pluralism will lead inevitably to conflict (Stolcke, 1995).

While many have treated racism as an aberration, a failure of modernity or an exception, or as external to democratic states, a few important writers, such as Hannah Arendt (1966), Zygmunt Bauman (1989, 1991), Gilles Deleuze and Felix Guattari (1987) and Michel Foucault (2003, 2007, 2008) have shown that, far from being external to the capitalist liberal–democratic nation-state, modern racism was a consequence of modernity. In light of such an argument, especially Foucault's understanding of racism becomes particularly useful. Foucault's reading of racism is inextricable from the concept of biopower, a concept that refers to the intense and direct involvement established between political dynamics and human life. Biopolitics, then, is a form of politics concerned with the life of its population as its new political object of governance, where population is seen as a biological and vital species whose life preservation becomes the primary objective of political action (Foucault, 2003). Considered a natural entity, the population escapes the sovereign's direct action and intervention, and comes to be acted upon in terms of apparatuses (*dispositif*)[1] of security.

Under this governmental mode of power that has population as its object and the apparatuses of security as its technique, we see the emergence of a completely different problem, no longer of fixing and demarcating the territory, but of allowing circulations to take place, of controlling them, sifting the good and the bad, ensuring that things are always in movement, in such a way that the inherent dangers of the circulation are cancelled out (Foucault, 2007, p. 65). Given that the field of interventions for security *dispositif* seems, therefore, to be organised around the question of how things should circulate or not circulate, it is not surprising that security and migration are tightly linked together. But why in such an obsessive way and coupled with cultural difference, or, in other words, why this return of racism (as culturally disguised)?

Foucault argues that biopower as a form of power promoting life could not have been integrated into the technologies of power without introducing means of division and hierarchisation, of subdividing populations into subspecies. The mission to cultivate life entails the imperative to destroy 'the other', however that is defined: the abnormal, the deviant, the diseased, the migrant and so on. Foucault argues that as biopower developed to ensure the survival of the population as a whole, the modern Western states have become racist, appealing to a clear distinction between a homogeneous 'us' and a heteronomous Other, mobilising entire populations against races perceived as threats to their purity and their health. As Shein (2004, p. 6) notes, 'viewing enemies as biological dangers is crucial to Foucault's argument regarding racism and biopower because it explains the identification of external and internal threats to the population'. Under a biological metaphor of the social body, killing one's enemies is therefore no longer only a right (as it was under sovereign forms of power), but rather, an obligation, because they are thought to impede the survival of the organism. It is 'a racism that society will direct against itself, against its own elements and its own products. This is an internal racism of permanent purification, and it will become one of the basic dimensions of social normalisation' (Foucault, 2003, pp. 61–62). The merging of external security with internal security (see Bigo, 2000) is also not a surprising development according to this interpretation, when notions of security and the defence of society are invoked to preserve the destiny of a species, justifying and legitimising violence.

Reading security as an apparatus in a modern biopolitical governmentality means understanding security as a constitutive feature of Western democracies (instead of framing security as outside politics, or as an exception). The governmentality approach emphasises how the exception to the rule does not lie outside the modern state, but is, rather, well embedded within it (see Ewald, 1991;

Salter, 2008). The implications of this analysis are that if the security apparatus and racism as a biopolitical technology are constitutive elements of our democracies instead of exceptional features, the options for countering some of their effects and the role of restorative justice therein must be adequately thought and understood, but it is unlikely that simple solutions will suffice. Other scholars have contributed further to our understanding of security, in ways that might be more fruitful for conceiving the contribution of restorative justice. I will more specifically link here the framework of 'immunisation' with recent literature on conviviality.

Security as immunity: convivial politics?

The Italian philosopher Roberto Esposito (2008, 2012) has complemented the Foucauldian analysis of biopower with the 'paradigm of immunisation'. The notion of immunity encompasses attempts that are made to draw a mark between self and other, communal and foreign, normal and pathological, and order and disorder, especially in times of crisis and anxiety. Esposito's particular thesis is that immunity is a reaction to community. Community, for him, refers to a common *munus*, which can mean both gift and obligation towards another. This is an explicit attempt to counter the definitions of community as something which we share and have in common, or a common belonging, identity and ownership. Defined as a common obligation towards one another, as a giving up of the proper, as a being in common, community exposes each of us to a contact with another, in the face of which a process of immunisation is activated. For Esposito (2008), therefore, we have to think the idea of community (*communitas*) and that of immunity (*immunitas*) as reciprocal. He argues that 'if *communitas* binds individuals to something that pushes them beyond themselves, *immunitas* reconstructs their identity by protecting them from a risky contiguity with the other, relieving them of every obligation towards the other' (Esposito, 2012, p. 49).

According to Esposito, while immunity in itself is necessary for the protection of life and safeguards the individual and collective body, if it is carried past a threshold (with regard to risk and insecurity), it becomes a form of autoimmunity, slowing down and eventually destroying the growth and development of a collective body. Using, therefore, immunological analogies, he argues that 'a surplus of defence with regard to elements outside the organism turns against the organism, with potential lethal effects' (2012, p. 62). Moving from the realm of disease to the realm of immigration, according to Esposito, confirms this tendency: the fact that the flows of immigrants are thought to be one of the worst dangers for our societies suggests how central the immunitary question is becoming. Under this frame, new walls and dividing lines are erected against something amorphous that seems to threaten our biological, social and environmental identity. But an extremely fenced and walled community would be, according to Esposito's arguments, only a 'perversion of the idea of community into its opposite' (2012, p. 43).

In reflecting further on the fact that security has become not only one among the different existing governmentalities, but an obsession, Esposito (2012) points out that we are not simply dealing with an increase in the attention we pay to danger, but rather, the usual relation between danger and protection has been reversed: no longer does the presence of risk generate the demand for protection, but the demand for protection artificially generates the sensation of risk. This has been pushed to the extreme by the idea of a preventative war, where war is no longer the exception or a last resort, but the sole form of global coexistence. In this anthropological frame, dominated by the persistence of insecurity-politics, it is fear, argues Esposito, that becomes the (only) glue that holds society together. Elisabeth Young-Bruehl (2006, p. 62) has argued how dangerous and problematic it is when vague phrases such as 'war on drugs', 'war on terror' or 'war on crime', where no enemies are named, start to circulate, because 'the door is open to limitless war outside all rules of war'. Other scholars have pointed to similar problematic developments in the realms of preventative justice (Zedner, 2007; Ashworth and Zedner, 2014) or the preventative state (Janus, 2004) that lead us further into security societies.

Reading security as an immunitary apparatus in a modern biopolitical governmentality frame bridges the gap between 'security as an exception' and 'security as a routine' by showing how the exception becomes the routine and the routine the exception, and how they co-constitute each other. There are additional advantages of reading security within an immunitarian frame, which points to as problematic not the idea of security itself, but its obsessive and autoimmunitarian tendencies. In other words, just as there is danger in pursuing security to the point of destruction of community, there is just as much danger in the idea that we can do away with the pursuit of security completely. Another concept that mirrors to a certain degree the notions of community/immunity as proposed by Esposito is conviviality. Originating from Ivan Illich's work *Tools for conviviality*, conviviality is based on the Latin roots of 'living with'. Using the notion as an alternative to the notions of multiculturalism, identity and culturalised politics, Paul Gilroy (2004, p. xi) has described the process of conviviality as processes of 'cohabitation and interaction that have made multiculture an ordinary feature of social life'. Conviviality, therefore, for Gilroy, is a social pattern in which different metropolitan groups dwell in close proximity and where their racial, linguistic and religious particularities do not add up to insuperable problems of communication. Rather, they become unremarkable, ordinary, mundane.

The notion is also an alternative to the more celebratory and politically correct viral notion of diversity, which, while attempting to challenge the links of conflict (or deficit) and interculturality, makes diversity seem, naively, a sheer matter of curiosity and strengths represented best under a rainbow type of metaphor. Conviviality, on the other hand, has been characterised further by a fine balance between building relations across difference and keeping a distance, both avoidance of contact and engagement, boundary-crossing and interethnic solidarities accompanied by local conflicts, ethnic exclusion and immunitary forms of boundary maintenance, conflict and friendliness. Yearning for human togetherness, and tensions and conflict constituting community life, all have been shown to coexist, relating at the same time also to people's basic need for protection and security (Vigneswaran, 2014), especially under the uncertainties which characterise and shape local convivial interactions.

Thus, besides curiosity and openness towards 'the other', it has been argued that indifference to ethnic or cultural differences might also be a mode of 'dealing with diversity' (van Leeuwen, 2010). This becomes especially visible in super-diverse contexts, where pragmatism often takes the lead, as treating people differently according to their backgrounds becomes almost meaningless in such contexts because everybody comes from elsewhere (Vertovec, 2007). Differences are therefore acknowledged as a matter of fact, and the superficial acceptance of the others does not always translate into a deeper interest in each other, because actively engaging with differences might go beyond one's capacity and might be grounded in attempts to avoid tension and conflict. Neal *et al.* (2013) describe these 'mundane competencies for living cultural differences' as 'cool conviviality' or 'light engagement'. Noble (2009) refers to acceptance of people who are different as 'unpanicked multiculturalism', contrasting it with the 'panicked multiculturalism' which dominates public discourses.

Being slightly more pessimistic about the 'cool conviviality', research on social capital has also shown that rising diversity will in time reduce trust and lead to social isolation, where inhabitants withdraw from collective life (Putnam, 2007, pp. 149–151). The most important implication of Putnam's research on social capital is that diversity in the long run will not necessarily cause different group solidarities, but will reduce solidarities altogether. Another problem, which is rarely problematised enough, thus emerges as striking: withdrawal from social life and collective and cooperative action. Scholarship that deals with social capital and cooperative actions has argued that trust is an essential element of cooperation. Distinguishing between subjective and objective conditions of trust, Susan Dimock (1997) argued that while subjective conditions of trust depend on personal knowledge of the person to be trusted, objective conditions must be in place for our relations to people who are strangers to us, something she calls 'metatrust' or a 'trust-in-trust' (p. 51). When considering withdrawal from social life, then, we are talking about 'metatrust', not the familial, or localised, trust which we can argue, on the contrary, is an extremely promoted type of trust under capitalism, with families and small communities being responsibilised and empowered to support each other and deal with their affairs. Research that has focused largely on the impact on diversity on *metatrust* has almost always argued that it is not diversity in itself, but unequal diversity and socio-economic inequality, that reduces metatrust (see Alesina and La Ferrara, 2002; Uslaner, 2003; Gesthuizen *et al.*, 2009; Portes and Vickstrom, 2011). These findings seem to suggest that only robust welfare state institutions and their universal public services (as compared with needs-testing, selective or means-testing) increase metatrust, and as a result, lead to cooperation (see Ragazzi, 2015). Nevertheless, even under optimal conditions, cooperation does not appear to be something that occurs organically and naturally, but requires constant labour as well as technical and semi-formal organisation (social craftsmanship).

Reclaiming justice: emancipatory politics

Arguably, the securitisation approach and the governmentality approach to security are helpful in diagnosing how security takes difference for a spin, in both exceptional terms and constitutional terms. Beyond the contribution of their diagnoses, both approaches have been criticised for their lack of normative commitment and concrete proposals in relation to security. They have also been criticised for thinking about security in an exclusively negative way, one willing to wish it away through de-securitisation and the other claiming that we are doomed to live with it everywhere. While both the immunitary reading of security and the convivial approach provide a more balanced approach, further normative approaches can be useful when thinking about security. Such an approach, coming from the Aberystwyth school of security, proposes that the axis of security studies should be the emancipation of individuals from what Ken Booth has termed the conditions of insecurity (1997, 2004). According to this approach, the study of security must be oriented towards the identification, analysis and redressing of the insecurities affecting individuals and groups in particular contexts (Booth, 2004, p. 7), where insecurity is seen as constituted of a network of oppressive relations and structures (economic, social and political) that determines the lives of individuals and groups.

There are obvious similarities in this approach to what Nancy Fraser (1996) has called the political aspect of justice. According to her, overcoming injustice means dismantling institutionalised obstacles that prevent some people from participating on a par with others as full partners in social interaction. This idea of emancipation can also be linked to Slavoj Žižek's call for a new global solidarity based in emancipatory struggle, a struggle in which 'it is not the cultures in their identity which join hands, it is the repressed, the exploited, the suffering, that "parts of no–part" of every culture which come together in a shared struggle' (2008, pp. 133–134). In similar terms, Judith Butler (2004) has argued for moving beyond identity politics by proposing the recognition of 'precariousness' as a shared condition of all human life. Only a recognition of shared precariousness, according to her, introduces strong normative commitments of equality and invites a more robust universalising of rights that seeks to address basic human needs for food, shelter, and other conditions for persisting and flourishing. Linking the existential conception of 'precariousness' with the more political notion of 'precarity', Butler argues that life requires various social and economic conditions to be met in order to be sustained as a life. It implies that one's life is always in the hands of others, a dependency on people we know, barely know, or know not at all. And it is, in her view, the differential allocation of precarity that forms the point of departure for a politics that exceeds the categories of identity.

More direct efforts have been made by scholars to either challenge the primacy of security discourses by emphasising counter-values like ambiguity

(De Lint and Virta, 2004) or 'living with risk' (O'Malley, 2004), by focusing on everyday security (Crawford and Hutchinson, 2016) or by promoting a notion of positive security that relies on human connectedness, local capacity building and spiritual order (Schuilenburg and van Steden, 2014). Scholars within criminology have also argued and suggested that restorative justice may be able to provide an approach to justice that can bridge a moral approach for confronting the past with a risk-based, instrumental and security-oriented approach to governing the future (Shearing, 2001; O'Malley, 2006; Crawford, 2015). Nevertheless, the restorative justice scholars have been cautious not to emphasise this link too strongly and too often. Or, if the link is to be celebrated, it must come with some qualifications.

Conclusions: or which path for restorative justice?

To conclude this chapter, I would like to elaborate more concretely some ideas that point to possible ways we can imagine restorative justice to contribute to security in intercultural settings. Based on both the discourses and approaches identified above, and the results of the ALTERNATIVE project, I can envision this contribution as following two main directions.

The first would be to challenge the primacy of security as a political project altogether and to focus instead on the primacy of justice. Recent trends in crime control and management indicate, worryingly, a move towards a 'security society' even at the heart of the criminal justice system, whereby crime is being redefined from an action that breaks the law to one of the other threats and risks in society that lead to insecurity, a risk that must be forestalled. When justice is governed by the utilitarian rationale of protecting the public, it dissolves into the pursuit of security and becomes preventative. Beyond penal justice, the discourse on social justice also clearly offers more robust and normative principles when compared with the discourse of security. As Lucia Zedner (2009, p. 12) argues, the pursuit of security signals an urgency and importance that stifle debate as to priorities, resources and countervailing interests. To invoke security is a move to foreclose debate as to the wisdom of a policy or the necessity of a measure. Symmetric engagement of restorative justice and security should therefore be treated with prudence. The emergency character of securitisation, the limitations of debate and the speed imposed on decision making are hardly compatible with a restorative approach based on inclusive, non-violent and inevitably slow communication, deliberation and dialogic approach (Ragazzi, 2015). Nevertheless, the need to counteract securitised dynamics is at its highest precisely when these dynamics are making restorative justice difficult. As discussed in this chapter, security feeds predominantly on the affect of fear, so other affects, such as trust and solidarity, need to be constantly promoted. Securitisation also feeds on dualistic (hierarchical and divisionary) frames of responsibility (good and evil, self and other); thus, counteracting those frames through dialogic processes that nurture complexity and shifting of subject positions becomes paramount, and restorative justice is well placed to engage in these ways.

Under obsessive concerns with security, we end up anticipating problems and avoiding them altogether, opting out and immunising (through gated communities, private schools, hunkering down and fortification) instead of doing things together to change situations, which makes social policies and social justice seem old-fashioned, not necessary and not cost-efficient. Once a normative agenda has been agreed on for the prevention of securitisation, restorative justice can contribute to influencing the conditions of success for the restoration of communication, trust and cooperative action for justice, treating restorative justice processes in intercultural settings as essentially public goods. When we look at the connection between the justice system and rising socio-economic inequalities in Europe during the last 30 years, its main problem is probably not simply the pain it delivered, but its cooptation as a tool of social control and class warfare by the social bloc hegemonised by corporate financial interests. Restorative justice, therefore, has to promote the emancipatory power of an intensive universalism in social provision and share a substantial part of the agenda of critical criminology (Ragazzi, 2015).

The proliferation of restorative justice as a technology of managing conflict may be desirable only if it accords with Christie's (1977) goal of public participation as a social activity which leads to endless norm-clarification rather than speedy crime prevention (and management). Restorative justice seems, therefore, more likely to be in need of being realigned with the emancipation approach of the security studies, which argues that the study of security must be oriented towards the identification, analysis and redressing of the insecurities affecting individuals and groups in particular contexts (Booth, 2004), rather than with the social management of crime approach. Thus, while on the one hand restorative justice requires a small state in the criminal justice sense, challenging processes of colonisation and juridification, on the other hand, it requires a strong welfare state. John Braithwaite (2000, p. 233) has argued that restorative justice stutters when the welfare state is not there to support it, because its central notions (responsibilisation, empowerment, reintegration, reparation, participation and transformation), despite all arguments that claim the opposite, depend on elements of a strong welfare state.

On the one hand, it has become clear from the comparative analysis of the ALTERNATIVE sites (see Ragazzi, 2015) that in countries with strong leadership and steering by public institutions combined with effective socio-economic redistributive policies, where we see lower levels of active participation, on the one hand, and de-securitisation of issues, on the other, restorative justice seems to act as a complementary corrective, contributing (through improved communication and dialogue) towards a more effective representation of interests and identities of stakeholders, including a partial reappropriation of conflicts, strengthening public provision via consultation and more effective representation where these are weak in order to counter the further colonisation of the lifeworld, funding-driven logic, cutting civic organisations off from their bases, and so on. On the other hand, in countries where higher levels of active participation and mobilisation in the presence of weaker social public provision are potentially open to exclusionary practices, are associated with heightened perceptions of insecurity and are more prone to securitising dynamics, restorative justice (in particular, peacemaking circles or social forms of mediation) might contribute towards strengthening social solidarity between stakeholders, building, bridging and restoring trust, by increasing the sense of fairness in the process and improving the perceptions of safety.

Second, despite its focus on the primacy of justice (and social equality), restorative justice can contribute to elaborating alternative ideas of how security can be pursued. I argue that it is necessary to move away from, or at least correct, an idea of security based on an excessive focus on technology, surveillance and control, which produce feelings of insecurity, and instead towards an idea of security that is less paranoiac and nourishes human relations through participation, encounter and dialogue, moving towards more positive and sustainable ideas of security, based on elaborating norms, restoring relations, building trust and promoting cooperation. This focus can shatter the current immunitary tendencies that characterise both the security discourse and social insecurity. Therefore, by challenging the idea of 'cultural difference' as insecurity, while recognising the impact of the uncertainty these differences create in social environments, restorative justice can contribute to the unveiling of relations of power in communities and especially focus on the differences which are conditioned by political inequality or economic exploitation, thus moving beyond a 'culturalised politics', while at the same time working on the reduction of uncertainty that may result from sustained open communication and restoration of trust, empowering alternative discourses and local leaders able to challenge the credibility of securitising actors, and de-coupling socio-economic inequality from cultural diversity through cooperative action for social justice.

Finally, security discourses (especially in intercultural communities) risk pushing towards the isolation and hunkering down of communities into immunitary forms of coexistence, where inhabitants withdraw from collective life. Therefore, the role of restorative approaches as a counteracting force for these tendencies and in becoming a revitaliser of communities is extremely important. The multiplication and transformation of common spaces become important, especially in the light of the role of public space in the proliferation of conflict. The 'community' that is to be revitalised (or created) must nevertheless be different from the close bounded community usually understood as a 'common being', and more like a convivial 'being together' or 'being in common'. Notions that challenge not the idea of difference but constant and perpetual division and hierarchisation in societies, such as *communitas*, conviviality and precarity, must be developed and elaborated. Alternative ways of living together, or doing things together, will not just happen organically, given the forces and forms of power that push and pull communities in certain directions. It is, rather, more likely that forms of social craftsmanship will be strongly needed, and this is where the role of restorative justice becomes important, in countering at the same time societal divisions and societal withdrawal by nourishing trust. As elaborated above, to do this, the starting point seems to be putting things into a perspective of social justice and embedding subjectivities in a system of political economy. Understanding justice as multidimensional shows how questions of distribution, recognition and representation cannot be understood separately, and therefore, there are multiple levels where social craftsmanship can take place: at the level of material production and redistribution issues, at the level of framing of subjectivities, and at the level of participation, cooperation and solidarity.

Note

1 By the term 'apparatus', Foucault (1980, p. 194) means the network or system of relations that can be established among these heterogeneous and diverse phenomena: 'discourses, institutions, architectural forms, regulatory decisions, laws, administrative measures, scientific statements, philosophical, moral and philanthropic propositions', which are linguistic, extra-linguistic and non-linguistic.

References

Agamben, G., 2005. *State of exception*. Chicago: The University of Chicago Press.

Alesina, A. and La Ferrara, E., 2002. Who trusts others? *Journal of Public Economics*, 85(2), pp. 207–234.

Arendt, H., [1951] 1966. *The origins of totalitarianism*. New York and London: Harcourt Brace.

Ashworth, A. and Zedner, L., 2014. *Preventive justice*. Oxford: Oxford University Press.

Balibar, E., 1991. Racism and nationalism. In: E. Balibar and I. Wallerstein, eds, *Race, nation, class: Ambiguous identities*. London: Verso, pp. 37–67.

Banton, M., 1996. The cultural determinants of xenophobia. *Anthropology Today*, 12(2), pp. 8–12.

Barker, M., 1981. *The new racism: Conservatives and the ideology of the tribe*. London: Junction Books.

Bauman, Z., 1989. *Modernity and the Holocaust*. Cambridge: Polity.

Bauman, Z., 1991. *Modernity and ambivalence*. Cambridge: Polity.

Bigo, D., 2000. When two become one: Internal and external securitisations in Europe. In: M. Kelstrup and M. Williams, eds, *International relations theory and the politics of European integration: Power, security and community*. London: Routledge, pp. 171–204.

Booth, K., 1997. Security and self: Reflections of a fallen realist. In: M. C. Williams and K. Krause, eds, *Critical security studies: Concepts and cases*. Minneapolis: University of Minnesota Press, pp. 83–121.

Booth, K., 2004. Realities of security: Editor's introduction. *International Relations*, 18(1), pp. 5–8.

Braithwaite, J., 2000. The new regulatory state and the transformation of criminology. *British Journal of Criminology*, 4, pp. 222–238.

Braithwaite, J. and Rashed, T., 2014. Nonviolence and reconciliation among the violence in Libya. *Restorative Justice*, 2(2), pp. 185–204.

Butler, J., 2004. *Precarious life: The powers of mourning and violence*. London: Verso.

Buzan, B., Waever, O. and de Wilde, J., 1998. *Security: A new framework for analysis*. London: Lynne Rienner.

C.A.S.E. Collective. 2006. Critical approaches to security in Europe: A networked manifesto. *Security Dialogue*, 37(4), pp. 443–487.

Ceyhan, A. and Tsoukala, A., 2002. The securitisation of migration in Western societies: Ambivalent discourses and policies. *Alternatives: Global, Local, Political*, 27(1), pp. 21–39.

Christie, N., 1977. Conflicts as property. *British Journal of Criminology*, 17(1), pp. 1–15.

Crawford, A., 2015. Temporality in restorative justice: On time, timing and time-consciousness. *Theoretical Criminology*, 19(4), pp. 470–490.

Crawford, A. and Hutchinson, S., 2016. Mapping the contours of 'everyday security': Time, space and emotion. *British Journal of Criminology*, forthcoming 2016.

De Lint, W. and Virta, S., 2004. Security in ambiguity: Towards a radical security politics. *Theoretical Criminology*, 8(4), pp. 465–489.

Deleuze, G. and Guattari, F., 1987. *A thousand plateaus. Capitalism and schizophrenia*. Minneapolis: The University of Minnesota Press.

Dimock, S., 1997. Retributivism and trust. *Law and Philosophy*, 16(1), pp. 37–62.

Esposito, R., 2008. *Bios: Biopolitics and philosophy*. Minnesota: University of Minnesota Press.

Esposito, R., 2012. *Terms of the political. Community, immunity, biopolitics*. Fordham: Fordham University Press.

Ewald, F., 1991. Insurance and risk. In: G. Burchell, C. Gordon, and P. Miller, eds, *The Foucault effect: Studies in governmentality*. Chicago: University of Chicago Press, pp. 197–210.

Faist, T., 2004. The migration–security nexus. International migration and security before and after 9/11. Willy Brandt Series of Working Papers in International Migration and Ethnic Relations 4/03, Malmo University.

Foucault, M., 1980. The confession of the flesh. In: C. Gordon, ed. *Power/knowledge: Selected interviews and other writings*. New York: Pantheon, pp. 194–228.

Foucault, M., 2003. Society must be defended. *Lectures at the Collège de France, 1975–1976*. London: Penguin.

Foucault, M. 2007. Security, territory, population. *Lectures at the Collège de France, 1977–1978*. London: Palgrave Macmillan.

Foucault, M., 2008. The birth of biopolitics. *Lectures at the Collège de France, 1978–1979*. London: Palgrave Macmillan.

Fraser, N., 1996. Social justice in the age of identity politics: Redistribution, recognition, and participation. Paper presented at the Tanner lectures on human values delivered at Stanford University, 30 April – 2 May.

Gesthuizen, M., Van Der Meer, T. and Scheepers, P., 2009. Ethnic diversity and social capital in Europe: Tests of Putnam's thesis in European countries. *Scandinavian Political Studies*, 32(2), pp. 121–142.

Gilroy, P., 1987. *There ain't no black in the Union Jack: The cultural politics of race and nation*. London: Hutchinson.

Gilroy, P., 2004. *After empire: Melancholia or convivial culture?* London: Routledge.

Grillo, R., 2003. Cultural essentialism and cultural anxiety. *Anthropological Theory*, 3(2), pp. 157–173.

Gullestad, M., 2004. Blind slaves of our prejudices: Debating 'culture' and 'race' in Norway. *Ethnos*, 69, pp. 177–203.

Hannerz, U., 1999. Reflections on varieties of culturespeak. *European Journal of Cultural Studies*, 2, pp. 393–407.

Huysmans, J., 1995. Migrants as a security problem: Dangers of 'securitizing' societal issues. In: R. Miles and D. Thranhardt, eds, *Migration and European integration: The dynamics of inclusion and exclusion*. London: Pinter, pp. 53–72.

Illich, I., 1973. *Tools for conviviality*. New York: Harper and Row

Janus, E.S., 2004. The preventive state, terrorists and sexual predators: Countering the threat of a new outsider jurisprudence. *Criminal Law Bulletin*, 40, p. 576.

Lentin, A., 2005. Replacing 'race', historicising 'culture' in multiculturalism. *Patterns of Prejudice*, 39(4), pp. 379–396.

McSweeney, B., 1999. *Security, identity, and interests: A sociology of international relations*. Cambridge: Cambridge University Press.

Neal, S., Bennett, K., Cochrane, A. and Mohan, G., 2013. Living multiculture: Understanding the new spatial and social relations of ethnicity and multiculture in England. *Environment and Planning C: Government and Policy*, 31(2), pp. 308–323.

Noble, G., 2009. Everyday cosmopolitanism and the labour of intercultural community. In: A. Wise and S. Velayutham, eds, *Everyday multiculturalism*. Basingstoke: Palgrave Macmillan, pp. 46–65.

O'Malley, P., 2004. *Risk, uncertainty and government*. London: GlassHouse.

O'Malley, P., 2006. Risk and restorative justice: Governing through the minimisation of harms. In: I. Aertsen, T. Daems and L. Robert, eds, *Institutionalising restorative justice*. Cullompton: Willan, pp. 216–236.

Policar, A., 1990. Racism and its mirror images. *Telos*, 83, pp. 88–108.

Portes, A. and Vickstrom, E., 2011. Diversity, social capital, and cohesion. *Annual Review of Sociology*, 37(1), pp. 461–479.

Putnam, R., 2007. E pluribus unum: Diversity and community in the twenty-first century. The 2006 Johan Skytte Prize Lecture. *Scandinavian Political Studies*, 30(2), pp. 137–174.

Ragazzi, M., 2015. Report on comparative analysis in the action research sites. Deliverable 8.5. ALTERNATIVE project. KU Leuven.

Salter, M.B., ed. 2008. *Politics at the airport*. Minneapolis: University of Minnesota Press.

Schuilenburg, M. and van Steden, R., 2014. Positive security: A theoretical framework. In: M. Schuilenburg, R. van Steden and B. Oude Breuil, eds, *Positive criminology: Reflections on care, belonging and security*. Den Haag: Eleven, pp. 19–33.

Seidel, G., 1986. Culture, nation and 'race' in the British and French New Right. In: R. Levitas, ed., *The ideology of the New Right*. Cambridge: Polity.

Shearing, C.D., 2001. Punishment and the changing face of the governance. *Punishment and Society*, 3(2), pp. 203–220.

Shein, A., 2004. A Foucauldian explanation of racism beyond Foucault's. Cited in Ball, S. J., 2013. *Foucault, power, and education*. New York: Routledge.

Stolcke, V., 1995. Talking culture: New boundaries, new rhetorics of exclusion in Europe. *Current Anthropology*, 36(1), Special Issue: Ethnographic Authority and Cultural Explanation, pp. 1–24.

Strathern, M., 1995. Comments: Talking culture. *Current Anthropology*, 36(1), p. 16.

Taguieff, P.A., 1990. The new cultural racism in France. *Telos*, 83, pp. 109–122.

Todorov, T., 1993. *On human diversity: Nationalism, racism and exoticism in French thought*. Cambridge: Harvard University Press.

Uslaner, E.M., 2003. Trust, democracy and governance: Can government policies influence generalised trust? In: M. Hooghe and D. Stolle, eds, *Generating social capital: Civil society and institutions in comparative perspective*. New York: Palgrave Macmillan, pp. 171–190.

Van Leeuwen, B., 2010. Dealing with urban diversity: Promises and challenges of city life for intercultural citizenship. *Political Theory*, 38, pp. 631–657.

Vertovec, S., 2007. Super-diversity and its implications. *Ethnic and Racial Studies*, 30, pp. 1024–1054.

Vigneswaran, D., 2014. Protection and conviviality: Community policing in Johannesburg. *European Journal of Cultural Studies*, 17(4), pp. 471–486.

Wikan, U., 1999. Culture: A new concept of race. *Social Anthropology*, 7(1), pp. 57–64.

Young-Bruehl, E., 2006. *Why Arendt matters*. New Haven, CT and London: Yale University Press.

Zedner, L., 2007. Pre-crime and post-criminology. *Theoretical Criminology*, 11(2), pp. 261–281.

Zedner, L., 2009. *Security*. Oxford: Routledge.

Žižek, S., 2008. *Violence*. London: Profile Books.

3 In the name of security

Justice under threat or restored?

Tim Chapman

Introduction

Following the daily news, it seems that we live in dangerous times. By 'we' I am referring to those of us who live in Western democratic countries with developed economies. Many people fear the arbitrary violence of political extremists and the undefined threat posed by migrants and refugees. Less immediately, there is a general anxiety over the instability of the global economy and the risks to a sustainable global environment. National governments seem relatively impotent in the face of global economic and environmental issues. However, they are forced to respond to terrorism and migration. A politics of fear has emerged, emphasising that it is the responsibility of governments to protect their citizens from these risks. The primary strategy has been to strengthen security through the exercise of the state's coercive powers: for example, a stronger and more visible presence of armed police in public places, more intrusions into the privacy of individuals, and the construction of physical defences such as walls at borders.

This chapter inquires into whether this response weakens or excludes responses to conflicts in intercultural contexts based upon the values of justice and inclusion. Northern Ireland is used as an example in which a politics based upon fear of the other and securitisation dominates. Yet it is also a society in which restorative justice is developing to offer people the opportunity to address issues that concern them in relation to justice and social cohesion and inclusion.

Risk society

The globalisation of the economy has produced rapid changes in the free movement of capital, labour and information. For Beck (2007), this has created a 'risk society' in which people are preoccupied with security, which they expect to be delivered by their governments. Environmental risks, global financial risks and the terrorist risk are often conflated in the public's perception of migration. Climate change, war in the Middle East and in Africa, and the growing economic inequality between the developed countries and the less developed countries have resulted in the mass migration of people from the poorer areas, which often also experience political oppression and war, to the richer and more stable Western countries. The mobility of people across national borders may become the defining characteristic of modern society for years to come.

People who have lived in a country for generations tend to define their identity through a sense of belonging to a place and through a sense of citizenship and membership which entitles them to privileges over those who are defined by their experience of displacement and movement (Nail, 2015). This dichotomy between the static and those on the move can often produce and sustain conflicts within society. These may take the form of competition over scarce resources such as jobs and housing or of the difficulties arising from people of diverse cultures living in close proximity.

Beck (2007) identifies the origin of the risk society with the openness and uncertainty in modern society of a created future rather than one already defined by religion or tradition. Many risks are produced by the exploitation of rapid developments in science and technology, as Beck (1992, p. 183) asserts 'the sources of danger are no longer ignorance but knowledge'. Most discourse on risk and how to control it is highly political and dominated by mass media, politicians, social movements, writers and lawyers.

> The risk discourse is a process of selection in which one risk is given great emphasis while others are ignored. The reason why certain forms of risk are emphasised at the expense of others is that they fit a larger totality of conceptions, especially of a moral nature, that vary from culture to culture. There is no reason to believe that our conceptions of risk are detached from such social contexts. One aspect that often also applies is that a danger does not capture our attention before someone is found who can be blamed for it.
>
> (Svendsen, 2007, p. 52)

The result of this process of selection is that certain groups of people are chosen as sources of threats to wider society. They are often those groups who already suffer most from the risks that globalisation creates: the poor, the migrant, and marginalised ethnic groups.

The theory of precarity (Butler, 2004) connects insecurity with sustaining a form of power based upon the politics of fear. The process of 'precarisation' (Lorey, 2012) generates a significant section of the population who are preoccupied with security. This state of insecurity justifies forms of state control designed to protect people against threats. Standing (2010) sees those living with precariousness as constituting a new class, the 'precariat'. Their lives are characterised by insecurity, uncertainty, debt, humiliation and exclusion from active participation in politics, careers and civil society.

Feeling anxious, angry and alienated, without any stake in the future, they can be seen as a dangerous class. Once people give up on the hope for security, they may feel that they have nothing to lose. This disinhibits behaviour that would be defined as anti-social or criminal or makes them vulnerable to the influence of extremist politics. Those living with precariousness fear others living under the same conditions, and this fear can result in conflict and violence (Butler, 2004). It is this sense of precariousness and exclusion from exerting any influence over global forces that is increasingly exploited politically by both extremist and mainstream politics, as witnessed in 2016 during the 'Brexit' referendum in the UK and the presidential election campaign in the USA.

The political response to minority groups labelled as dangerous has been analysed critically through 'securitisation theory'. The language of securitisation aspires to be objective and evidence based. For example, MI5 in the UK assesses the current threat from international terrorism as 'severe'. As a consequence, steps taken to protect the public are seen as managing an objective risk rather than as political action. However, this security discourse can also include highly emotive language, such as the British prime minister's reference to 'swarms' of migrants trying to enter the UK. As Balzacq (2005, p. 177) comments, 'thus, inasmuch as security is a *logos*, that is, a linguistically manifested agency, no issue is essentially a security problem. (In)security is not an objective condition, a state of affairs that predates discourse.'

Political authority is required to establish a security discourse (Buzan *et al.*, 1998; Watson, 2009), which allows a 'state of exception' (Agamben, 2005) through which emergency measures, outside of the normal functioning of democratic decision making and scrutiny under the rule of law, are introduced. For example, after the terrorist events of 11 September 2001 in the USA, the US Patriot Act was enacted to allow the state to disregard the legal status and rights of any individual suspected of threatening the national security.

Securitisation is rarely effective in making people feel safe. As Wæver (2000, p. 253) states,

> security action on the behalf of identities typically decreases the sense of security even for those defended because problematising the security of an identity and triggering attempts to define and complete it tend to expose its contingency, incompleteness and impossibility and thus lead to further action.

Not only is the promise of complete security impossible to achieve, but the presence of visible security mechanisms (closed circuit television (CCTV), armed security forces, etc.) reminds people that they are living in a dangerous place (Guittet, 2008).

The theory of securitisation is useful in understanding how British governments responded to the violent civil conflict in Northern Ireland. Byrne (2013, p. 2) writes:

> In 1969 the Stormont government in conjunction with the British Army took the decision to construct temporary security barriers and fences as a response to the sectarian violence and disorder. These temporary structures were not initially referred to as 'peace walls' but were considered lines that demarcated territory and provided people with a sense of security. In 1971 a

> Working Group on Parades and Processions, consisting of senior politicians, military representatives and civil servants, conducted a review of the 'peace lines' in Belfast. The group knew the risks it was running from the beginning: It is an ugly thing, its continued existence creates an atmosphere of abnormality which is psychologically damaging. It emphasises and institutionalises division … and it can too readily become a crutch for the community with the abnormal becoming normal, and the search for solutions set aside for another day … we must assert that no community can continue to rely indefinitely on such methods.

Thirty-five years later, the 'peace walls' are higher and more substantial. The government aims to remove them by 2023 (25 years after the peace agreement).

During the conflict (Bew and Gillespie, 1993; McKittrick and McVea, 2000) in Northern Ireland, emergency laws were passed introducing internment without trial temporarily, increasing the powers of the police to detain people suspected of terrorist acts, establishing trials without juries and changing the rules of evidence in courts (Blackburn, 2014). There was visible evidence of security throughout the country: armoured vehicles, soldiers in full combat uniform and equipment patrolling ordinary streets, regular road blocks where car passengers' identities were checked and vehicles searched, routine bodily searches entering shops and public buildings, observation towers on hills in the countryside, and helicopters often hovering in the skies shining bright beams of light into residential areas. In addition to this overt security, the security services gained information through covert surveillance and informers within paramilitary organisations.

In spite of these security measures, buildings were destroyed by bombs and over 3000 people were killed, with many more injured and traumatised. Rather than reassuring the public, the visible security reminded them of the dangers. Furthermore, many people experienced the security measures as oppressive of their freedom and human rights. Eventually, the security forces, especially through their covert intelligence, convinced the IRA that it was never going to achieve its objective of ending British rule of Northern Ireland by force. This led to Sinn Fein committing itself to a democratic strategy to achieve its political ends.

Securitisation can never succeed in protecting people from all violence. It can be argued that it can lead eventually to the cessation of violence and the effective management of conflict. This, at least in part, explains its attraction for governments. Terrorism represents a challenge to the authority of government and its competence to maintain order. Thus, restoring people's confidence in the government's ability to govern becomes the primary purpose of a security policy, rather than either protecting the public or resolving the conflict that is causing the violence.

Dean, writing about Foucault's (2007) concept of 'governmentality', perceives risk as 'a way of representing events in a certain form so they might be made governable in particular ways, with particular technologies and for particular goals' (1999, p. 177). Simon (2007) in the field of criminology refers to this as 'governing through crime'. The way the state manages offenders and others defined as dangerous is a means of governing or exercising power over the whole population. Building on a sense of public unease, security professionals achieve a position of authority, which is difficult to challenge without access to confidential data. There is also an expanding private security industry that has a strategic economic interest in risk, in maintaining people's fears and in increasing its political influence.

Esposito understands the growing dependence upon security delivered by the state as 'the political trade-off between two fears: a reciprocal fear of each man toward the other and a fear that must push the state itself to impede the destructive proliferation of the first fear' (2013, p. 30). For Esposito, political action can lead the security system, designed to protect individuals, to become so strong that it threatens to destroy what it should be defending. As Beck (2006) explains, it is not terrorism that threatens democracy but the state's reactions to the threat of terrorism that threaten it.

While securitisation did contribute to the paramilitary organisations' ceasefires in Northern Ireland and created the opportunity for the negotiations that eventually led to the peace agreement, it did not address the underlying cultural and relational conditions that caused and sustained the conflict. The 'state of exception' (Agamben, 2005) that allowed the state to disregard people's rights, to adapt and distort the process of justice, and to contravene the normal accountability mechanisms of democracy has left a lasting legacy which continues to have a serious impact upon the social cohesion, political stability and economic prosperity of Northern Ireland. The use of informers within paramilitary organisations has caused great distress and a strong sense of injustice among victims who have realised that the security forces chose not to prevent their loved ones from being killed so as to protect a valuable source of intelligence. Other victims have seen people who are suspected of harming them being given a guarantee that they will not be prosecuted. The strategic gains of securitisation may be short term compared with the enduring effects of many personal injustices on individuals and families and ultimately, on the functioning of society.

Parallel to the strategy of securitisation by the state in Northern Ireland during the conflict, a strategic approach to security in both Republican and Loyalist working-class areas emerged out of the paramilitary organisations. Normal policing was impossible due to the fact that the police were not accepted as legitimate by many residents and were targets of paramilitary attacks. Their need to protect themselves through armoured vehicles and fort-like police stations meant that they could not develop the relationships with local people that are vital in preventing crime.

Paramilitary organisations filled this policing vacuum. Local people brought their complaints about crime to them, and they consequently dealt with the offenders through a tariff of punishments (Kennedy, 2001) including warnings, beatings, gunshot wounds through various limbs ('kneecapping'), expulsion from the community and ultimately, in a few cases, killing. Strategically (McEvoy, 2003; Monaghan, 2004), this practice of offering protection from crime gained them credibility with and authority over their communities. It reduced the risk that local people would cooperate with the police out of fear of crime. However, similarly to the state securitisation, these practices were both ultimately ineffective in reducing crime and oppressive to people's rights.

Many community groups sought alternative methods to divert young people from offending (Chapman and Pinkerton, 1987; Chapman, 1995). They were motivated by the perception that the criminal justice system had failed to protect them and that shooting children was not just. It was out of a realisation of the ineffectiveness of both the state's and the armed groups' attempts to provide security that the community-based restorative justice projects were created.

'*You can't shoot poverty*': the development of community-based restorative justice

Community restorative justice projects began to be established in the mid-1990s in a number of mainly Loyalist and Republican areas. Eriksson (2009) traces their origins to disillusionment with paramilitary punishments within both Republican and Loyalist organisations. There was clearly a contradiction between the organisations' armed struggle against the oppression of their community and the fact that the armed groups were abusing the rights of members of their own community. But the strongest argument was based upon the logic of problem solving. These draconian punishments did not work.

Activists had to persuade the paramilitary organisations to give up, or at least substantially reduce, their reliance on violence to provide security to their communities. Their approach was to ask what causes crime and then to assert that violence cannot address the underlying causes of crime; poverty, family problems, alcohol abuse and so on. As Harry Maguire, director of Community Restorative Justice Ireland, regularly states when arguing for a restorative justice approach, 'You can't shoot poverty', thus proving the limitations of the strategy.

Community-based restorative justice projects were developed in the most deprived areas of Northern Ireland and demonstrated to local people that crime and anti-social behaviour could be addressed through dialogue and mediation. As a result, paramilitary punishments decreased. Here was an example of a strategy based upon security being replaced successfully by an approach founded upon the value of justice.

The *Review of the Criminal Justice System in Northern Ireland* (Criminal Justice Review Group, 2000) stated that community-based restorative justice should be enabled to address low-level crime committed in local communities. However, because community restorative justice had its origins in paramilitary punishments and because ex-prisoners were taking a lead in the schemes, the government refused to fund the schemes or permit its agencies to cooperate with them. Concerns were also raised regarding the coercion of parties to a restorative process and the possible abuse of human rights.

It was only when Sinn Fein changed its policy on policing in 2007 that progress was possible. In 2007, protocols (Northern Ireland Office, 2007) for community-based restorative justice schemes were finally agreed. The principles underpinning the protocols were designed to conform to international standards and rights. The schemes agreed to be subject to regular inspections by the criminal justice inspectorate, to participate in an independent complaints mechanism and to undertake appropriate training.

These were all reasonable safeguards. However, the critical provision related to referrals. Community schemes had up to that point taken referrals directly from members of the community. Prior to the protocols, community-based restorative justice schemes were dealing with thousands of cases each year. The new arrangements required all referrals to community restorative justice schemes to come through the police and the Public Prosecution Service (PPS) after they had completed their investigation and assessment of each case. Table 3.1[1] shows how many cases were sent to the Public Prosecution Service by the Police Service for referral to a community-based restorative justice (CBRJ) project. The second column shows how many cases were actually referred to a CBRJ project. Over a period of five years, only nine cases were considered suitable for community-based restorative justice.

If the strengths of community restorative justice include the capacity to respond quickly and effectively to the concerns of local people regarding low-level crime and anti-social behaviour, these arrangements are severely reducing this capacity.

Colonisation of the lifeworld by the system

This account of community restorative justice and its relationship with the state in Northern Ireland can be understood as an example of what Habermas (1987) defines as the colonisation of the lifeworld by the system. Habermas's theory of communicative action provides a means of understanding the nature of restorative justice and why it tends to be marginalised by the criminal justice system. 'Lifeworld' is a concept that Habermas uses to describe everyday social life in civil society. It includes family life, and cultural and social activities. It sustains the social integration of society and the socialisation of individuals.

Table 3.1 Cases referred by the police for a possible community-based restorative justice (CBRJ) process and actual cases approved by the Public Prosecution Service (PPS) for referral to a CBRJ project

Year	*Number of suspects referred from the police to the PPS*	*Number of suspects referred from the PPS to CBRJ projects*
2010/2011	10	6
2011/2012	6	2
2012/2013	4	1
2013/2014	0	0
2014/2015	2	0
Total	22	9

The state and the market are not integrated by communicative action but through instrumental or strategic action. They are oriented towards achieving planned outcomes and avoiding unwanted consequences. In modern societies, the trend has been to increase both the regulatory power of state bureaucracies and the penetration of the market into the daily lives of ordinary people. Habermas refers to this trend as the colonisation of the lifeworld by the system.

McEvoy and Eriksson (2008) argue that the state saw community-based restorative justice as a threat to its need to control and own justice, and as a result, sought to regulate community justice initiatives. Habermas (1987) refers to this as 'juridification'. It would be inaccurate to represent community restorative justice as a pure product of the lifeworld. Communities are, of course, subject to political competition for power and control. These politics have had an impact on community restorative justice in both Republican and Loyalist communities. Furthermore, community projects are not impervious to the market. They have to 'sell' their services to funders in order to survive.

While community restorative justice is a product of the lifeworld, it is more useful to understand restorative justice in terms of its use of communicative action rather than whether it is community based or within the state. The power of the system to colonise the lifeworld is based upon its power to impose its strategic approach and outcomes and consequently to weaken the communicative action facilitated by community-based schemes.

Van Ness and Strong (2010, p. 46) distinguish the roles of government and of the community in relation to justice. They argue that government is responsible for preserving a just order, whereas community is responsible for establishing a just peace. Order can be measured in the achievement of instrumental goals measurable by crime statistics and is thus the result of strategic action. Peace is less tangible. It is derived from the quality of relationships between people living in community and from how they set about resolving conflicts and breaches of norms. Community restorative justice aimed to reduce the culture of violence within some Northern Irish communities, to restore relationships, and to clarify and reinforce the norms of the community (Eriksson, 2009).

A state system emerging from 30 years of violent conflict during which its legitimacy was challenged will be eager to demonstrate its ability to govern and to maintain order. It is in the interest of the state to promote the credibility of the Police Service of Northern Ireland (PSNI) as a modern, diverse and effective service, particularly in those areas where it has come under most criticism in the past and where community restorative justice projects are most active. In order to achieve this, the PSNI needs to demonstrate to the community that it can improve its clear-up rate of reported crime, that it can bring offenders to justice, and in so doing, that it is protecting the public. It is also important that the PSNI establishes itself as the only legitimate criminal law enforcement agency in Northern Ireland.

It was made clear to the community restorative justice schemes that unless they signed up to the protocols, they would not be funded or supported by statutory agencies. The state also imposes its strategic priorities: to improve relations between the police and alienated communities, to cut public spending and to reduce reoffending. These are legitimate goals relating to governmentality. However, they undermine the ability of restorative justice to operate effectively in the lifeworld.

In seeking funding support from statutory agencies, these projects are increasingly involved in youth work, social work and prisoner resettlement. Each of these tasks is important, but they are not core restorative justice tasks. They support the state's strategy to reduce reoffending. They support the value of security over the value of justice. Such a strategy prioritises system integration (actions consistent with a strategy) over social integration (actions consistent with people living at ease with each other).

Yet, there is evidence that social cohesion and social capital are key factors in controlling crime (Braithwaite, 1989; Bursik and Grasmick, 1993; Putnam, 2000). The enforcement of the law through the criminal justice system is necessary to protect the rights of citizens and to address serious acts of harm, which are beyond the capacity of community-based responses. However, the criminal justice system is an expensive and blunt instrument to deal with most crime and anti-social behaviour, which is local and not serious. The harm that is caused by such crime to individuals and communities cannot be satisfactorily repaired strategically by punishment or restitution. The use of state powers to enforce compliance to the law is no substitute for encouraging citizens' commitment to making things right when they have done wrong. Furthermore, by restricting the ability of community organisations to engage constructively in issues of justice, the state may actually be rendering community life less safe.

Habermas (1987) maintains that, as the lifeworld becomes weaker through domination by the system, social pathologies emerge such as a decrease in shared meanings and mutual understanding, an erosion of social bonds, an increase of feelings of helplessness and lack of belonging, an unwillingness to take responsibility for actions, and a consequent destabilisation and breakdown in social order. Those who are active in local communities in Northern Ireland will be familiar with these pathologies. A mapping exercise on behalf of Belfast City Council (Belfast City Council, 2007) found that deprived areas suffered from trauma and exclusion as a legacy of the conflict. The research concluded that these factors resulted in communities feeling overwhelmed and hopeless.

The risk is that a previously vibrant civil society and community life in Northern Ireland will lose its energy and creativity. People increasingly become passive recipients or consumers of state services rather than active participants in the process of justice. Relationships with and responsibilities to neighbours in specific situations become reduced to observing the law.

Reimagining, reprioritising and restoring justice

The argument of McEvoy and Eriksson (2008) that the state is very reluctant to delegate its control over delivering justice resonates with Christie's (1977) thesis that conflict is a resource to society that is stolen by the state and its professionals.

While it is clear that all governments should take responsibility for protecting the safety of their citizens, there are great dangers in relying on what has been described as securitisation. An over-emphasis on security can result in heightening people's fears rather than reassuring them. There is also a danger that securitisation will undermine the very values – human rights, the rule of law and justice – it is designed to protect, and may facilitate totalitarian politics.

The field of peace-building has emphasised the critical role of justice (Galtung, 1981; Reardon, 1988, 2000; Harris and Morrison, 2013). Similarly, in the context of Northern Ireland, Eyben *et al.* (2002) place equity along with diversity and interdependence as key principles of good community relations. Would there be less need for strategic action by the state to increase security if justice rather than security were the primary focus in addressing harmful conflicts, especially in intercultural settings? If so, what, then, does justice mean in this context?

A real situation facing a community in Belfast studied through the ALTERNATIVE project will serve as an example of the dilemmas that arise from different theories of justice. In 2012, the government announced that a high school located in a large housing estate was to close as a result of a strategy to rationalise provision and reduce costs. The school had played a significant role in the lifeworld of the community over many years. Generations of residents shared a common education. The school had provided employment to local people. It provided a centre for a range of community activities. After an unsuccessful campaign to save the school, the community association and local politicians pressed the government to use the site of the school for social housing. Ninety-eight new houses will be built in the estate and will be available at reasonable rents. The question that faces the local community is: to whom will these high-quality homes be allocated?

This question can be addressed through different discourses of justice. Rawls (1971, 2003) argues that the authorities should not take into consideration the class or status of the parties in deciding what is just. The distribution of the houses should be on the basis of equality of access to goods, and those in greatest need should benefit first. This form of justice is followed by the state's bureaucratic method of assessing and scoring need and allocating housing according to the highest score. In this way, the system is, as Rawls suggests, 'blind' to favouring people on any other basis than need. This is a positive corrective principle to the view that people should be privileged due to their status, power or money. As far as Rawls is concerned, as long as the houses are allocated fairly according to procedures designed to comply with the universal principles of equality of access and human rights, there can be no injustice. In this discourse, 'injustice is simply the absence of justice' (Shklar, 1990, p. 15).

Nozick (1974), on the other hand, believes that if property has been gained legitimately, individuals are entitled to use it within the rule of law to achieve their goals. In acknowledging the social processes that lead to a sense of entitlement, he would have some sympathy with the belief that the local community have earned some degree of privilege through their longstanding residence in the neighbourhood, their citizenship and tax paying. Social housing has always been seen as an entitlement in more deprived working-class communities. Not only do residents feel that they belong in the community, but they feel that their community belongs to them.

This conflict between entitlement derived from a sense of belonging and entitlement based upon equality of opportunity and need has created a dilemma for the local community-based restorative justice project. How should they understand and respond to this conflict?

As MacIntyre (1981) points out, both models take for granted that individuals rather than groups or communities are concerned with the issue at stake. He introduces the notion of desert, which, he maintains, can only be assessed in the context of a shared understanding of what is good not only for the individual but also for society, rather than what is right, as Rawls would argue.

For the formal state system, following Rawls, there is a fair system, which distributes a scarce and valued resource according to need. The state will also value the bureaucratic integrity of the system for allocating houses. From the community's point of view, these principles and procedures may undermine social integration. The community-based restorative justice project fears that, if this issue is not resolved satisfactorily and local people are not allocated a 'fair share' of the homes, people who are not seen as members of the community will not be made welcome and may become victims of hate crime. There is an element of sectarianism and racism implicit in their viewpoint. Yet they do not hold the same views about private houses to let. Social housing has a different meaning and connects historically to a sense of entitlement in working-class communities.

This dilemma highlights the tension within concepts of justice between the right and the good. Rawls' formulation of fairness, impartiality and neutrality would exclude discussion and judgements of what arrangement would lead to the common good. This is based upon the belief that moral, cultural or religious dispute has no place in a process of justice and that to avoid such dispute preserves the peace. However, this local community believes that to ignore these areas of contention will only lead in the future to conflict, which will be met by a security response by the state.

In such a situation, Habermas (1996, pp. 26–27) would recommend: 'The only way out of this predicament is for the actors themselves *to come to some understanding* about the *normative regulation of strategic interaction*' (author's italics).

By following this approach, the activists could prepare residents for possible future dialogues with newcomers so that conflict may be avoided. While Rawls' elaboration of justice as fairness (1971) was found to be of limited value to the community in this situation, it should be acknowledged that his later writing (Rawls, 1993) developed the notion of overlapping consensus as an outcome when faced with moral or cultural dissent. Following Honneth (Fraser and Honneth, 2003), the project can attempt to engage the community in recognising not only their own needs, rights and worth but also the needs, rights and value of others. The community can be prepared to recognise the other's worth rather than to see strangers as a threat. In this sense, the restorative project's mission is to prepare the ground for a process of dialogue between the current residents and the new residents in which there can be an equitable exchange of cultural capital (Bourdieu, 1993). This is a process that allows equal respect to each culture, but within the boundaries of a common set of the values and the norms required for diverse people to live together in peace. A justice that provides equality of recognition to different communities of identity and at the same time opens up membership to the other as a person entitled to rights (Benhabib, 2004) will avoid struggles for cultural domination.

So far, the argument in this chapter has been that addressing conflicts in inter-cultural contexts requires more than a security response. It is clear that what is required is an answer to the question posed by Ferrara (1999, p. x):

> What notion of justice can ensure the integration of a society of free and equal citizens who subscribe to different conceptions of the good by means of helping these citizens to solve their controversies of interest and value without appealing to any standpoint, criterion or principle external to the parties involved in the contention?

Restorative justice processes are designed not simply to consider how to restore justice and to repair what has been lost or damaged by an injustice, but also to consider what obligations the people must undertake to be accepted as members of the community (cf. Braithwaite, 1989). In return for fulfilling these obligations, the community reintegrates the other, and through this process, social inclusion is reconciled with social cohesion. This is illustrated by the following example of a restorative process studied in the ALTERNATIVE project.

In a Loyalist community in Belfast, two neighbours are in dispute. One is a local resident and the other is an Eastern European family. The dispute arose in July, when it is hot and many locals sit and have parties in their gardens, and when Protestants celebrate their cultural and political identity through putting up flags. The Eastern European family complained about rubbish falling into their garden and some bunting blowing in the wind and falling over the fence into their property. The local woman responded that they were not respecting her culture. Other residents in the street supported the local woman.

There was a risk of an escalation into violence. The house and car of the Eastern European family was damaged maliciously, and another house in the street occupied by a foreign family was vandalised. Outsiders assumed that the foreign nationals were the victims and that the local woman was at fault.

A worker from a local community organisation, who had been trained in restorative practices, was asked by a representative of the Eastern European community to intervene. The worker visited the foreign family first to listen to their story. He said that he just wanted to understand their perspective and was not taking responsibility for dealing with the complaints. They told him their story of how they had been harmed by their neighbour's actions. They had called the police, but no action was taken. The worker then spoke with the local woman next door.

Having listened to both sides of the story, the worker called a meeting inviting the local politician, another activist, two police officers, neighbourhood wardens, the local woman and her supporters, the Eastern European family, another family from the same country to support, and a family from another country who lived in the same street. Unfortunately, the original foreign family were unable to attend the meeting at the last moment, as they had to go away for a while.

During the meeting, everyone had the opportunity to tell their story and question each other. It was agreed that there were faults on both sides and that, although it had an ethnic dimension, it was really a dispute between two neighbours, both of whom were prone to conflict. The local people invited the foreign families to a local celebration and asked them to bring their food to the barbecue to share with the others. People shook hands and committed to being better neighbours in future. When the original foreign family returned, the local woman went to them, shook hands and invited them to the street party. All parties agreed that it had been a just process, which succeeded in avoiding violence and improving the security of the street.

This story illustrates that a restorative process can be very effective in not only resolving conflict but also improving community relations. The key was a reliance on communicative action. The police could only take action if a crime had been committed. Both the local community and the foreign nationals were inclined to define the conflict as cultural or racist. This would have both politicised and escalated the conflict and would probably have resulted in violence. The communicative action focused on the real issues of a specific situation rather than the general political discourse of foreign immigrants.

This is just one example of a restorative process, which addressed a conflict in an intercultural context. There were many other examples of effective processes in the community. We cannot say that a restorative process will be successful in every case. But it is important for ordinary people to take part in exemplary events in which ideas and values are implemented so as to achieve a satisfactory result. This is what Ferrara refers to as 'the force of *what is as it should be* or the force of the *example*' (author's italics) (2008, pp. 2–3) It is important, because to experience an event as it should be opens people's minds and will to the possibility that the way they have always addressed conflict could be transformed, or at least improved. It broadens people's horizons (Gadamer, 1989).

What, then, are the critical elements of this form of justice in relation to conflicts in intercultural contexts?

A focus on injustice

The legal system tends to focus on the question of what is the best way of delivering or doing justice. This has led to a concentration upon a universal set of principles and a search for a fair process, which can be applied to every case. While justice is based upon general abstract principles designed to ensure fairness, injustice is concrete, felt and experienced in specific contexts and through the narratives of individuals and groups. A formal concept of justice has also led the system to attend to facts or evidence and to focus on the offender, while neglecting or discounting the experiences, feelings and needs of victims. Ordinary people are more concerned with the question of what is the best way to undo injustice.[2]

Bauman (2007), writing about people's anxieties over health, observed that illness has come to be seen as a constant, present threat that requires permanent vigilance and precaution. He contrasts this with the view that an illness can be a single incident which is treated and from which one can recover. The restorative process enables parties to examine a specific injustice and the harm it has caused, come to a common understanding of it and agree how to undo it. This avoids it becoming overwhelming and requiring professional power and resources.

Conflicts in intercultural contexts often involve one group committing an injustice against another group. The aggrieved group feels that it has been wronged and needs that wrong to be recognised and addressed. As Gaita (2000, p. 92) stated, 'to be wronged is a distinctive and irreducible form of harm'. A restorative process takes each wrong seriously as a concrete experience rather than seeing it through universal principles of justice. It resists reducing and simplifying conflict to culture or ideology by mediating it through dialogue or, as Benhabib (2004) puts it, through democratic iterations.

Accommodate social groups

A process of justice that addresses conflict in intercultural contexts should accommodate social groups rather than attending only to individuals. It should also attend to the social context and the historical factors shaping the injustice. Benhabib (1986, p. 341) shifts the focus in encounters with the 'concrete other' from rights and entitlements typical of liberal society to needs and solidarity: 'The moral categories that accompany such interactions are those of responsibility, bonding and sharing. The corresponding moral feelings are those of love, care, sympathy, and solidarity, and the vision of community is one of needs and solidarity.' This requires a form of justice in which different groups encounter one another and communicate.

Strive for parity of participation

Fraser (Fraser and Honneth, 2003) maintains that overcoming injustice involves reforming the institutional obstacles to full participation in social life. Any process of justice that addresses conflict in intercultural settings will need to ensure that those most affected by the conflict are enabled to participate actively in its resolution. Sen (2009) also connects the process of justice with a democratic orientation that requires the engagement of informed people in interactive discussion so that different voices are heard. This discourse transforms justice from something one receives, or not, from a fair or unfair system to an action that people do when they experience what they perceive as an injustice in their lives. Similarly, Young (1990, p. 91) argues for the democratisation of justice:

> I have defined justice as the institutionalised conditions that make it possible for all to learn and use satisfying skills in socially recognised settings, to participate in decision making, and to express their feelings, experience, and perspective on social life in contexts where others can listen.

Develop capability

A participative approach requires people to have access to opportunities, resources and capabilities that enable them to participate actively in questions of justice rather than be passive recipients of the services of institutions and the protection of professionals. There is a need in a pluralist and rapidly changing society to develop people's capacity to negotiate their way through the 'sometimes overlapping and sometimes conflicting obligations that claim us and to live with the tension to which multiple identities give rise' (Sandel, 2009, p. 34). The resources that enable people to do so are found in 'the places and stories, memories and meanings, incidents and identities, that situate us in the world and give our lives their moral particularity' (Sandel, 2009, p. 34).

Nussbaum (2011) has developed this capabilities approach to doing justice. She asks the question: what is each person able to do and to be? Capabilities are the 'totality of the opportunities she has for choice and action in her specific political, social and economic situation' (Nussbaum, 2011, p. 21). This discourse of justice is based upon policies that protect and support human agency rather than treating people as passive recipients or consumers. 'In the absence of action, rights are mere words on paper' (Nussbaum, 2011, p. 65) The capability approach is confirmed by Marmot's (2009) research findings that a more just distribution of capabilities will lead to more participation in civil society as well as a more equal distribution of health. People need to be given the opportunity to practise and learn the skills of dialogue; not only advocating to have their needs attended to but also listening to the needs of others.

Communicative action

Through dialogue rather than dispute, a more multidimensional, thicker understanding of injustice emerges. This may highlight the areas of difference, but it also opens space for agreement: 'thinness and intensity go together, whereas with thickness comes qualification, compromise, complexity and disagreement' (Walzer, 1994, p. 6).

Rorty (1997), building upon Walzer's notion of thick morality, argues that people can expand their sense of justice beyond loyalty to the interests of their own group to a wider loyalty of fellow citizens. In doing so, parties in conflict create a sense of community, even if only temporarily, which may be the beginning of widening their horizon of 'people like ourselves' (Rorty, 1997, p. 18). Ferrara (1999, p. 118) conceives of a superordinate identity or enlarged point of view being formed at the intersection of contending identities, which facilitates the fulfilment of justice. His thinking suggests that the idea of an obligation or duty to the other emerges not so much from empathy for the other as from seeing oneself through the eyes of the other. Justice emerges through reflective judgement oriented towards this superordinate identity.

Enable people to move towards those whom they fear

The state systems for security and justice assume that citizens wish to be protected from what they fear and that they do not have the resources and capabilities to address harm and injustice. People tend not to trust those whom they fear and to avoid them. Yet, this attempt to immunise oneself usually makes the threat seem more dangerous and more strange. As Svendsen (2007, p. 98) states, 'Fear and mistrust become self perpetuating.'

In restorative processes, parties are invited to move towards the people whom they fear, and to meet with them and to enter into dialogue with them. Through this process, they explore the reality of what they fear, and they are enabled to reclaim definitional power over what is and is not a risk to them. By reaching mutual understanding and making some commitments on how they should act towards each other in the future, a measure of trust is restored. Trust, a tangible resource in society as a form of social capital (Fukuyama, 1996), is a more flexible and efficient way of managing the unpredictability of life than constantly calculating risk (Svendsen, 2007).

Any dangerous activity requires safety procedures and equipment. Seamus Heaney (1966), the Irish poet, writes of the temporary necessity of scaffolding when building:

> Masons, when they start upon a building,
> Are careful to test out the scaffolding;
> Make sure that planks won't slip at busy points,
> Secure all ladders, tighten bolted joints.
> And yet all this comes down when the job's done
> Showing off walls of sure and solid stone.

This metaphor has been used by others (Vygotsky, 1986; Bruner, 1990; White, 2007) writing about the support that people need to make difficult transformations. The practice of respecting each person equally provides a kind of scaffolding for people to cross the intercultural frontiers of conflict.

Equal respect

When justice relies on the good judgement of the parties most closely involved, the 'ideal of equal respect' is critical, according to Ferrara (1999, p. 202). By this he means that 'no one should be treated in a way that directly or indirectly suggests that his or her human dignity is of less import than that of anyone else' (Ferrara, 1999, p. 203). This entails ensuring that each party has the resources and support to participate actively in a challenging process in which they will have equal opportunity to express themselves and question others (Habermas, 1996, p. 107). A process founded on equal respect will facilitate the search for common ground.

The ideal of equal respect is based upon the value of human life inherent in each individual and the fact that injustice is an obstacle, which must be overcome if individuals are to pursue a life well lived. This value has the advantage of framing the identity of the parties in a conflict in terms of their future life narrative, who they want to be, rather than their identity in relation to the conflict, who they are being (an aggrieved victim or a defensive perpetrator). Rather than a dispute as to who is right and who is wrong, who is good and who is bad, the dialogue enables an overlapping consensus to emerge on the question of what must be done so that we can live in peace and move on with our lives.

Forget your perfect offering[3]

No form of justice is ever perfect, or, as Derrida stated, 'that is why the call for justice is never fully answered. That is why no one can say "I am just"' (1997, p. 17). But it can be 'good enough' for those who participate in it.

Notes

1 Table 3.1 has been provided with permission by Lauren Hogg from her PhD thesis 'The Impact of State Intervention on the Work of Community-based Restorative Justice Projects in Northern Ireland', Queens University Belfast.
2 I am grateful to Antony Pemberton of Tilburg University for the distinction between doing justice and undoing injustice.
3 From Leonard Cohen's song 'Anthem'.

References

Agamben, G., 2005. *State of Exception.* Chicago: University of Chicago Press.

Balzacq, T., 2005. 'The Three Faces of Securitization: Political Agency, Audience and Context', *European Journal of International Relations*, 11 (2), pp. 171–201.

Bauman, Z., 2007. *Liquid Times: Living in an Age of Uncertainty.* Cambridge: Polity.

Beck, U., 1992. *Risk Society: Towards a New Modernity.* London.

Beck, U., 2006. *Cosmopolitan Europe.* Cambridge: Polity.

Beck, U., 2007. *World at Risk.* Cambridge: Polity.

Belfast City Council. 2007. *Social Research Centre in Partnership with the Institute for Conflict Research, Mapping Exercise in Relation to ASB Pilot Final Report 3 July 2007.* Belfast City Council.

Benhabib, S., 1986. *Critique, Norm and Utopia.* New York: Columbia University Press.

Benhabib, S., 2004. *The Rights of Others: Aliens, Residents and Citizens.* Cambridge: Cambridge University Press.

Bew, P. and Gillespie, G., 1993. *Northern Ireland: A Chronology of the Troubles 1968–1993*. Dublin: Gill and Macmillan.

Blackburn, J., 2014. *Anti-Terrorism Law and Normalising Northern Ireland*. London: Routledge.

Bourdieu, P., 1993. *The Field of Cultural Production*. Cambridge, UK: Polity.

Braithwaite, J., 1989. *Crime, Shame and Reintegration*. Cambridge: Cambridge University Press.

Bruner, J., 1990. *Acts of Meaning*. Cambridge, MA: Harvard University.

Bursik, R. and Grasmick, H., 1993. *Neighbourhood and Crime: The Dimension of Effective Community Control*. Lexington, MA: Lexington Books.

Butler, J., 2004. *Precarious Life: The Powers of Mourning and Violence*. London: Verso.

Buzan, B., Wæver, O. and Japp de Wilde, 1998. *Security: A New Framework for Analysis*. London: Lynne Rienner.

Byrne, J., 2013. Another Wall of Shame in Belfast, EamonnMallie.com. http://eamonnmallie.com/2013/11/another-wall-of-shame-in-belfast/ (accessed 5 August 2016).

Chapman, T., 1995. 'Creating a Culture of Change: A Case Study of a Car Crime Project in Belfast'. In: J. Maguire, ed., *What Works: Reducing Re-Offending*. Chichester: Wiley, pp. 127–138.

Chapman, T. and Pinkerton, J., 1987. 'Contradictions in Community', *Probation Journal*, 34 (1), pp. 13–16.

Christie, N., 1977. 'Conflict as Property', *British Journal of Criminology*, 17, pp. 1–26.

Criminal Justice Review Group, 2000. *Review of the Criminal Justice System in Northern Ireland*. Belfast: HMSO.

Dean, M., 1999. *Governmentality: Power and Rule in Modern Society*. London: Sage.

Derrida, J., 1997. The Villanova Roundtable: A Conversation with Jacques Derrida. In: J. D. Caputo, ed., *Deconstruction in a Nutshell. A Conversation with Jacques Derrida*. New York: Fordham University Press.

Eriksson, A., 2009. *Justice in Transition*. Cullompton: Willan.

Esposito, R., 2013. *Terms of the Political: Community, Immunity, Biopolitics*. New York: Fordham University Press.

Eyben, K., Morrow, D., Wilson, D. and Robinson, B., 2002. *The Equity, Diversity and Interdependence Framework – A Framework for Organisational Learning and Development*. University of Ulster.

Ferrara, A., 1999. *Justice and Judgment*. London: Sage.

Ferrara, A., 2008. *The Force of the Example: Explorations in the Paradigm of Judgment*. New York: Columbia University Press.

Foucault, M., 2007. *Security, Territory, Population: Lectures at the College de France (1977–1978)*. New York: Palgrave Macmillan.

Fraser, N. and Honneth, A., 2003. *Redistribution or Recognition: A Political-Philosophical Exchange*. London: Verso.

Fukuyama, F., 1996. *Trust: The Social Virtues and the Creation of Prosperity*. New York: Free Press.

Gadamer, H.-G., 1989. *Truth and Method*, 2nd edn. London: Sheed and Ward.

Gaita, R., 2000. *A Common Humanity: Thinking about Love and Truth and Justice*. Abingdon: Routledge.

Galtung, J., 1981. 'Social Cosmology and the Concept of Peace', *Journal of Peace Research*, 18 (2), p. 183.

Guittet, E.-P., 2008. 'Military Activities inside National Territory: The French Case'. In: D. Bigo and A. Tsoukala, eds, *Terror, Insecurity and Liberty: Illiberal Practices of Liberal Regimes after 9/11*. London: Routledge, pp. 137–166.

Habermas, J., 1987. *The Theory of Communicative Action Vol 2: Lifeworld and System: A Critique of Functionalist Reason*. Boston: Beacon.

Habermas, J., 1996. *Between Facts and Norms: Contributions to a Discourse Theory of Law and Democracy*. Cambridge: Polity.

Harris, I. and Morrison, M., 2013. *Peace Education*. Jefferson, NC: McFarland and Co.

Heaney, S., 1966. *The Death of a Naturalist*. London: Faber and Faber.

Kennedy, L., 2001. *They Shoot Children, Don't They? An Analysis of the Age, Gender of Victims of Paramilitary 'Punishments' in Northern Ireland. A Report Prepared for the Northern Ireland Committee against Terror (NICAT) and the Northern Ireland Affairs Committee of the House of Commons*. http://cain.ulst.ac.uk/issues/violence/docs/kennedy01.htm (accessed 28 October 2015).

Lorey, I., 2012. *State of Insecurity: Government of the Precarious*. London: Verso.

McEvoy, K., 2003. 'Beyond the Metaphor: Political Violence, Human Rights, and "New" Peacemaking Criminology', *Theoretical Criminology*, 7(3), pp. 319–346.

McEvoy, K. and Eriksson, A., 2008. 'Who Owns Justice? Community, State and Northern Ireland Transition'. In: J. Shapland, ed., *Justice, Community and Civil Society: A Contested Terrain*. Cullompton: Willan.

MacIntyre, A., 1981. *After Virtue: A Study in Moral Theory*. Notre Dame: University of Notre Dame Press.

McKittrick, D. and McVea, D., 2000. *Making Sense of the Troubles*. London: Penguin.

Marmot, M., 2004. *The Status Syndrome: How Social Standing Affects Our Health and Longevity*. New York: Henry Holt.

Monaghan, R., 2004. '"An Imperfect Peace": Paramilitary "Punishments" in Northern Ireland', *Terrorism and Political Violence*, 16(3), pp. 439–461.

Nail, T., 2015. *The Figure of the Migrant*. Stanford: Stanford University Press.

Northern Ireland Office, 2007. *Protocol for Community-Based Restorative Justice Schemes*. Belfast: Criminal Justice.

Nozick, R., 1974. *Anarchy, State, and Utopia*. New York: Basic Books.

Nussbaum, M., 2011. *Creating Capabilities*. Cambridge, MA: Harvard University Press.

Putnam, R., 2000. *Bowling Alone: The Collapse and Revival of American Community*. Carmichael, CA: Touchstone Books.

Rawls, J., 1971. *A Theory of Justice*. Cambridge, MA: Harvard University Press.

Rawls, J., 1993. *Political Liberalism*. New York: Columbia University Press.

Rawls, J., 2003. *Justice as Fairness: A Restatement*. Cambridge, MA: Harvard University Press.

Reardon, B., 1988. *Comprehensive Peace Education*. New York: Teachers College Press.

Reardon, B., 2000. 'Peace Education: A Review and Projection'. In: B. Moon, S. Brown and M. B. Peretz, eds, *International Companion to Education*. New York: Routledge.

Rorty, R., 1997. *Justice as a Larger Loyalty*. In: R. Bontekoe and M. Stepianiants, eds, *Justice and Democracy: Cross-Cultural Perspectives*. Honolulu: University of Hawaii Press.

Sandel, M. J., 2009. *Justice: What's the Right Thing to Do?* London: Allen Lane.

Sen, A., 2009. *The Idea of Justice*. Cambridge, MA: Harvard University Press.

Shklar, J. N., 1990. *The Faces of Injustice*. New Haven and London: Yale University Press.

Simon, J., 2007. *Governing through Crime: How the War on Crime Transformed American Democracy and Created a Culture of Fear*. Oxford: Oxford University Press.

Standing, G., 2010. *The Precariat: The New Dangerous Class*. London: Bloomsbury.
Svendsen, L., 2007. *A Philosophy of Fear*. London: Reaktion Books.
Van Ness, D. W. and Strong, K. H., 2010. *Restoring Justice: An Introduction to Restorative Justice* (4th edition). New Providence, NJ: LexisNexis.
Vygotsky, L., 1986. *Thought and Language*. Cambridge, MA: MIT Press.
Wæver, O., 2000. 'The EU as a Security Actor: Reflections from a Pessimistic Constructivist on Post-Sovereign Security Orders'. In: M. Kelstrup and M. Williams, eds, *International Relations Theory and the Politics of European Integration: Power, Security, and Community*. London: Routledge.
Walzer, M., 1994. *Thick and Thin: Moral Arguments at Home and Abroad*. Notre Dame, IL: University of Notre Dame Press.
Watson, S. D., 2009. *The Securitisation of Humanitarian Migration. Digging Moats and Sinking Boats*. London and New York: Routledge.
White, M., 2007. *Maps of Narrative Practice*. New York: W. W. Norton.
Young, I. M., 1990. *Justice and the Politics of Difference*. Princeton, NJ: Princeton University Press.

4 Restorative justice

Doing justice and security?

Christa Pelikan and Ivo Aertsen

Introduction

In this chapter we will analyse, through the action research that took place in the ALTERNATIVE project, the role of restorative justice in becoming a counter-security discourse, and what is most important in being counter in the sense of doing both justice and security, that is, grounding a restorative praxis of justice and security.

We will propose 'participatory justice' as the counter-justice, the other justice we have been looking for in ALTERNATIVE, as well as 'participatory security/safety' as a counter-security. We derive these notions from the core elements of restorative justice and from adaptations of these elements that occurred in designing and performing action research in ALTERNATIVE. The radicalisation of the participatory element towards community ownership, on the one hand, and the extension of the reparative element towards transformation, on the other, have oriented the interventions of the action researchers. They are grounded in the lifeworld. This implies resorting to concrete experiences of wrongdoing, harm, conflict or injustice and the possibility of counteracting the tendency to react to conflicts repressively. It can provide an antidote to ideology-driven images, politics feeding on these images, and the fears evoked.

The descriptions of the societal ecology of the research sites have laid open the dynamics of those fears as produced by social and political upheavals, which vary at the four sites. In each case, they result in experiences of insecurity/uncertainty and injustice, oftentimes coming together.

Restorative justice and restorative practices offer ways to tackle these fears – to find a new societal balance and a new togetherness based no longer on people being in the same 'secure' situation, the same secure place with neatly separated compartments or social strata, but on their being together within their being different. This approach, espousing active participation and dialogue, is highly demanding, though. The readiness of people to enter these participatory processes is not self-evident; it has to be fostered and tended with care and caution.

If 'participatory justice' and 'participatory security/safety' appear as hallmarks of an alternative governmentality, its intricacies and its ramifications have to be traced carefully. This we have attempted through the presentation of case stories from ALTERNATIVE.

Action research in ALTERNATIVE

In the course of four years, teams of researchers in four European countries developed action research models in several settings characterised by cultural diversity and various kinds of conflict on the micro–meso–macro scale.

The action research in *Vienna* dealt with everyday conflicts at the micro-level between local residents and residents with a migrant background in public/social housing estates. Researchers explored the potential of active participation of citizens and of civil society organisations, aiming at enhancing perceptions of justice and safety.

The research programme in *Kisváros*, a small town in rural Hungary, dealt with different – if mostly undercurrent – sources of tension between the inhabitants (e.g. between old residents and newcomers, Roma and non-Roma, etc.). The action research focused on finding out how and at what points restorative theory and practice can be integrated into the existing institutional structure, with special attention to the justice and law enforcement system.

The researchers in *Serbia* worked with a mixed method approach (e.g. quantitative survey and qualitative in-depth interviews) on the perceptions and involvement of citizens from multi-ethnic communities in three border towns – Bačka Palanka, Prijepolje and Medvedja – with ethnically diverse populations (Serbs, Albanians, Croats and Muslims). The researchers gave special attention to victims of past abuses and observed their roles in democratic processes for peace-building and conflict resolution.

The researchers in *Northern Ireland* focused on the relationship between the state system and local communities in three research sites (south Belfast, east Belfast and Derry/Londonderry) in the context of the violent conflict and the restorative potential of promoting active citizenship and community development. Local capacity to resolve intra- and inter-communal conflict is being evaluated in projects dealing with problems between local community and gangs of youths, and between long-term residents and recent immigrants, and intercommunity sectarian conflict.

Justice and security at the four action research sites of the ALTERNATIVE project

We will start our considerations of justice and security by tracing relevant experiences in these fields at our research sites. And let's further introduce this section by looking at the ways the concepts of security and justice are 'caught' in words in the language of these research sites.

The English language differentiates security, safety and certainty. The Serbian language also discerns '*bezbednost*', that is, feeling safe in the physical sense (lack of war, bombardment, violence, incidents, etc.), and '*sigurnost*', which refers to safety in a broader sense. Hungarian does not differentiate – in that respect being similar to German, where there is '*Gewissheit*' to denote 'certainty', but security and safety are both '*Sicherheit*'. It is important to point out that in the Hungarian language 'trust' (*bizik*) lies at the root of the Hungarian word for security, '*biztonság*'.

It is the other way round with justice, where the German language differentiates between '*Recht*' and '*Gerechtigkeit*', the latter denoting a broader concept of justice, including social justice or distributive justice; the Serbian language does so as well. In the Serbian language, the word 'justice' can be translated in several ways: '*pravo*' (as a system of legal norms protected by the state), '*pravda*' (which refers to feelings of justice (the justice of the people); this can be linked to the legal (court) justice as achieved in the judiciary system, but also to justice achieved in another way) and '*pravicnost*' (which refers to fair treatment, equal treatment, respect of certain standards in procedures (e.g. court procedures), respect of human rights and freedoms etc., but also to feelings of justice (the justice of the people). It is interesting to observe that in other Slavic languages, Russian and Polish, '*pravda*' is also the word for 'truth' – although not in the Serbian language, which uses '*istina*' or '*vernost*'. The word for justice in Hungarian is '*igazság(osság)*' which also has its root in the word for truth. There is a different word for law/statute in Hungarian: '*törvény*'. These linguistic specifics provide some indication of the scope of understanding of these concepts within a language, but they do not yet tell us about what is called in anthropology the 'emic' use, meaning the insider or bottom-up perspective and the usage of words by the research participants. We learned about this emic use in the course of the action research.

The four action research sites are characterised by different perceptions and understandings of security and justice. Looking at the material gathered, the interviews conducted with social workers and with residents of social housing estates (*Gemeindebau*) in *Vienna*, we can state that, at first sight, security and/or safety issues are – almost – non-existent. We heard about some residents' fears of walking home late at night, but only two reports of physical attacks or of injuries resulting from such occurrences were mentioned in these interviews. There was a time when media reports of soaring crime rates were frequent, portraying social housing estates and especially 'The *Schöpfwerk*' as hotbeds of conflict and disorder, a result of the failed housing politics of the Social Democratic regime in the City of Vienna. In a few of the interviews with residents, these issues have been identified as predominantly media constructions. The plan to install CCTV in the housing estate is about preserving order and cleanliness in the estate and the hope of being able to trace and apprehend perpetrators, those depositing of their garbage or of bulky waste (Kremmel and Pelikan, 2015, pp. 20–24). Such cases would be dealt with by civil/administrative law and would not constitute criminal cases.

The topic of justice is mainly addressed as social justice, more specifically distributive justice. The issue of access to flats in the *Gemeindebau* stands out as arousing a lot of anger among the Old-Austrians. When these statements of residents of the *Gemeindebau* are analysed, it becomes evident that they are about a just distribution and allocation of entitlements. The prevailing opinion of residents is to blame newcomers for not having contributed to building the welfare state on whose grounds social housing in Vienna and access to flats in the *Gemeindebau* rest. ('We – and our parents – have built it, we have suffered and endured hardship – they just come and reap the benefits without any prior investment') (Kremmel and Pelikan, 2015, p. 92). Finally, in the course of working in the Women's Café (*Frauencafé*), the researchers perceived fear and uneasiness/uncertainty on the side of the Old-Austrians provoked by the large numbers of Turkish migrants, and especially by women wearing the headscarf. What is the threat emanating from these developments? We have identified it as shaking the world in which people have come to build their trust and which provides them with safe ground.

In *Kisváros* in Hungary, it is predominantly security as absence of crime, crime meaning theft and burglary, that the inhabitants of the village are concerned with. The threat to security is coming from newcomers and from Roma – 'Gypsy crime'.

The researchers refer to a survey that showed high levels of security, which were later discussed in a meeting – with some doubts uttered but also confirmation received. In the discussion about founding a new 'Civil Guard', providing security by successfully preventing and combatting theft and burglary comes up repeatedly.

But social justice or distributive justice is addressed – albeit less often – in the interviews as well: for example, when government is blamed for not securing the 'opportunity for me to plan my future', or failing to guarantee a level of prosperity, 'even for "those living below". In default of such a care "public security" will be endangered' (Hera *et al.*, 2015, p. 13).

Distributive justice plays an important role in the 'Charity case'. There, the pervasive rift between the Roma and the Hungarian residents becomes visible. Digging deeper, we can see the fears that produce and accompany the more recent developments regarding the situation of the Roma. The authors have dedicated quite some attention to this issue. In this chapter, we will try for an overall assessment and a bold conjecture. While the economic situation has decidedly worsened since the overthrow of communism, the European project with its emphasis on human rights has supported new claims for minorities, including the Roma, and this in turn has disquieted the 'old-Hungarian' population; it has raised fears. Whereas under communism discriminatory practices – especially in the school and housing system – existed, anti-discriminatory language and invectives were not allowed. One could sum up the situation of the Roma by stating that they knew their place. They did not aspire to reach beyond this place, they had jobs to earn a very modest living, and they had basic, albeit excessively poor, housing. In this place, they were tolerated; they were not valued and esteemed. If they did receive recognition, it was because they stayed in their place. Nowadays, their no longer remaining in 'their place' arouses fear and anger. These fears, we would like to venture, are also one of the forces that account for the tendency to avoid open confrontation – the 'culture of silence', as researchers have named this phenomenon (Benedek *et al.*, 2014, pp. 4–24).

Serbia has dedicated a lot of effort – researching and thinking – to the issue of security. In a post-conflict society, it is indeed a most pressing issue. In a highly pertinent analysis, researchers stated:

> We found that perception of security goes much beyond physical safety of people (in terms of freedom from crime, war or violence); it also refers to social, economic, legal and political safety, thus, a strong link with the concept 'human security' is noticed. The concept of human security refers to the protection of the vital core of all human lives in ways that enhance human freedoms and human fulfilment. It is identified as the protection of individuals from risks to their physical and psychological safety, dignity and well-being in a broader sense. Therefore, it has two main components: 'freedom from fear' and 'freedom from want'.
>
> (Nikolić-Ristanović and Copic, 2013, pp. 10–11)

The authors of the report on Serbia refer to the analysis of Rohne *et al.* (2008, pp. 12–13), who had stated that 'post-conflict societies often lack mechanisms and institutions for upholding the rule of law and dealing with the past abuses'.

Thus, in the Serbian case, we find the longing for human security in the broad sense stated above as 'freedom from fear' and 'freedom from want' closely connected to experiences of justice/injustice. There remains the unfulfilled dream of a society guided by the rule of law instead of – as is deplored repeatedly in the interviews conducted with people at the Serbian research sites – the 'political' taking precedence. The 'political' is the superiority of party politics, a kind of politics that overrides the concerns and the needs of those it is supposed to represent.

In *Northern Ireland*, the situation described in the baseline report of the research team of the University of Ulster is in many ways different from the one in Serbia, despite both sites representing post-conflict societies (Chapman *et al.*, 2013).

We start from a situation with overall high crime rates, especially crimes of violence, with hate crime constituting a considerable part of this. As a stark difference from the situation in Serbia, the role of the police in Northern Ireland has undergone thorough change during the last decades. The Police Service of Northern Ireland (PSNI) has made substantial progress in gaining the confidence of local communities. Police officers' training has improved, and they are becoming more effective at dealing with racially motivated hate crime. As the police become more sensitive to this issue, the black and ethnic minority communities will increase the reporting of such incidents. There are signs that these communities are making more efforts to integrate through forming associations and participating in diversity events.

While sectarian-motivated hate crime is decreasing, racially motivated crimes of violence are, as a tendency, increasing. Further, the authors contend, there is still a strong belief that much crime and anti-social behaviour is unreported, particularly in south Belfast Loyalist areas and areas where dissident Republican groups have influence. The existence or suspicion of armed groups continues to have a negative impact upon relationships between the police and local people in specific areas.

In this respect, we can perceive commonalities between Serbia and Northern Ireland: in the British Isles as well, 'the underlying political and relational causes of the conflicts remain active and pose an on-going threat to both the security and sense of justice of both communities' (Chapman *et al.*, 2015, p. 39). Thus, while day-to-day sectarian violence is relatively exceptional and almost tolerated, the underlying relationships which sustain sectarian divisions in Northern Irish society continue to lie beneath the surface and pose a constant threat to political progress and social cohesion.

Finally, the authors conclude, from the Loyalist point of view the biggest threat to their security is the perceived strategy of Republicans to deprive them of their British identity. It is the threat to identity that causes most insecurity and a sense of injustice.

Everywhere, we are thus confronted with fear: fear at various levels as analysed by the Serbian research team, fear of 'the other' arriving from outside in Vienna, fear of being deprived of one's privileged position, as in Vienna and in Kisváros, and fear of losing one's identity, as in Northern Ireland. Moreover, there are the fears of the old and the new 'others', the Roma in Kisváros and the migrants in Vienna, fears of being left at the margins and of being exposed to outright attacks and discrimination. All these fears affect experiences of both security and justice. As concerns these experiences, this is not a relationship of complementarity, one increasing at the expense of the other, as is indeed often the case when we observe processes of securitisation, or as is frequently referred to in international literature on global conflict and post-conflict societies (World Bank, 2011). At the research sites of the ALTERNATIVE project, justice and security make their appearance as parallel phenomena – and they are developing in parallel, becoming exacerbated or abated by and large together. These fears become the currency of political power play. They are also the basic 'material' restorative practices have to work with.[1] We will see in the following that the restorative approach aims at a transformation of security and of justice based on those lifeworld experiences and striving for 'maximum feasible participation'.

To summarise the yield of the explorations into the societal ecology: in post-conflict societies, in the Balkans and in Northern Ireland, experiences of injustice and insecurity – mainly developing in parallel – stem from the repercussions, or rather, the ongoing effect, of underlying tensions of past decades of war and violence. At the research sites of Kisváros in Hungary and Vienna, the sources of these experiences are changes in the socio-economic field and in the composition of the population of these places. We see a massive influx of people with a migration background in Vienna's social housing estates on the one hand, and on the other hand, the changed situation of the Roma; more precisely, the deterioration of their economic circumstances together with a rise in claims to equal treatment based on human rights.

These developments make the 'old residents' feel that they are losing secure ground and thereby the assurance of their, albeit modest, privileges. This creates fear and a tendency to put up one's defences and to blame whoever is 'at the top' for not sufficiently protecting these privileges, the most striking being the case of access to the *Gemeindebau*, where the requirement for having earned this access by partaking in previous investments in the building of the social welfare state is voiced vehemently. In Kisváros, we have to be aware of prejudices against and contempt for the Roma that have existed since centuries; we have identified the new fears that surfaced as stemming from the fact that they, 'the Gypsies', no longer 'keep their place'.

Then there is the intersection with the issue of preserving and defending identity; this is strong in Northern Ireland, where one's whole existence is built around these 'religious' identities. The ALTERNATIVE material from Serbia is much less concerned with this concept. Both the quantitative and the qualitative research are mainly addressing experiences of physical and psychological threat and/or hurt and damage. We would also like to contend that the fears we perceive in the Viennese *Gemeindebau* are not primarily about preserving one's identity. Rather, it is the fear of the others, who are becoming increasingly stronger – both in numbers and regarding the attention they receive.

The previous observations mainly refer to an overall experience of 'The time is out of joint', through wars and their repercussions and through social upheavals, turning over what has provided security and justice, namely, portioning out the dues, especially the benefits of the welfare state, according to the place individuals and groups of people have long occupied in society.

The promise of restorative justice to deal with fears of injustice and insecurity

Justice in ALTERNATIVE

Restorative justice and restorative practices offer ways to tackle the fears as highlighted above – to find a new societal balance and a new togetherness based no longer on people being in the same 'secure' situation, the same secure place with neatly separated compartments or social strata, but on their being together within their being different. It is about alternative understandings of security and justice and – we would like to contend – practices based on these understandings.

ALTERNATIVE's understanding of justice has been developed in confrontation with the principles guiding criminal justice. We have arrived at distinguishing three core elements of restorative justice, captured as differences. They are: lifeworld versus system-oriented, participation versus delegation, and reparation versus retribution/punishment.

In ALTERNATIVE, the three core elements of restorative justice have acquired a new scope. Justice has to reach beyond the level of differences to the criminal justice system and its rationale. It has to be understood much more broadly – and, as we have seen from the material presented above, it is indeed understood by the people we have been working with in this broader sense. Life-world orientation in striving for justice remains a constitutive element, though; it becomes even more pronounced.

The conflicts that we are supposed to deal with, emerging within intercultural settings, include everyday conflicts, exclusively so in Vienna, but in large numbers at the other research sites as well. The lifeworld element is not a counter-perspective to be introduced as different from the system-perspective; it is there from the very beginning – it just has to retain its place and its importance.

As concerns the reparative element – captured as different from retribution – this has also acquired a new meaning within the ALTERNATIVE project. The *reparative element* becomes transformative – that is, oriented towards the future. It is about transforming relationships and about transforming the societal structures in which these relationships are embedded. We have already seen this to some extent in 'classical' restorative justice procedures. Transformation goes beyond reparation and 'restoration' of wrongdoings of the past. It aims at the transformation of those relations where wrongdoing ensued and at transforming societal structures that engender acts of wrongdoing. In ALTERNATIVE, it is of paramount importance.

The participatory element, that is, the active involvement of the parties concerned, is an indispensable element of any restorative process. With restorative circles or peacemaking circles, active involvement acquires an additional quality; it is sharpened and radicalised. It takes the shape of community ownership.

We find pieces of theories of justice that are kin to this understanding. Habermas, in connection with justice and social justice, makes an important contribution by introducing the concept of deliberative justice. Within his discourse ethics, justice is achieved whenever the requirements of a discourse free from domination are met and provide the grounds for the decisions society rests upon: first of all decisions regarding the constitution, but also regarding all kinds of political decisions that become manifest as law-making in various fields of society. The core sentence referring to the discourse free of domination is: 'Only those norms can claim validity that could meet with the acceptance of all concerned in practical discourse' (Habermas, 1990, p. 66); 'In this view, one no longer needs to define principles of justice prior to the deliberating processes by which societies order their interests' (Pali, 2013, p. 8). Pali refers to further developments starting from a critique of Rawls' and Habermas' theories of justice. The historical context out of which the works of Nancy Fraser (and Iris Marion Young) evolved had to do with the emergence during the 1960s of struggles for civil rights, of emancipatory social movements against racism, of peace movements and of feminism. It also had to do with the emergence of new social movements, which, in reaction to the earlier ones, began to question the idea of justice more exclusively in terms of identity politics and social recognition. More specifically, in the 1980s, political theory in the West was characterised by a paradigm change from *redistribution*, a politics of structural equality, to *recognition*, a politics of difference. Fraser (1996) and Young (1990) have come to reflect on a *three*-dimensional theory of justice – redistribution (the 'what' of justice), recognition (the 'who' of justice) and (political) representation (the 'how' of justice).

In a similar vein and dwelling on the concept of representation, Agnes Heller (1987), developing Habermas' communicative ethics further, suggests that justice is primarily the virtue of citizenship, of persons deliberating about problems and issues that confront them collectively in their institutions and actions, under conditions without domination, oppression or coercion, with reciprocity and mutual tolerance of difference. The idea of justice here shifts from a focus on distributive and recognition patterns to procedural issues of participation in deliberation and decision making (Braithwaite and Parker, 1999).

Following that line, we will propose 'participatory justice' as the counter-justice, the other justice we are looking for in ALTERNATIVE. 'Participatory justice' can be understood as an abbreviation or, rather, condensation of the 'how of justice' as espoused by Nancy Fraser within the three-dimensional theory of justice. And it is indeed close to Habermas' deliberative justice and the way it has been further developed by Agnes Heller.

Security in ALTERNATIVE

Lucia Zedner (2007) diagnoses the arrival of what she calls a 'security society', a society in which the possibility of forestalling risks competes with and even takes precedence over responding to wrongs done. When justice is governed by the utilitarian rationale of protecting the public, it can also be viewed as a means to achieve security. In this perspective, justice dissolves into the pursuit of security.

Thinking of the question of how we are to achieve justice in a security society, Zedner (2007) explicitly argues that criminology should seek to elaborate and defend a conception of justice apposite to the problems and potential of the security society. Other scholars have emphasised embracing counter-values such as ambiguity (De Lint and Virta, 2004), 'living with risk' (O'Malley, 2004), a focus on everyday security (Crawford and Hutchinson, 2016), and a notion of positive security that relies on human connectedness, local capacity building and spiritual order (Schuilenburg and van Steden, 2014).

We prefer using the term 'safety', and Christa Pelikan has argued this previously in the context of the contribution to *Images of Restorative Justice Theory* (Pelikan, 2007).

The procedures of conflict regulation ought to restore the possibility for the members of society to experience having a 'place in the world' (Arendt, 1958), of being upheld and of belonging (Zehr, 2002; Wessels and Miedema, 2003). Safety is closely linked to this same experience. Safety is provided by keeping at bay threats to the life and the living together of people – coming from outside or from inside a social group. 'Conflict regulation contributes to safety by (re)establishing a peaceful living together of the parties to a conflict' (Pelikan, 2007, p. 36). Security is different from safety: safety pertains to protection from exterior and interior dangers, while security is about forestalling the risks that lie in the future (Legnaro, 1997).

What emerges from this characterisation of safety is that the quality of counter-security is parallel to counter-justice, derived from the element of participation. It is a participatory security that is to create and produce the experience of being held and of belonging.

Resorting to the lifeworld

Both the transformative and the participatory element, for example the construction of the future by relying on wider circles of participation, are grounded in the lifeworld element. In criminal justice, reference to the concrete lifeworld experiences of the other becomes the lever for a transformation of the norms set in legislation to the individual level. It means translating and 'bringing home' a norm that is presumed to be generally accepted, for example denoting a societal understanding of a '*Sollen*' (the 'ought').[2]

This might imply continuous discussion of these norms and their meaning in the lifeworld of the parties to a conflict. Attending to the concrete experiences of the 'doer and the done-to' (Benjamin, 2004) gives depth and plausibility to norms – or it exposes them as mere instruments of control by those in power.

In ALTERNATIVE, the lifeworld orientation implied the confrontation with 'the Other' from the outset, starting from the concrete experiences of sufferings and of anger, of fears and hopes. This quest for dialogue – and for confrontation – constitutes a risk, though. It is an offer opening a new path towards overcoming fear and uncertainty, but it is a true challenge, and it is not at all self-evident that this offer will be accepted by the stakeholders to a conflict. Strong apprehensions and fears might exist and keep people from venturing onto this path. It is indeed something extra-ordinary; that is, outside the well-used, ordinary paths they are used to treading, they are invited to try out something different.

In Kisváros, a lot of attention has been paid to the phenomenon of a 'culture of silence', denoting the preference of people to keep conflicts from entering the open in order to be dealt with through mediation and/or a peace circle. Overcoming these apprehensions requires a lot of patience, perseverance and trust in the persuasive powers of restorative practices.

In Vienna, we found opposite forces – the tendency to avoid open conflict, on the one hand, and a quest for togetherness, on the other hand. Here as well, the persuasive power of 'doing justice and security' grounds the hope the ALTERNATIVE team placed in restorative practices.

Participatory justice and participatory security: the interventions

In this section we will provide narratives of interventions to show the different modes of dealing with security and justice through participation.

Kisváros: the Charity case – striving for just distribution

The 'Charity case' can be read as an attempt to openly tackle the problem of injustices experienced by members of the Roma community in Kisváros, where the ALTERNATIVE team was offering residents the road to participatory justice. The case targeted the distribution of Red Cross donations for poor people. Charity distribution, in this form, has been running in Kisváros since 2010. After several charity provision actions had taken place, some local residents started to criticise the organisers regarding the distribution of the packages. It was claimed to be unfair, as people who did not deserve support or aid could get the packages while the people in real need were not considered at all.

The protagonists of the conflict were, on the one side, Edit, an unemployed Roma woman who works occasionally in the social work projects of the local government. She used to work in the Roma Self-Government back in the early 1990s but was still an opinion leader within the Roma community. The other actor, Ági, was the main organiser of the charity action event. She is a district nurse in mother- and childcare who also knows most of the families in the village, including the Roma community.

The Foresee Research Group, responsible for introducing restorative practices in Kisváros, succeeded in bringing together a peace circle to address the conflict that had ensued. In the course of the peace circle, definitions of 'poverty' and disadvantage were in the foreground. Ági acted defensively out of fear of being regarded as racist; she introduced her understanding of 'relative' poverty,[3] which regarded those who 'keep up appearances' but are hard put to do so also as eligible for receiving a charity package. Edit, on the other hand, voiced the unequal and oppressed position of the Roma, claiming: 'Roma are now only on their own. They are afraid to tell their opinions, because they are afraid of atrocities they can get as answer' (Hera *et al.*, 2015, p. 25). In addition, she pointed to discrimination against Roma families regarding the distribution of the charity packages. It proved difficult to arrive at mutual recognition of different concepts of poverty and, following from that, different concepts of distributive justice. The deficits of information that became visible as one of the reasons for the experience of injustice proved more amenable to working towards a shared solution. There, it was possible to arrive at concrete steps and concrete tasks for the participants to take care of in order to achieve improvements (Hera *et al.*, 2015).

The practical implementation of the solutions agreed upon did not work smoothly, though; only one of the participants in the peace circle really worked at advertising the new charity event, which in the end did not take place at all. However, although the conflict was not completely resolved within the circle, Ági experienced a positive transformation of the conflict in the circle. She had found some common points with the 'other party', with Edit, the woman representing the Roma community. The experience of this circle became the node for her involvement with restorative methods and their application in certain conflict situations arising from her professional work.

*Vienna: the Women's Café (*Frauencafé*) – striving for community ownership*

The *Frauencafé* had been established as one of the outcomes of a long-lasting, complex conflict mediation process, led by '*wohnpartner*', a sub-organisation of Vienna's large administrative housing agency, culminating in large group mediation. It was about conflicts between Old-Austrian and mostly Turkish residents in one of Vienna's social housing estates that had escalated over the course of more than a year. The proposal to have a regular get-together of women of both Turkish and 'Old-Austrian' origin came from the side of the Turkish women and was supported by *wohnpartner*. It finally turned out to be a fortnightly event that brought together women living in the estate, 'Old-Austrians' as well as Turkish and a few other Muslim women – up to 40 people – for having breakfast together, talking, and planning various events and activities. In autumn 2013, a major conflict emerged, visible and tangible as accusations by women of a more traditional and religious bent directed at those who were not strictly adhering to religious prescriptions. In 2014, ALTERNATIVE started to initiate interventions and action research in the Women's Café, with the intention of exploring whether a restorative justice approach would be feasible and 'desirable' for the women meeting there, using the opportunity of the café to get in contact and to establish relationships of mutual understanding and mutual support.

The research team had recruited an experienced facilitator of restorative circles, and together they designed workshops for the Women's Café. They were intended to serve the 'double' purpose of further exploring the women's willingness to address the conflict – the rift that had occurred within the group of women of Islamic faith – and of enhancing their capacity to handle the conflict of their own accord.

Gerda, the facilitator of peace circles, started to carefully find her way into the group of women and to find an incident from which to approach the 'main' big conflict at stake, the one between liberal and orthodox/traditional Muslim women. This incident had happened in connection with a lecture and discussion on Christian Christmas rituals that had taken place in Advent and had resulted in the exodus of a group of Muslim women, who had experienced this lecture as an onslaught on their own religious beliefs. In a first meeting of the group, preparing for the circle, there was understanding of the position and of the feelings of the Muslim women on the side of the Austrians ('yes, this was too much and too long, we better take care of this by ourselves not by inviting somebody some expert from outside!' (Kremmel and Pelikan, 2015, p. 49)). In the second meeting, which was attended by Austrians only (with one Turkish woman present, but leaving early), there was a string of complaints about the Muslim women being unwilling to get acquainted with Austrian customs and a general voicing of feeling threatened by their ever-increasing presence. There was now complete denial of any significant exodus of Muslim women at the Advent lecture; on the contrary, they were accused of having been unjustly offended by the information that had been presented. Gerda had experienced this session as quite satisfactory because the women had started to vent feelings, fears and apprehensions. Katrin, in her position as participating researcher, found it strenuous and exciting. But *wohnpartner*, and more specifically the head of team 21, responsible for the *Frauencafé*, was disquieted and alarmed. *Wohnpartner* called off the procedure, or rather, they informed the ALTERNATIVE team that they would not continue to work with Gerda. They thought that the women were left in the dark and the unleashing of anti-Turkish feelings could result in an avalanche of xenophobia. More transparency and more safety were called for. After Gerda had to terminate her commitment as the restorative circles' facilitator, the researchers had to clarify their position vis-à-vis *wohnpartner* and the *Frauencafé* anew. The task of facilitating the circle was taken on by the social workers of *wohnpartner*. The ALTERNATIVE team was to assist in further designing and planning the next steps of the circle. The observing role remained with the researcher.

But now the researchers decided to pay even more attention to the situation of *wohnpartner* as a stakeholder with political aims and with responsibilities towards the residents of the *Gemeindebau* and towards the *Frauencafé*. One the one hand, their fears had to be considered as well, next to the fears of the Muslim women and the Austrian women. On the other hand, the ALTERNATIVE researchers wanted to hold on to basic tenets of restorative justice and to convey the aim of 'maximum feasible participation' (the maxim of the War on Poverty of the 1960s in the USA; cf. Moynihan, 1969).

During the following weeks, the facilitators from *wohnpartner* with the assistance of the ALTERNATIVE team – and drawing on Dominic Barter's restorative circles design as introduced by Gerda[4] – developed a new version of restorative circles. This was to take care of the specific situation of women of different ethnic and religious backgrounds living together in the *Gemeindebau*, as well as of the position and the political traditions of *wohnpartner* as part of the administration of the City of Vienna.

The new model for restorative circles (*Gemeinschaftskreise*) was to attend to the core requirement of any restorative approach, namely, the active participation of those affected by a conflict, further sharpened and intensified to become the goal of 'community ownership'. In this way, the circles should contribute to the participants becoming able to tackle 'their' conflicts of their own accord, trusting in their own capacities and their command of the necessary means and instruments to do so. In the course of the preparation of a circle, great importance was placed on providing prospective participants of a restorative circle with sufficient information about the basic goals of the circle procedure and about its potential benefits as well as the risks incurred. This happened through individual talks, taking place before the circle procedure took place, and the opportunity to get individual coaching whenever it proved desirable for one of the participants. The steps of the procedure ought to be made transparent and understandable; this understanding should ground the acceptance of the procedure by the potential participants and ultimately their assuming ownership of the procedure. One could state that participation and transparency are basic preconditions of initiating a restorative circle.

The outcome of this specific circle, as it was realised in the form of a restorative circle finally taking place, was astounding. It has to be said that no representative of the 'orthodox' Muslim women participated. Notwithstanding this serious setback, one could see in the course of the circle a heightened capacity of listening to the other, and therefore a heightened ability to understand the 'other'. Moreover, an increased trust of the group and its members in the capacity of finding ways of dealing with conflicts was observed. And finally, an increased experience and 'feeling' of togetherness and mutual responsibility was seen. This found its ultimate expression in the whole group becoming involved in a project to assist refugees.

Conclusion: what is participatory justice? Tensions and contradictions

We have put forward the promise of restorative approaches to deal with fears of injustice and insecurity, and with the more general experience of uncertainty, uneasiness and perturbation.

In Kisváros, the ALTERNATIVE team felt confronted with the 'culture of silence', the reluctance to speak up and to bring conflicts into the open. In the Charity distribution case an attempt was made to stage a confrontation, to speak out on feelings of being discriminated against and feelings of being unjustly accused of promoting and of supporting unfair distribution, ultimately acting out of racism. A tiny movement was made towards listening to and recognising the 'truth' of the other, thereby easing tensions and reducing mutual fears and misgivings. Despite the fact that the implementation of the agreements achieved was lacking, the circle gave the participants a taste of what participatory justice could look like.

In Vienna's Women's Café, the offer to approach the 'big conflict' with the orthodox Muslim women via a restorative circle met with difficulties of a different kind. Feelings of fear and xenophobic sentiments were vented in the course of the second preparatory meeting and caused the 'leading' organisation, *wohnpartner*, to try for a path of their own, which at first sight appeared to leave less room for 'community ownership' and provided more guidance by the facilitators. But when analysing the adaptation of Dominic Barter's restorative circles for tackling conflicts in the intercultural setting of the *Gemeindebau* in Vienna, we perceive a careful and creative way of taking care of and caring for the parties to the conflict, their concrete socio-economic situation and their life-worlds. Getting as close as possible to the individual experiences of fear and uncertainty, and offering the possibility to make the other side get a glimpse of understanding, opens the door towards an experience of shared and participatory safety. It is a safety that rests upon continuous exchange of feelings of insecurity – and of feelings of good will.

The tensions within the group of Muslim women that came as a consequence of an orthodox brand of Islam surfacing with new anxieties and insecurities thriving, and ultimately the failure to include these women, point to the limits of the restorative justice approach.

To conclude: what are the chances for a counter-justice and a counter-security, and what does it look like? It is about instigating processes that might appear both attractive and – at least in certain circumstances – strange. It is about carefully opening the opportunity for people – in intercultural settings – to try out these processes. This often requires active support from the informal environment of the stakeholders, or from civil society organisations, or from society's institutions. The last might have an important responsibility in this respect. We have the choice: to actively support and initiate dialogical processes by providing a safe space and adequate facilitation, or to leave things as they are and to 'wait and see'. Finally, we need to be aware that one might encounter doubts and resistance – which one has to acknowledge and take into account. It is about learning, changing, transforming and opening paths towards transformation.

As a variation to this conclusion, we want to quote Ingeborg Bachmann, the Austrian poet: '*Die Wahrheit ist dem Menschen zumutbar.*' This quote, from a speech in 1959 (Bachmann, 1984), is now the epitaph of her grave. The speech continues by talking about the pain we go through when confronting the truth by alluding to this pain bearing fruit. Translated and adapted, it could read: People can reasonably be expected to face the truth and to engage in participatory justice and safety.

Notes

1 Brunilda Pali (2015) has conceptualised this conglomerate as 'uncertainty' – and this is indeed less prone to become the currency of political power play. It lacks the emotional appeal and the drama that characterised the notion of 'fear'. It refers to the mere fact that one cannot predict what the future will hold in store. It consists in large part of an erosion of those traditions that assured a certain amount of predictability.

2 Claudia Mazzucato, referring to the philosophy of law, arrives at the same conclusion: 'Norms in criminal law should therefore (tend to) communicate in the same "gentle", yet effective, way as examples do: they should involve their addressees in a normative dialogue on how to reconcile "is" and "ought"'. German Sociology of Law from its beginning, and most prominently since Max Weber (2002), was concerned with '*Sein*' and '*Sollen*', with Jürgen Habermas (1996) and Niklas Luhmann (1969) arriving at different notions (cf. also Ludwig, 1999).

3 Which is close to the concept of relative deprivation introduced by Robert K. Merton (1968) based on Emile Durkheim.

4 Dominic Barter had started to work with and further develop a restorative circles approach in the 1990s in Brazil and has exerted considerable influence in Europe (cf. Dzur, 2017; Mazzetti, 2013).

References

Arendt, H., 1958. *The Human Condition.* Chicago: The University of Chicago Press.

Bachmann, I., 3rd edn. 1984. *Rede anlässlich der Verleihung des Hörspielpreises der Kriegsblinden, 1959* (Speech on the occasion of getting the prize for her audio-drama). Werke, Bd. 4: Essays, Reden Schriften, Zürich: Piper, p. 277.

Benedek, G., Hera, G., Gyorfi, È., Balla, L. and Szegö, D., 2014. *Grasping Action and Research.* ALTERNATIVE Deliverable 5.3.

Benjamin, J., 2004. Beyond doer and done-to. An intersubjective view of thirdness. *The Psychoanalytical Quarterly*, 73, pp. 5–46.

Braithwaite, J. and Parker, C., 1999. Restorative justice is republican justice. In: G. Bazemore and L. Walgrave (eds), *Restorative Juvenile Justice: Repairing the Harm of Youth Crime*. Monsey: Criminal Justice Press, pp. 102–126.

Chapman, T., Campbell, H., McCord, J. and McCready, P., 2013. *A Baseline Research Report into Issues and Needs in Three Sites Where the Community Is Experiencing Conflict*. ALTERNATIVE Deliverable 7.4.

Chapman, T., Campbell, H., Wilson, D. and McCready, P., 2015. *Exploring and Crossing the Frontiers of Society: Restorative Approaches to Conflict between Groups*. ALTERNATIVE deliverable 7.6.

Crawford, A. and Hutchinson, S., 2016. Mapping the contours of 'everyday security': Time, space and emotion. *British Journal of Criminology*, 56(6), pp. 1184–1202.

De Lint, W. and Virta, S., 2004. Security in ambiguity: Towards a radical security politics. *Theoretical Criminology*, 8(4), pp. 465–489.

Dzur, A., 2017. Conversations on restorative justice: A talk with Dominic Barter. *Restorative Justice: An International Journal*, 5(1), pp. 116–132.

Fraser, N., 1996. *Social Justice in the Age of Identity Politics: Redistribution, Recognition, and Participation*. Paper presented at the Tanner lectures on human values delivered at Stanford University, 30 April–2 May.

Habermas, J., 1990. *Moral Consciousness and Communicative Action*. Cambridge, MA: MIT Press.

Habermas, J., 1996. *Between Facts and Norms: Contribution to a Discourse Theory of Law and Democracy*. Cambridge, MA: MIT Press.

Heller, A., 1987. *Beyond Justice*. New York: Basil Blackwell.

Hera, G., Benedek, G., Szegö, D. and Balla, L., 2015. *Comprehensive Final Report on RJ in Intercultural Communities*. ALTERNATIVE Deliverable 5.5.

Kremmel, K. and Pelikan, C., 2015. *Towards Restorative Circles: Action Research Interventions in Vienna's Social Housing Estates*. ALTERNATIVE Deliverable 4.4.

Legnaro, A., 1997. Konturen der Sicherheitsgesellschaft: Eine polemisch futurologische Skizze. *Leviathan*, 25, pp. 271–284.

Ludwig, M., 1999. *Sein und Sollen. Eine Untersuchung zur Abgrenzung der Rechtsnormen von den Sozialen Normen bei Max Weber und Eugen Ehrlich*. Marburg: Tectum Verlag.

Luhmann, N., 1969. Normen in soziologischer Perspektive. *Soziale Welt*, 20, pp. 24–48.

Mazzetti, S., 2013. Dominic Barter im Gespräch mit Sissi Mazzetti. Restorative Circles. Ein Ansatz aus Brasilien, der Raum für den gemeinschaftlichen Umgang mit schmerzhaften Konflikten schafft. In: TOA – Servicebüro für Täter-Opfer-Ausgleich und Konfliktschlichtung (ed.), *Restorative Justice. Der Versuch, das Unübersetzbare in Worte zu fassen*. DBH Materialien nr. 71, pp. 24–38.

Mazzucato, C., 2016. *Restorative Justice and the Potential of 'Exemplarity': In Search for a 'Persuasive' Coherence within Criminal Justice* (forthcoming).

Merton, R. K., 1968. *Social Theory and Social Structure*. New York: Free Press.

Moynihan, D. P., 1969. *Maximum Feasible Misunderstanding. Community Action in the War on Poverty*. New York: Free Press.

Nikolić-Ristanović, V. and Copic, S., 2013. *Dealing with Inter-Ethnic Conflicts in Serbia and the Place of Restorative Justice and Victims*. ALTERNATIVE Deliverable 6.1.

O'Malley, P., 2004. *Risk, Uncertainty and Government*. London: GlassHouse.

Pali, B., 2013. *Theoretical Analysis Report. Alternative Epistemologies of Justice and Security*. ALTERNATIVE Deliverable 1.1.

Pali, B., 2015. Restorative governmentalities in intercultural Europe. Towards a counter-security discourse? Unpublished paper. Leuven: ALTERNATIVE.

Pelikan, C., 2007. The place of restorative justice in time and space. In: R. Mackay, M. Bosnjak, J. Deklerck, C. Pelikan, B. van Stokkom and M. Wright (eds), *Images of Restorative Justice Theory*. Frankfurt/Main: Verlag für Polizeiwissenschaft, pp. 5–56.

Rohne, H.-C., Arsovska, J. and Aertsen, I., 2008. Challenging restorative justice: State-based conflict, mass victimisation and the changing nature of warfare. In: I. Aertsen, J. Arsovska, H.-C. Rohne, M. Valinas and K. Vanspauwen (eds), *Restoring Justice after Large-Scale Violent Conflicts*. London: Routledge, pp. 3–46.

Schuilenburg, M. and van Steden, R., 2014. Positive security: A theoretical framework. In: M. Schuilenburg, R. van Steden and B. Oude Breuil (eds), *Positive Criminology: Reflections on Care, Belonging and Security*. Den Haag: Eleven, pp. 19–33.

Weber, M., 2002. *Wirtschaft und Gesellschaft*. 5. Aufl. Tübingen: Mohr Siebeck.

Wessels, B. and Miedema, S., 2003. Towards understanding situations of social exclusion. In: H. Steinert and A. Pilgram (eds), *Welfare Politics from Below. Struggles against Social Exclusion in Europe*. Aldershot: Ashgate, pp. 61–75.

World Bank, 2011. *Conflict, Security and Development. World Development Report 2011*. Washington DC: The World Bank.

Young, I.M., 1990. *Justice and the Politics of Difference*. Princeton: Princeton University Press.

Zedner, L., 2007. Pre-crime and post-criminology. *Theoretical Criminology*, 11(2), pp. 261–281.

Zehr, H., 2002. Journey to belonging. In: E. G. M. Weitekamp and H.-J. Kerner (eds), *Restorative Justice. Theoretical Issues*, Cullompton, Devon: Willan, pp. 23–32.

5 Restorative justice and urban citizenship

A comparative dialogue between Vienna and Brussels

Erik Claes and Katrin Kremmel

Introduction

From its early beginning, the development of restorative justice theory and practice has found its gravitational centre in its response to criminal justice. Restorative justice principles and values propose restorative responses to crime, rather than punishment (e.g. Bosnjak, 2007; Pelikan, 2007; Domenig, 2011). Through mediation practices, conferencing and sentencing circles, victims and offenders are given a voice, so that they themselves may define what they most need in the aftermath of crime (e.g. McCold, 2006; Raye and Roberts, 2007; Stuart and Pranis, 2006).

Less developed and less theorised are the potentials of restorative practices in complex, urban settings that bring in issues of poverty, intercultural tensions, density and lack of urban space. Applying restorative justice principles and values to these urban settings requires an exploration of the field far beyond criminal justice and raises a whole set of conceptual, as well as practical, challenges. Since urban contexts are so specific, so differentiated and often unpredictable, one of the main questions is how to refine and even reinvent the conceptual building blocks of restorative justice in order to guide key actors in these specific settings. Another important, more practical issue revolves around the question of whether firmly established restorative practices like mediation or peacemaking circles can be simply replicated in urban settings.

In this chapter, we will explore the potential of restorative justice in urban settings. We will especially focus on conceptual challenges regarding restorative justice, but will also reflect upon concrete, restorative interventions stemming from action research. Our research findings are drawn from two specific urban research sites in Europe: the social housing estates in Vienna ('*Gemeindebau*') and an urban quarter in the heart of Brussels. How should we redefine restorative justice theory in order to make it fit with both urban contexts? What do we learn when we compare our efforts to transform new concepts and approaches in concrete interventions? And how can we further enrich this theoretical framework through a comparative examination of these interventions? These questions determine the focus of this chapter. But in order to address these questions, a brief presentation of both research projects is needed.

Action research in Vienna and Brussels: comparison of both research sites

From 2013 to 2015, a team of the Institute of the Sociology of Law and Criminology (IRKS) explored community-building and restorative practices in close collaboration with the partner organisations '*wohnpartner*' and the community centre 'Bassena', in order to align restorative justice concepts with the urban challenges of living together in social housing complexes. Both partner organisations introduced the team of researchers and restorative practitioners to residents. The team conducted qualitative interviews with residents and social work professionals in order to deepen their field analysis. They invited the residents to participate in communicative capacity-building workshops and restorative circles workshops. During these workshops, the team tested restorative techniques in a specific urban setting. And, finally, they experimented with participatory filmmaking. Youngsters living in the housing estate were invited to make a documentary on how they live and position themselves in the *Gemeindebau* (see Kremmel and Pelikan, 2013, 2014a, 2014b, 2015).

From January 2014 till November 2015, a research team from Odisee, department of social work, weekly visited the Anneessens quarter in the centre of Brussels. Anneessens is a small, multi-diverse, densely populated (25,000 km^2) and poor neighbourhood 500 metres from 'la grand place', and 'la Bourse'. The research approach of the Belgian team was quite similar to the methodology of the researchers in Vienna. With the help of the community centre Buurtwinkel, the Belgians found access to a complex web of social networks that was broadened and deepened by 40 'walking interviews'. For each interview, the researchers accompanied one habitant on a walk through the quarter. The latter easily assumed the role of a guide, showing, explaining and reading into the streets and squares the problems, the conflicts but also the potentials of the neighbourhood. Similarly to the Vienna team, the Belgian researchers used multi-media techniques to enter intimately into the lifeworld of the habitants. They organised two digital storytelling trajectories, enabling nine habitants to make their own short digital movies on their views of the quarter (Claes *et al.*, 2015). Digital storytelling with a personal outcome for each participant (a short movie) is a participative practice used in a variety of disciplines (oral history, educational sciences). By giving participants the tools to combine a short story with a series of strong, evocative images, and with the recording of their own voice, an individual and collective process of empowerment and ownership unfolds (Couldry, 2008; Gyabak and Godina, 2011; Lambert, 2013; Malita and Martin, 2010; Yang and Wu, 2012).

Another similarity between Vienna and Brussels pertains to the character of both urban sites. Both sites bear the visible imprint of social housing policies of social-democratic majorities in their respective city-halls. In Vienna, one-third of the population lives in *Gemeindebau* (Kremmel and Pelikan, 2014a). Social housing is also part of the urban environment of Anneessens. The most visible traces of post-war social policy are symbolised in two completely worn-out social housing blocks.

Despite these similarities both research projects also reveal a few differences in approach. The first difference concerns the status of the research methodology. While the Vienna team used the interviews and the participatory filmmaking exclusively as a tool for better reading the urban, intercultural setting in which they intervened, the Belgian team designed their walking interviews and digital storytelling process as part of an alternative restorative programme, a staged process steered by a broader conceptual framework on restorative justice in an urban setting. Another difference relates to the broader political setting of the research sites. Whereas in Vienna the social housing estates are strongly regulated by top-down social welfare politics, the Anneessens quarter leaves much more space for civic grass-roots initiatives. Institutional complexities in Brussels, resulting in a huge regulatory deficit, favour the emergence of a multitude of grass-roots initiatives transforming abandoned public spaces, finding creative solutions for pressing social needs, and so on. A third difference revolves around the research focus. While the research team in Vienna analysed the potentials and limits of restorative ways of dealing with conflicts within different social housing complexes across the city, the Brussels team chose a wider focus. They did not exclusively focus on the social housing complex in Brussels, but attempted to map different conflict zones spread over the whole quarter. Consequently, their interviewees were not limited to the residents of the social housing estate, but comprised habitants all over the neighbourhood.

Given these similarities and differences, there is a strong reason to embark on a comparative analysis between both research sites. Both are driven by the same general aim: to stretch restorative theory and practice beyond its classic ideas, assumptions and tensions and to make it sensitive to pressing urban issues, as well as promising opportunities.

In the second section of this chapter, we will formulate a few challenges that come to the surface when we try to stretch the restorative justice framework to the complex urban settings of the *Gemeindebau* and the Anneessens quarter. Elaborating these challenges permits us to dig into the peculiarities of both research sites.

In the following section, we present two conceptual fields as promising entrances for aligning restorative justice with urban complexities. The first entrance is an intersectional approach to interculturality. The second entrance revolves around the intertwinement of urban citizenship and three basic ingredients of restorative justice.

In the last section, we explore the interpretive and guiding force of our idea of urban citizenship by revisiting a few cases and interventions from the research sites in Vienna and Brussels (and herewith fully address our central research question).

Stretching restorative justice to urban settings

How should we readjust the classic restorative justice framework to the complexities of urban settings? Which key concepts are in need of refinement? And which notions clearly are to be abandoned? In the following, we will map a few challenges that flow from the field analyses of both research sites in Vienna and Brussels. These challenges come to the surface when we try to stretch the restorative justice framework to complex urban settings.

Bracketing the language of criminal justice

Since restorative justice theory and practice have defined themselves in response to criminal justice, the key concepts of this alternative framework are still to a large extent tributary to the criminal justice language: victims, offenders and criminal wrongdoing are central reference points around which restorative justice has organised itself (e.g. Johnstone and Van Ness, 2007; Sullivan and Tifft, 2006; Weitekamp and Kerner, 2002). But are these reference points adequate in order to implement restorative justice philosophy in urban settings?

Looking at existing neighbourhood disputes in Viennese social housing estates, we come to notice that these disputes predominantly centre on divergent ideas of how to use the semi-public spaces of the courtyards, noise disturbances due to insufficient acoustic insulation, garbage disposal and vandalism. None of these issues fall within the responsibilities of the criminal justice system. Feelings of victimisation do, of course, exist, and at times to a very high degree, since the trouble occurs 'at home', the place where one would usually go to escape trouble. Nevertheless, there are neither 'victims' nor 'offenders' as defined by criminal law, since none of the mentioned acts is actually criminalised by legal regulations (see Haller and Karazman-Morawetz, 2004; Haller *et al.*, 2008; Kremmel and Pelikan, 2014a).

Having examined the views of 40 habitants regarding the living conditions of the Anneessens quarter, the Brussels team reached similar conclusions. A majority of the interviewees associated public spaces with conflicts revolving around the use of and unequal access to certain spaces, due to drug and alcohol abuse, and garbage disposal. In the lived experiences of the interviewees, conflicts are often framed as struggles between groups in the different forms of appropriation of public spaces. The interests of drug and alcohol users and their strategies of appropriation compete with the needs of playing children and caring mothers.

These research findings come as no surprise. In contemporary cities, urban spaces are crossroads of concurring and competing interests in the use of public space. Especially in dense and diverse areas, multiple tensions exist between communities, within communities, between generations, between habitants and real estate firms, and between the interests of citizens and their local authorities, to mention but a few conflict lines.

Some of these conflicts result in the use of violence to claim or settle one's interests. Often tensions and hostilities smoulder and can surface in strategies when boundaries need to be marked again. Sometimes these conflicts pop up through insulting language, blunt racism or thrown stones (Huysmans and Claes, 2015).

Starting from these common-sense insights regarding urban realities, we could reasonably articulate a first theoretical challenge. Alternative, restorative practices that are grounded in dialogue and mutual recognition can no longer simply depart from the lifeworld experiences of a victim-position and an offender-position, for the simple reason that urban tensions do not exclusively crystallise into criminal behaviour. In these conflicting settings, it is often impossible, and even undesirable, to clearly identify victim and offender roles.

Moreover, the pivotal concept around which restorative justice practices should be reframed is the notion of urban tensions and conflicts. When can we rightly say that a tension takes the shape of a conflict? What are the themes around which these tensions arise? Where are they surfacing? Who is concerned? How are the stakeholders experiencing these conflicts, and how are they defining them?

From private troubles to social issues

Restorative justice practices are often praised for their psychological benefits. Establishing a dialogue between victims and offenders responds to deep emotional needs of both victims and offenders. Restorative meetings may lead to empowering processes, because the voices of both parties are heard in a setting of mutual respect (see Sawin and Zehr, 2007). Empirical research tends to confirm these beneficial effects (Sherman, 2006), which surely enhances the legitimacy of restorative justice, but one tends to forget the deeper structural causes that lead to criminal behaviour.

In urban settings, behaviour that is seen as socially disruptive (vandalism, street violence, drug-dealing ...) begs for contextualisation in broader processes of social deprivation. In the social housing estates of Vienna, as well as in the Anneessens quarter, social needs are pressing.

Compared with inhabitants living in other types of housing, the residents of social housing estates in Vienna have lower educational attainment, lower per capita income and higher unemployment rates (IFES, 2007). In 2008, almost 30 per cent of the tenants lived below the poverty line. In 2003, 4600 eviction orders were issued and 9900 tenants were in danger of becoming homeless. This is twice the number of tenants of private or cooperative housing who were confronted with this situation. Overall, the social composition of the tenants changed from the 1970s onwards; the proportion of socio-economically disadvantaged households increased. The demographic composition of the residents of the public housing estates regarding their ethnic and cultural background has also changed. We face an intersection of the social homogeneity of comparative economic deprivation and being dependent on social assistance, on the one hand, and ethnic heterogeneity, on the other hand. The latter adds the lack of resources due to language and cultural barriers and the exclusion resulting from this to an already existing disadvantaged position. Migration and social deprivation merge and contribute to a tendency of social downward mobility. This affects the lifeworld of people. There is the experience and the 'feeling' of more social inequality, and there is more insecurity and lack of safety (see Reinprecht, 2012).

A similar intersection can be observed in Anneessens. In line with demographic transitions in Brussels since the 1990s, Anneessens reflects a cosmopolitical, multi-linguistic city counting a majority of minorities. Like most quarters in the old industrial zones around the canal, Anneessens is marked by a young population (48 per cent are younger than 30 years old). At the same time, this dense, diverse and young population is experiencing massive social deprivation. Income derived from labour reaches only 37 per cent of the population of Anneessens. The ratio of long-term unemployed in this quarter is around 63 per cent. The average income of habitants of Anneessens is 50 per cent lower than the average income in the rest of Belgium.

Given these demographic realities of both the Viennese *Gemeindebau* and the Anneessens quarter, a second challenge with regard to restorative justice in urban settings comes to the surface. If we want to successfully stretch restorative practices to these areas, then rethinking restorative justice inevitably comprises reflection on how to transform conflicts into dialogues around fair redistribution of social needs and rights.

Repositioning restorative justice

Restorative justice has consolidated its identity as an alternative framework in constant opposition to, or in dialogue with, the logic of the traditional criminal justice system, its classic legal safeguards and its penal interventions. As a response to the formal, abstract, complexity-reducing character of criminal justice interventions, restorative justice seeks to bring in the lifeworld experience of victims, offenders and communities. Opposing itself to the paternalistic, top-down logic of a state-based criminal justice system, restorative justice defines itself as a participatory democratic experiment, giving victims, offenders and communities the chance to invent peacemaking solutions. And, finally, in response to the retributive, punitive force of the traditional criminal justice system, restorative justice seeks to remedy harm by calling the offender to take responsibility for the harms inflicted on victims and community (Walgrave, 2008).

In urban settings, restorative justice initiatives and values are confronted with logics and changes that transcend the criminal justice system. One of these logics, which has made its imprint on urban spaces, is neoliberal capitalism. In his book *Rebel Cities*, David Harvey (2013, p. 15) argues that 'The increasing polarisation in the distribution of wealth and power is indelibly etched into the spatial forms of our cities, which increasingly become cities of fortified fragments, of gated communities and privatized public spaces kept under constant surveillance.'

The imprint of capitalism on urban living can easily be identified in Brussels. The traces of a neoliberal market are omnipresent in the city. Real estate speculation and targeted investments in specific urban zones produce strong social inequalities in the use and appropriation of the urban space. In Brussels, this becomes visible in the contrast between poor, densely populated quarters around the canal, on the one hand, and green, comfortable urban spaces at the borders of the city, on the other. Some spaces attract massive investment and offer flourishing opportunities for the wealthy. Others are considered to be economically uninteresting. They are abandoned and left to the poor and the precarious. Unequal distribution of resources and life chances, reproduced into the urban geography of Brussels, creates an enormous potential for conflicts and tensions, especially since abandoned quarters around the canal have become transit zones for massive fluxes of newcomers migrating to Brussels since the 1990s. These changes partly explain an increase of frustrations, resentment and tensions within socially deprived groups (Vandecandelaere, 2015).

Another important social dynamic that calls for repositioning restorative justice revolves around the political framing of social conflicts in urban environments. In Vienna, social housing is one of the most important pillars of the welfare system, as about a third of the city's inhabitants live in social housing estates. Compared with other European cities, this percentage of people living in buildings built and owned by the city is rather high. Also, social housing estates were and still are constructed all over town – marginalised city outskirts or inner-city districts are practically non-existent in Vienna. Together, these facts seem to contribute to a relatively low stigmatisation of people living in social housing estates.

In 2006/2007, an EU Directive initiated a parliamentary process that eventually led to the long-discussed admission of third-country nationals to social housing estates. Ever since, the urban neighbourhoods of social housing estates in Vienna have turned into increasingly intercultural fields (this is not to say that they weren't intercultural before, though). Troubles and tensions (due to illegal garbage disposal, noisy children, vandalism and so forth) between neighbours have since been increasingly framed with reference to cultural differences. Vienna, however, stands out on the European map, since its city government still largely desists from the securitisation of residents of social housing estates to legitimise counter-measures of surveillance and control. While the Austrian Freedom Party (FPÖ) insists on framing conflicts (and their alleged potential of violence) as risks to the living comfort of 'Old-Austrian' inhabitants, brought about by their neighbours with a migration background, the long-ruling social democrats (SPÖ) in the city government deny the existence of any conflict at all. Nevertheless, they instituted *wohnpartner*, an organisation responsible for conflict mediation and community building in all social housing estates as a social response to social troubles (see Kremmel and Pelikan, 2014a).

If this is the broad social narrative regarding urban settings, then we have to reposition restorative justice on different levels. (1) Restorative narratives have to be embedded in a larger framework of critique and resistance regarding neoliberal capitalism and the future of the welfare state. (2) Restorative justice has to revisit its skills, sources, talents and values deployed in order to give citizens the tools to deconstruct reductionist strategies of 'othering'. (3) It should offer alternative ways of construing conflicts and transforming these through urban participative practices that address those powerful social and political forces that maintain social inequalities.

In this chapter, we aim to enrich restorative justice by offering two accounts. The first is an intersectional approach to interculturality, which allows us to get a differentiated view of conflicts in intercultural settings. The second account revolves around urban citizenship and aims at transforming conflicts through common civic practices that resist forces of social and political exclusion.

Towards an 'alternative' restorative framework

Restorative justice: some key elements

Pinpointing restorative justice to its essential concepts is not a sinecure. Many restorative justice theories and models exist, and sometimes they compete in their claims and ambitions. The research teams of both the Vienna site and the Anneessens site departed from a core idea of restorative justice defined by Pali and Pelikan (2010). Both authors identify three elements that recur in the theory and practice of restorative justice: the lifeworld element, the participative element and the restorative element.

Restorative justice stresses the lifeworld element because it sees crime and conflict not only as unlawful behaviour, but also as a disturbance of human interactions, as a web of frictions and frustrations that begs to be told and heard by the stakeholding parties. A respectful restorative response aims at constructing a safe space in which these personal stories can be told and respectfully listened to. The underlying restorative intuition comes down to the idea that the exchange of stories in a dialogical setting generates a context in which conflicting parties can be moved by each other's story. Finding appropriate practices that embody this lifeworld element is one of the key steps to conflict transformation (see Pali and Pelikan, 2010, pp. 11–12).

Restorative justice stresses the participative element for the simple reason that restorative justice is shaped by democratic ideals of ownership, participation and deliberation. It strongly believes that conflicting parties are affirmed and even growing in their dignity, self-respect and autonomy if they are given a stake in responding to crime or conflict. Participation in finding solutions for conflicts, or in negotiating conflicting interests, is seen as an expression of shared ownership. Conflicting parties are becoming the owners of their conflicts and thereby regain some control over their lives (see Pali and Pelikan, 2010, pp. 11–12).

Finally, restorative justice conceives its practices with the aim of restoring 'something'. What this restorative element precisely contains is not always clear. To many restorative justice advocates, it means the desistance from punishment in criminal justice. Also, a common idea is that the response to crime is something constructive, something that gives victims and offenders, or the conflicting parties, a chance to open new perspectives for the future. By doing so, restorative justice focuses on mobilising moral emotions such as empathy, repentance, forgiveness and hope. These emotions risk being obscured in a punitive climate that is dominated by fear, resentment and retribution. In rediscovering these restorative emotions, proponents of restorative justice hope to transform conflicts into new chances for human interactions in the future. Exchange of personal narratives (the lifeworld element) and actively participating in finding a response to conflicts are seen as important vehicles in releasing and channelling these restorative emotions (see Pali and Pelikan, 2010, pp. 11–12).

One of the main challenges of the research projects in both Vienna and Brussels is to link these three key elements to urban settings outside of the narrow context of crime and criminal justice and to make these restorative justice elements fully responsive to complex urban intercultural settings. Both research projects imported new conceptual fields into the framework of restorative justice. We will briefly discuss them in the following paragraphs.

An intersectional approach to interculturality

Since 'intercultural conflicts' are allegedly identified as issues troubling our times, we find it crucial to critically reflect on the term and to attend to the concept of 'interculturality'. Bluntly put, 'intercultural conflicts' do not exist, since cultures cannot enter into conflict – but people do, and their identities can be described in cultural terms (Foss *et al.*, 2012). This means that we acknowledge the important role 'culture' comes to play for people when they construct their narratives about who they are, but we do not think of culture as being the sole defining element. We understand identity as being constructed (through self- and external ascriptions) and not as a given essence.

In order to grasp the notion of 'interculturality' without promoting homogenising perceptions of social groups and essentialising some of their cultural traits, we make use of an intersectional approach (e.g. Du Gay and Hall, 1996; Grzanka, 2014; Solomos, 2014). We consider an intersectional understanding of interculturality to be viable for restorative justice theory and practice, since it allows a reading of social contexts that attends to the complexity of everyday life in urban spaces. Identities are multidimensional and relative, in that they consist of different dimensions, which come to the fore depending on the contexts we find ourselves in (I was born in the province of Vorarlberg and I live in Vienna, I am Austrian when I travel to Germany, and during holidays in Asia I identify myself as a female, middle-class European citizen).

From these observations, it follows that in each 'intercultural' setting, 'culture' is only one among many categories through which people may differ from each other. Other categories, like class, age, gender, sex and so on, also shape our ways of relating to each other and of constructing our identities. The risk inherent in the predominant focus on 'cultural differences' is of overlooking not only the influence of these other categories on organising differences between people, but also the possibilities they create for solidarity between individuals who might seem divided by different cultural backgrounds. We (the researchers in Vienna) thus dedicated ourselves to looking closely at people's narratives and interactions in order to identify the many dimensions or categories through which people differ from and identify with each other.

During our workshops in Viennese social housing estates, we were able to observe how people deployed different aspects of their identities to negotiate belonging and forge alliances. The observations we made during the bi-weekly breakfast sessions of a group of women (the Women's Café), consisting of members of the Austrian majority and migrant women mostly from Turkey, serve as vivid examples to illustrate these theoretical arguments (see also Kremmel and Pelikan, 2014b, 2015).

The group of women had initially got together after a series of serious incidents and conflicts in their housing estate, in order to improve communication between them. This being the explicit aim of the group, in the beginning they mostly conceived of each other as speaking different languages, but slowly – as they got to know each other better – aspects they had in common came to the fore. Shared experiences of motherhood, and along with these the concrete needs for assistance with childcare for some, and the longing for grandchildren for others, created the ground for practices of mutual support.

To contrast these observations, we will shortly quote a conversation between three members of the Women's Café at one of the breakfast meetings at this point: Michaela (a retired secretary, whose husband had passed away recently), Esra (the social worker who had supported the group since its beginning; she had migrated from Turkey to Vienna 15 years ago) and Cemre (a 16-year-old girl wearing a headscarf and looking for a job since she had lost her last employment as a hairdresser).

> MICHAELA TO CEMRE: So, where do you feel more at home, here in Austria, or in Turkey?
>
> CEMRE: I don't feel at home neither here nor there. (Turning towards Esra) That's how it is for us, isn't it?
>
> ESRA (in a very calm voice): Are you asking me? No, I belong here.
>
> (Kremmel, 2014)

Let's take a close look at this short quotation to grasp what the women were communicating about when we read their exchange through an intersectional lens: Michaela clearly feels affected by the strong suspicion that Cemre could have been discriminated against at her former workplace. She therefore tries to empathise with Cemre and, in her well-intentioned efforts, confronts the girl with an exclusionary logic of belonging by asking her where she feels more at home: here OR there?

With her answer, Cemre does not commit to these exclusionary terms, and she straightforwardly denies belonging to any state territory at all. She suggests that she belongs to a certain group – the 'us' she refers to is the 'we' of the migrants prone to be homeless, in which she also includes Esra.

Yet Esra, in turn, refuses to include herself in this 'we' Cemre introduced. Instead, she refers to herself, a migrant woman in Austria. By stating that she actually feels that she belongs to where she lives, she insists on the possibility of creating a sense of belonging to a place where one migrated to and where others might perceive one as a foreigner.

Looking at intercultural contexts with an intersectional lens prevents us from taking intracultural alliances for granted. It helps to better understand how people construe their identities and differences through interaction and dialogue with each other. It may have also an effect on restorative practice in an immediate way, since the discovery of 'shared intersections', and the shared needs and interests that come with them, may build common ground between people where before there seemed to be none.

Therefore, such an intersectional approach might have an impact on essential ingredients of the restorative justice framework. Conflicts are often defined in terms of competition of interests or opinions, or as a struggle for power over vital resources. The intersectional approach helps us to understand how conflicts might also emerge when people build their identities through a variety of interactions with others. Conflicts receive their meaning and shape through processes of identity affirmation by overstressing a single defining category. Some people, or groups, have an interest in maintaining conflicting relations in order to forge their individual or collective identities.

Further, the intersectional approach invites us to rethink the lifeworld element of restorative justice. Bringing personal narratives to the fore has been seen as one of the key-levers in the process of conflict transformation. The intersectional approach brings about an understanding of the complexities and ambiguities of these narratives in the forging of people's identities. It encourages us to better understand how and under which conditions lifeworld experiences of conflicting parties might open up identity constructions and create unexpected alliances and shared experiences.

Urban citizenship

Next to this intersectional approach to interculturality, a second conceptual field can be woven into the restorative justice framework. This conceptual field revolves around the notion of urban citizenship[1] and has been elaborated by the research team in Brussels.

Having analysed various recent grass-roots initiatives, the researchers came up with an idea of citizenship that refers to informal urban, participative practices (Claes, 2014; Lamote and Ampe, 2013). The initiators of these practices often focus on small, sharply delineated, but fresh and innovative city projects, for which they mobilise social support in their networks. These projects address urgent social needs that open up possibilities for urban innovation. Sometimes they raise a critical voice against city capitalism, or ineffective local policies. Three dimensions of urban citizenship emerged from analysing these grass-roots initiatives. Urban citizenship refers to participatory practices through which citizens stimulate the development of each other's human capabilities (first dimension). As clearly analysed by Nussbaum (2011), these capabilities are multiple and mutually interdependent. Urban citizenship also refers to aspirational practices through which citizens learn together how to make their hopes and aspirations concrete (second dimension). As argued by Appadurai (2013), these learning practices are crucial to reinforce the capacity to change the future. And, finally, urban citizenship also contains a critical aspect. The practices to which it refers embody the capacity to collectively raise a counter-voice which makes needs and unequal access to rights visible in public spaces (third dimension). These practices express, to use Lefèbvre's notorious phrase, 'the right to the city' (Harvey, 2008; Lefèbvre, 1996; Plyushteva, 2009). A nice example that reflects these three dimensions emerged from a small non-governmental organisation (NGO), *Cultureghem*, in Brussels. Social workers invented mobile kitchens enabling children, parents, market visitors and schools to meet and learn how to easily get access to cheap and healthy food. Pushing these kitchens into public space creates a collective event around which people from completely different backgrounds connect and activate each other's capability to enjoy healthy food (first, participatory dimension). While learning to find cheap but healthy food on the market, children and their parents discover concrete strategies to change their eating patterns. Therefore, educational programmes attached to the mobile kitchens also embody the second dimension of urban citizenship (second, aspirational dimension). And, finally, the mobile kitchens are also critical signposts (third dimension). Their presence in urban public space raises a critical voice about the unequal access to healthy food due to unequal distribution of wealth, and the disproportional impact of junk food industries on contemporary consumerist societies.

In a next step, the Belgian research team made efforts to reinterpret the three basic ingredients of restorative justice in light of this notion of urban citizenship.

Regarding the lifeworld element, the research team in Anneessens fully embraced the idea of exchanging stories and lived experiences of stakeholders. These stories reveal different perspectives on how conflicts are lived, defined and contextualised from the first-person perspective of the narrator. In line with restorative justice theory, the team believed that the exchange of these stories has the power to generate mutual respect and understanding. The theoretical focus on urban citizenship invited the team to design a narrative practice in which the stories of conflicting parties make needs and rights visible, in which these stories might reveal deeper and shared aspirations as a basis for collective change of urban life. And this narrative environment should not only be a private, confidential one; it should also have a public counterpart, allowing discussion in public space on the basis of particular stories.

The research team in Anneessens thus developed the idea of adding other participatory activities than talking, negotiating and deliberating. If the aim of restorative justice in urban settings is to develop practices of urban citizenship out of conflicting relations, then citizens should be doing more than just deliberatively communicating. Facilitating solidarity around capabilities, around aspirational capacities, as well as around making one's needs and rights visible in the city, requires new interventions that focus not only on dialogue and communication, but also on collective action, on collectively transforming public space in order to make the power of hope more operational, more concrete and more visible. This, inevitably, implies that urban restorative justice practices should be explicitly output oriented. The idea of aspirational citizenship, then, implies creating a conflict-transforming environment in which hopeful ideas grow into city projects with a specific social impact.

So far the theory. But what is the interpretive and transformative power of this citizenship-based framework when we project it on the series of interventions both in Brussels and in Vienna?

From theory to practice

Walking citizens

Let us first focus on the research site in the Anneessens quarter. The walking stage successfully incarnated the idea of urban citizenship, since the interviewees during the walk performed their engagement as responsible citizens. The process of walking, guiding, reflecting, judging and dialoguing empowered the interviewees in their capacity to mentally as well as spatially appropriate their living space. The walks were also loyal to the spirit of restorative justice, since they have strong affinities with the preparatory stage of a mediation process. The position of the researcher melts with the role of the mediator, to the extent that the former listens, asks open questions, and opens space for trust and self-revelation (Huysmans and Claes, 2015).

What is missing, however, is a collective dialoguing process through which stakeholding parties are invited to discover conflicting views as a lever for redistributing and negotiating capabilities, making rights visible, or turn aspirations into city projects. The idea of citizenship-based restorative justice bounces here on the limits of its interpretive and action-guiding powers.

Digital storytelling and urban citizenship

As mentioned above, the multi-staged interventions of the Anneessens research team also contained a digital storytelling experiment that followed the walking stage. The researchers initiated two trajectories organised for small groups of citizens. How did this process of digital storytelling relate to the idea of urban citizenship? The researchers discovered that this stage offers a much stronger embodiment of a citizenship-based restorative practice. In contrast with the walking stage, these trajectories created a platform for a collective and communicative process between habitants. The personal challenge of each participant was to create a personal story, with a few sentences and some personal images or pictures. At the same time, this challenge was embedded in a context of discussion, listening, commenting and creatively helping each other. Both trajectories were quite diverse with regard to age, sex, socio-economic status, origins and length of time in the quarter. Accordingly, it was to be expected that colliding views would emerge during the sessions. Also particular for both digital storytelling trajectories was that they combined multi-media storytelling with a focus on living in and frequenting the urban environment of Anneessens. Both processes created imaginary scenes in which the participants could express themselves on their urban environment as citizens, and at the same time experience the appreciation of their fellow participants.

Moreover, when comparing both processes of digital storytelling, the intertwinement of restorative justice and urban citizenship serves as an interesting interpretive lens in order to deliver the deeper meaning of these processes as they unfolded during the sessions. Two thought lines should suffice to make our point here.

1 In both groups, setting up the dynamics of storytelling with regard to living in Anneessens proved to be quite conflicting. It was not that the participants were parties in conflict (they were not quarrelling or verbally violent), but their views on the quarter were in friction. It was also interesting to discover that most of the discussions circled around the use of public space by youngsters. Some argued that their impolite, sometimes aggressive behaviour was due to lack of parental responsibility. This view clashed head-on with those who were sensitive to the precarious life chances of both parents and children, their urge to survive, and their limited conceptual and linguistic skills restricting them in their ability to cope with the complexities of urban living.

   Intertwining urban citizenship and restorative justice served here as a fruitful interpretive scheme in that it called us to focus not only on a burning issue (disturbing behaviour of youngsters) but also on the frictions that emerge when habitants try, each from their own point of view, to make sense and to acquire a kind of ownership of their view on pressing urban issues. During the digital storytelling sessions, the participants were fully activating their human capability to control one's environment according to a certain conception of a good and meaningful life (Nussbaum, 2011, p. 34).

2 In both processes of digital storytelling, the participants were encouraged to enter into a moment of personal self-reflection. They were asked to tell a short personal story about their life in Anneessens. They were asked to shape their engagement as citizens in a truly authentic way. Again, fusing the language of aspirational citizenship and restorative justice helps to deepen the meaning of digital storytelling. Using this language, we can now say that the facilitator of the digital storytelling sessions invited the participating habitants to radicalise their ownership with regard to the conflicting material that came to the fore. By 'radicalising' we mean that the participants were encouraged to link their views on urban issues to their personal aspirations, their deepest convictions and their characteristic affective attitudes. A minimalistic narrative structure, a few evocative images, but most of all the unique voice of each participant are

the ingredients for making this ownership true. The result of this process of linking one's views on certain issues back to one's deepest aspirations is clearly visible in the outcome of the processes, in the digital stories (Digitaal verhaal Jonas, Elke, Sow, 2015).

Urban citizenship and the shift towards participatory research

One of the striking similarities between the research experiences of the Vienna team and the Brussels team is a strong reflective awareness of the role of the researcher and the impact of his/her interventions on the field. Both teams were strongly aware of the power relations involved in research interventions. The researchers in both teams took a critical stance towards an examining, objectifying and detecting researcher's perspective through which the inhabitants would have been reduced to study-objects, sources of data, respondents obedient to the research of an intervening team. Both teams fully acknowledged the importance of equalising interactions and added an element of reciprocity into the production of knowledge.

The Vienna team developed this democratic awareness through the methodology of participatory filmmaking. The Brussels team started to reflect upon their spatial position (as a distant observer with zero accountability) in parks and other public spots, and to reflect upon other spatial possibilities that attract respectful encounter between equals, as well as modesty, and proximity. As a consequence of this, they decided to build a mobile chalet that served three social functions (encounter, storytelling and presentation of digital stories) (Claes *et al.*, 2016). The chalet (called *Insjalet*) enabled them to welcome habitants in their mobile café, to meet them as full equals, to invite them to tell, draft and draw their stories of their neighbourhood (narrative atelier), and to show their digital stories to their co-habitants (mobile cinema).

Both types of interventions interrupt the vertical relation between researcher and respondent, and offer a participative, equal and reciprocal environment in which all the stakeholders involved have the right to stand behind the camera and to reappropriate public space through producing images, authentic opinions and confronting questions.

Bringing both types of participatory research together, and reflecting on this, inevitably leaves its imprint on the idea of urban citizenship. Researchers are unable to bring urban citizenship to intercultural settings without engaging themselves in a civic practice which is characterised by dialogue, mutual respect and equal positions as co-creators of meaning and knowledge.

Conclusions

So far, the comparative analysis of the Vienna sites and the Anneessens quarter enabled us to remould restorative justice theory by means of (a) an intersectional approach to interculturality and (b) urban citizenship. Particularly the last concept allows us to construct a framework of citizenship-based restorative justice. In order to align restorative justice with urban settings and its pressing social issues, restorative justice practices should aim at (1) reconnecting conflicting groups in order to redistribute or negotiate fair access to human capabilities; (2) transforming conflicts and tensions into collective projects that empower people to aspire to a better future; (3) finding a common ground between groups in order to make common needs and rights visible. Upgrading urban citizenship as the central goal of restorative practices promises to give proponents of restorative justice a strong framework to connect vulnerable groups with less vulnerable groups beyond their conflicts, to facilitate a platform on which they can open up possibilities and claim their say in the regulation of public space. Implementing the idea of urban citizenship in restorative justice opens the possibility of urban restorative practices which critically address the oppressive power of city capitalism. Embedded in such a citizenship-based framework, the restorative power of storytelling, participation and hope for a new beginning has the potential to mobilise a counter-force against the arrogance of huge financial interests or top-down political decisions.

Note

1 For a literature overview in the growing field of citizenship studies see Caglar (2015) and Varsanyi (2006).

Bibliography

Appadurai, A., 2013. *Condition de l'homme global*. Paris: Payot.

Bosnjak, M., 2007. Some thoughts on the relationship between restorative justice and the criminal law. In: R. Mackay, M. Bosnjak, J. Deklerck, C. Pelikan, B. van Stokkom, and M. Wright. eds, *Images of Restorative Justice Theory*. Frankfurt am Main: Verlag für Polizeiwissenschaften. pp. 93–112.

Caglar, A., 2015. Anthropology of citizenship. In: J. D. Wright, ed., *International Encyclopedia of the Social & Behavioral Sciences*. 2nd edn. Oxford: Elsevier. pp. 637–642.

Claes, E., 2014. Growfunding en stedelijk burgerschap. On-en offline solidariteit, *Alert: Tijdschrift voor Sociaal Werk en Politiek*, 2014.2, pp. 32–41.

Claes, E., Huysmans, M. and Gulinck, N., 2015. Digital storytelling en herstelrecht. Wonen in een Brusselse wijk Anneessens, sociaal.net, 16 April 2015. http://sociaal.net/analyse-xl/digital-storytelling-en-herstelrecht/ (accessed 23 June 2017).

Claes, E., Huysmans, M. and Gulinck, N., 2016. Levensverhalen komen bovendrijven. Met een mobiele chalet door Brussel, sociaal.net, 4 July 2016. http://sociaal.net/analyse-xl/insjaletherstelrecht/ (accessed 23 June 2017).

Couldry, N., 2008. Mediatization or mediation? Alternative understanding of the emergent space of digital storytelling. *New Media & Society*, 10 (3), pp. 373–391.

Digitaal verhaal Elke, 20 May 2015. sociaal.net/column/het leven-in-de-anneessenswijk.

Digitaal verhaal Homme, 12 November 2015. sociaal.net/column/het leven-in-de-anneessenswijk.

Digitaal verhaal Jonas, 16 April 2015. sociaal.net/column/het leven-in-de-anneessenswijk.

Digitaal verhaal Sow, 19 November 2015. sociaal.net/column/het leven-in-de-anneessenswijk.

Domenig, C., 2011. Restorative Justice – vom marginalen Verfahrensmodell zum integralen Lebensentwurf. In: Service Büro für Täter-Opfer-Ausgleich und Konfliktschlichtung, ed., 2011. *Restorative Justice. Der Versuch, das Unübersetzbare in Worte zu fassen*. Köln: JVA Druck + Medien, pp. 8–23.

Du Gay, P. and Hall, S., eds, 1996. *Questions of Cultural Identity*. London: Sage.

Foss, E., Hassan, S. C., Hydle, I., Seeberg, M. L. and Uhrig, B. 2012. Report on conflicts in intercultural settings. ALTERNATIVE: deliverable 2.1. Available at: www.alternativeproject.eu/publications/public-deliverables/ (accessed 13 June 2016).

Grzanka, P. R., ed., 2014. *Intersectionality. A Foundations and Frontiers Reader*. Philadelphia: Westview.

Gyabak, K. and Godina, H., 2011. Digital storytelling in Bhutan: A qualitative examination of new media tools used to bridge the digital divide in a rural community school. *Journal of Computers and Education*, 57, pp. 2236–2243.

Haller, B. and Karazman-Morawetz, I., 2004. *Konfliktlösungsmodelle für Großwohnanlagen*. Vienna: Report of the Institute for Conflict Research.

Haller, B., David, E., Lercher, K., Schranz, H. and Tomaschitz, W., 2008. *'Hot Spots' sozialer Konflikte und Gebietsbetreuung in Wiener Wohnhausanlagen*. Vienna: Report of the Institute for Conflict Research.

Harvey, D., 2008. The right to the city. *New Left Review*, 53, pp. 23–40.

Harvey, D., 2013. *Rebel Cities: From the Right to the City to the Urban Revolution*. London: Verso.

Hull, G. A. and Katz, M.-L., 2006. Crafting an agentive self: Case studies of digital stories. *Research in the Teaching of English*, 41(1), pp. 43–81.

Huysmans, M. and Claes, E., 2015. Conflictbeleving en herstelrecht in Brussel. *Tijdschrift voor Herstelrecht*, 15(3), pp. 53–68.

IFES (Institute for Empirical Social Studies), 2007. *Lebensqualität im Wiener Gemeindebau*. Vienna: Stadt Wien – Wiener Wohnen.

Johnstone, G. and Van Ness, D. W., eds, 2007. *Handbook of Restorative Justice*. Cullompton: Willan.

Kremmel, K. Unpublished field notes from 13 October 2014. Vienna: IRKS.

Kremmel, K. and Pelikan, C., 2013. Theoretical research report on activating Civil Society. ALTERNATIVE: deliverable 4.1. Available at: www.alternativeproject.eu/publications/public-deliverables/ (accessed 13 June 2016).

Kremmel, K. and Pelikan, C., 2014a. Living together in the Gemeindebau in Vienna: On tensions, conflicts, fears and hopes. ALTERNATIVE: deliverable 4.2. Available at: www.alternativeproject.eu/publications/public-deliverables/ (accessed 13 June 2016).

Kremmel, K. and Pelikan, C., 2014b. Ways towards the resolution of conflicts? A Study of the existing ways of handling conflicts in social housing estates in Vienna. ALTERNATIVE: deliverable 4.3.

Kremmel, K. and Pelikan, C., 2015. Towards restorative circles: Action research interventions in Vienna's social housing estates. ALTERNATIVE: deliverable 4.4.

Lambert, J., 2013. *Digital Storytelling: Capturing Lives, Creating Community*. New York: Routledge.

Lamote, F. and Ampe, S., 2013. We are a growfunding platform. Concepttekst.

Lefèbvre, H., 1996. *Writings on Cities*. E. Kofman and E. Lebas (ed). Oxford: Blackwell Publishing.

McCold, P., 2006. The recent history of restorative justice. Mediation, circles, and conferencing. In: D. Sullivan and L. Tifft, eds, *Handbook of Restorative Justice: A Global Perspective*. New York: Routledge, pp. 23–50.

Malita, L. and Martin, C. 2010. Digital storytelling as web passport to success in the 21st century. *Procedia Social and Behavioral Sciences*, 2, pp. 3060–3064.

Nussbaum, M., 2006. *Frontiers of Justice*. Cambridge, MA: Harvard University Press.

Nussbaum, M., 2011. *Creating Capabilities. The Human Development Approach*. Cambridge, MA: Harvard University Press.

Pali, B. and Pelikan, C., 2010. *Building Social Support for Restorative Justice*. Leuven: European Forum for Restorative Justice.

Pelikan, C., 2007. The place of restorative justice in society: Making sense of developments in time and space. In: R. Mackay, M. Bosnjak, J. Deklerck, C. Pelikan, B. van Stokkom, and M. Wright, eds, *Images of Restorative Justice Theory*. Frankfurt am Main: Verlag für Polizeiwissenschaften, pp. 35–55.

Plyushteva, A., 2009. The right to the city and struggles over urban citizenship: Exploring the links. *Amsterdam Social Science*, 1 (3), pp. 81–97.

Raye, B.E. and Roberts, A.W., 2007. Restorative processes. In: G. Johnstone and D. W. Van Ness, eds, *Handbook of Restorative Justice*. Cullompton: Willan, pp. 211–227.

Reinprecht, C., 2012. Die Zukunft des Wiener Gemeindebaus und die Transformation des Sozialen. In: F. Bettel, J. M. Permoser and S. Rosenberger, eds, *Living Rooms – Politik der Zugehörigkeiten im Wiener Gemeindebau*. Vienna: Springer, pp. 205–221.

Sawin, J.L. and Zehr, H. 2007. The ideas of engagement and empowerment. In: G. Johnstone and D. W. Van Ness, eds, *Handbook of Restorative Justice*. Cullompton: Willan, pp. 41–58.

Sherman, L.W., 2006. Effects of face-to-face restorative justice conferences: A quasi-experimental analysis. *Journal of Social Issues*, 62 (2), pp. 281–392.

Solomos, J., 2014. Stuart Hall: Articulations of race, class and identity. *Ethnic and Racial Studies*, 37(10), pp. 1667–1675.

Stuart, B. and Pranis, K., 2006. Peacemaking circles. Reflections on principal features and primary outcomes. In: D. Sullivan and L. Tifft, eds, *Handbook of Restorative Justice: A Global Perspective*. New York: Routledge. pp. 121–133.

Sullivan, D. and Tifft, L., eds, 2006. *Handbook of Restorative Justice: A Global Perspective*. New York: Routledge.

Vandecandelaere, H., 2015. *In Molenbeek*. Antwerp: Epo.

Varsanyi, M.W., 2006. Interrogating 'urban citizenship' vis-à-vis undocumented migration. *Citizenship Studies*, 10 (2), pp. 229–249.

Walgrave, L., 2008. *Restorative Justice, Self-interest, and Responsible Citizenship*. Cullompton: Willan.

Weitekamp, E. G. M. and Kerner, H., eds, 2002. *Restorative Justice. Theoretical Foundations*. Cullompton: Willan.

Yang, Y.-T. C. and Wu, J. J., 2012. Digital storytelling for enhancing student academic achievement, critical thinking, and learning motivation: A year-long experimental study. *Journal of Computers and Education*, 59, pp. 339–352.

6 Counteracting social exclusion through restorative approaches

Gábor Héra

Introduction

The chapter introduces some of the academic debates on the concept of social exclusion, identifying its core elements, and highlighting the main points by concretely referring to the situation of the Roma minority in Hungary. After this introductory background, the chapter presents the findings of action research that was conducted in a small Hungarian town and analyses the mechanism of exclusion that affected the local Roma. At the end of the chapter, emphasis is laid on the coexistence of exclusion and the lack of open communication between the Roma and non-Roma groups of the community under investigation. The author argues that the approach of restorative justice is an adequate answer not only for addressing the lack of open communication between different groups but also for supporting vulnerable groups and thereby counteracting social exclusion.

The concept of social exclusion

Originally the subject of public discourse in France during the 1960s, the term 'exclusion' became widespread only after the social and political crises in the 1980s (Silver, 1994), and was later on enthusiastically adopted across Europe. Between 1975 and 1994, the focus of the anti-poverty programs shifted from 'poverty' to 'exclusion' (Room, 1995; Silver, 1995), and the term (and the importance of social inclusion) was incorporated into various documents, policy papers and recommendations of the European Union. The term 'exclusion' is still a widespread concept nowadays. The acceptance and extensive application of the term is typical not only within the EU, since several international organisations such as the UN, the World Bank, the United Nations Educational, Scientific and Cultural Organization (UNESCO), the United Nations Development Programme (UNDP) and the International Labour Organization (ILO) have also been increasingly using the concept (Estivill, 2003).

Reflecting on the political origins of the concept, Murard argues that the concept of exclusion is not

> rooted in the social sciences, but an empty box given by the French state to the social sciences in the late 1980s as a subject to study. The empty box has since been filled with a huge number of pages, treatises and pictures, in varying degrees academic, popular, original and valuable.
>
> (2002, p. 41)

Despite the process of 'filling', the concept is still contested, it has multiple meanings, and, as Saraceno put it, 'what social exclusion means is about far from being univocally achieved' (2001, p. 3). Atkinson and Hills also emphasise (while citing Weinberg and Ruano-Borbalan) that 'observers in fact only agree on a single point: the impossibility to define the status of the "excluded" by a single and unique criterion. Reading numerous enquiries and reports on exclusion reveals a profound confusion amongst experts' (1998, p. 13). Other scholars also point to the lack of an adequate definition and scientific conceptualisation of the term (Shaaban, 2011; Jehoel-Gijsbers and Vrooman, 2007; Levitas *et al.*, 2007). Yet others underline that the picture is also blurred because the words changed their meanings when crossing borders, thus creating dissimilarities in interpretation (de Haan, 1999; Ferge, 2002; Estivill, 2003). The lack of an exact definition can be recognised even by the titles of scientific articles, such as 'Social exclusion: A concept in need of definition?' (Peace, 2001) and 'The problematic nature of exclusion' (Sibley, 1998).

Notwithstanding all these difficulties, some common grounds of the definitions can be identified, and thereby core elements of social exclusion can be specified. The first core element could be the *multidimensional* aspect of the term. As Shaaban summarises, scholars identified several realms of everyday life – usually the economic, cultural, social and political dimensions – where inequalities arise (2011, p. 120). Thereby, the concept of social exclusion encompasses not only lack of paid work or income poverty but – among many other things – lack of access to education, information, childcare and health facilities, accessibility of public provisions, poor living conditions, and so on. A similar distinction is made by Silver, who argues that social exclusion 'is multidimensional in that it marries the material and non-material, economic and social dimensions of disadvantage' (2006, p. 4). It is important to underline that social exclusion emerges in more than one dimension at the same time, resulting in inequality and negative consequences for quality of life, well-being and future life chances (Sen, 2000; de Haan, 1999; Miliband, 2006; Levitas *et al.*, 2007).

> Another important characteristic of social exclusion is *dynamics* – the phenomenon underlying what is beyond the current status and the process through which people become excluded. This attribute refers to the changing and interactive nature of social exclusion along different dimensions and at different levels over time [...]. The experience of social exclusion is unequally distributed across socio-economic and ethnic groups and that it is not a static state experienced by the same social groups at all times in all places.
>
> (Mathieso *et al.*, 2008, p. 13)

For example, stereotypes about the 'Roma people'[1] and the consequences of their potential stigmatisation probably differ in Canada (where the first Roma migrants arrived just a few years ago) and in Hungary (where the Roma people have lived since the thirteenth century). At the same time, one can presuppose that Roma people's experience of their own social exclusion is different nowadays from what it was during socialism or even before. Exclusion happens in time and can change during centuries, decades or even years, during the lifetime of a single person.

The dynamic aspect is additionally relevant given that the exclusion from social relationships results in further deprivations and thereby further decrease of living opportunities. De Haan underlines that 'the central definition of the notion of social exclusion [...] stresses the processes through which people are being deprived, taking the debate beyond descriptions of merely the situation in which people are' (1999, p. 5). Estivill also gives a similar description, stating that social exclusion

> designates an accumulation of confluent processes which, through successive ruptures, have their origins in the heart of the economy, politics and society, and which distance and render inferior individuals, groups, communities and spaces in relation to centres of power, resources and the prevailing values.
>
> (2003, p. 115)

This approach supports the understanding of social exclusion as 'succession, and cumulation, of breaks and disadvantages in an individual's life' (Saraceno, 2001, p. 15).

Finally, the *relational* aspect of the concept shifts the emphasis to the importance of social relationships and the need for comparison with others. According to this perspective, an observer cannot decide whether a person is socially excluded by looking at his/her circumstances themselves in isolation – one has to take the others also into consideration. Sen cites Adam Smith in order to explain the relational aspect:

> By necessaries I understand not only the commodities which are indispensably necessary for the support of life, but whatever the custom of the country renders it indecent for creditable people, even the lowest order, to be without.... Custom has rendered leather shoes a necessary of life in England. The poorest creditable person of either sex would be ashamed to appear in public without them.
>
> (Sen, 2000, p. 7)

Social exclusion on the macro level – the Roma minority in Hungary

In this section, I will illustrate the core elements of exclusion by referring to the case of the Roma minority in Hungary, identified as 'the poorest of the poor'

(*National Social Inclusion Strategy*, 2010, p. 6) and as the main victims of social exclusion par excellence.

Focus on the dynamics aspect – history of the Roma in Hungary

The Roma in Hungary do not belong to the newly arrived groups of migrants; sources from the thirteenth and fourteenth centuries have already mentioned the arrival and the presence of the Roma in Hungary (Dupcsik, 2009). Between the fifteenth and seventeenth centuries, the Roma found their place in the Hungarian society; during the war against the Ottoman Empire, in particular, the lack of craftsmen and the military preparations created some opportunities for them to work. However, the economic, political and social transformations in Hungary after the beginning of the eighteenth century brought some significant changes into the relationship between the Roma and the rest of the society. According to Nagy (2004), this was the period when non-Roma started identifying the Roma with those things that they feared, such as exclusion, poverty, homelessness, starvation and existential uncertainty. Kemény underlined that the 'enlightened' absolutism characteristic of the era of Maria Theresia tried to 'regulate anything that was still unregulated' (Kemény, 2005, p. 15). Many rules came into force about restrictions on marriage, travelling, begging, clothing, using the Romani language and so on. Mezey considered these regulations as a rough attack against the lifestyle and social structure of the Gypsies that 'resulted in an anti-Roma campaign' (1998).

The following century brought positive changes into the life of the Roma again. As Kemény put it,

> at the time of the 1893 census, the situation of Roma was significantly better than it had been in earlier decades or centuries. [...] Hungary's national income doubled or even tripled between 1867 and 1900. This growth had a tangible effect on Roma livelihoods.
>
> (2005, p. 41)

However, after World War I, the situation of Roma worsened again in terms of employment and due to the political ideology and the growing discriminatory tendencies; according to estimations, up to 1,500,000 Roma were persecuted because of their origins during the Nazi era in Europe (Hancock, 2004). As Bársony estimates, about 60,000–70,000 of them were Hungarian Roma, of whom 10,000–12,000 died (Bársony and Daróczi, 2007).

The next decades brought some positive changes again. The ideology of communism and the necessity for a labour force during the enforced industrialisation in socialist Hungary after World War II provided full employment, mainly for the Roma men, and thereby enhanced their opportunities for social integration (Kocsis and Kocsis, 1999). As the Roma could only partially fulfil the requirements of the labour market because of their educational, health and housing difficulties, nationwide campaigns began in Hungary in order to reduce these disadvantages. Although certain drawbacks of these programmes can be identified, the living conditions of the Roma improved significantly during this period.

This brief look at the history of the Roma minority in Hungary shows clearly that their level of inclusion/exclusion was a continuously changing and interactive process.

Focus on the relational aspect – Roma after the collapse of socialism

The employment rate of Roma has dramatically declined since socialism collapsed. Among the Roma, semi- and unskilled work were dominant, and these positions were the first to cease when the system changed. In 1989, the proportion of employment dropped from 67 per cent in 1989 (Kertesi, 2005) to 31 per cent in 1993 among the 15–49-year-old Roma population. There has not been any increase in the employment rate of Roma during the last 20 years; the rate of paid employment of Roma aged 20 to 64 is significantly lower (reaching about 35 per cent) compared with the non-Roma (nearly 50 per cent) (Fundamental Rights Agency of the European Union, 2012, p. 16).

Similar, and even quite dramatic, tendencies can be recognised in the field of education. In 2003, 40 per cent of the youth population in the 20–24 age group attended college or university, while this rate was only 1.2 per cent among the Roma youth (Kemény *et al.*, 2004, p. 89). Other research findings (Ferge *et al.*, 2002; Ladányi and Szelényi, 2002; European Network against Racism, 2011; Gábos *et al.*, 2013) point unambiguously at the relational aspect of social exclusion by emphasising the differences between the Roma and the non-Roma.

Focus on the multidimensional aspect – Roma after the collapse of socialism

Further research programs have described the poor housing conditions of Roma households. According to the survey in 2003 (Babusik, 2004, pp. 30–39), 20 per cent of the Roma live in social housing buildings originally not designed for living in. National research conducted between 2003 and 2010 shows that the infrastructure of Roma households is very poor (Babusik, 2007; Marketing Centrum, 2010; Letenyei and Varga, 2011). According to the Fundamental Rights Agency survey, about 45 per cent of Roma lived in households that lacked at least one of the following basic housing amenities: indoor kitchen, indoor toilet, indoor shower or bath, and electricity (Fundamental Rights Agency of the European Union, 2012, p. 23).

Another dimension of deprivation is health and/or access to health services. As studies emphasised, Roma people with poor health conditions did not have access to quality, specialist medical care within the health care system (Babusik, 2004).

Taking into consideration the findings of further programmes regarding negative attitudes towards the Roma, researchers suppose that the exclusion of the members of the minority from social relationships and interactions is also widespread. According to a survey conducted in 2011, two-thirds of Hungarians would not let their kids play with Roma children (NOL, 2011). In 2009, 58 per cent of the population believed that crime is in the blood of the Roma (Gimes *et al.*, 2009). In the same year, the percentage of those who agreed with the statement 'there are respectable Roma but the majority of them are not respectable' was 82 per cent (Gimes *et al.*, 2009). Negative attitudes towards Roma are obvious in everyday life; media, national broadsheets, websites and tabloids (Bernáth and Messing, 2011). Even documentary films (Strausz, 2014) strengthen such stereotypes and contribute to racist prejudices. Anti-Roma feelings are supported by radical movements and political parties (Gimes *et al.*, 2008; Juhász, 2010a, 2010b; Pytlas, 2013). Lack of tolerance and the exclusion phenomenon were highlighted not only by research but also by a series of hate-murders resulting in the deaths of six Roma and multiple injuries (Human Rights First, 2010).

These data reflect clearly the multidimensional aspect of social exclusion of the Roma from the labour market, high-quality education, the health care system and appropriate housing conditions.

Focus on the meso level – conflicts and exclusion in a small Hungarian town

In this section, the dynamics aspect of social exclusion at a meso level as 'the process by which individuals and social groups belong to, or are detached from, relevant and meaningful social networks' (Saraceno, 2001, p. 2) is further analysed at a local level, by focusing on a small town in Hungary where 'the social processes that include some groups and exclude others' (de Haan, 1999, p. 16) can be further identified.

Such an inquiry has been enabled by action research which focused on conflicts as a unit of analysis, and during which the researchers formed 'partnerships with community members to identify issues of local importance, develop ways of studying them, collect and interpret data, and take action on the resulting knowledge' (Smith *et al.*, 2010, p. 408), aiming 'to effect desired change as a path to generating knowledge and empowering stakeholders' (Bradbury-Huang, 2010, p. 93).

The colleagues of the Foresee Research Group, the Hungarian partner of the ALTERNATIVE project, were responsible for the action research that was implemented in a small Hungarian town – called 'Kisváros'[2] – between the end of 2011 and May 2015. During these years, they built up good relationships and mutual trust with the community, got in contact with the local residents, evolved personal relationships with them and thereby were often personally involved in the everyday life of the community.

Without trust, Foresee would have not been able to analyse the key issues of the action research: the conflicts and conflict handling strategies in Kisváros. Due to the mutual trust, the action research was successful, as at the end of the almost four-year-long field work a clear picture emerged about harms in the village, reasons behind disputes or misunderstandings, and a general understanding of discontents, including information about the way social exclusion works at the meso level.

Background – description of the village

Kisváros, where the action research was implemented, is an average settlement, with about 3000 inhabitants. It has its own soccer field, kindergarten, primary school, small library and church. A family doctor is available. Local grass-roots organisations – Home Guard, soccer club, a club for retired residents, a choir and so on – are active. Roma residents also live in Kisváros, but their number is not significant; in 2001, about 4 per cent of the people considered themselves Roma (Központi Statisztikai Hivatal, 2012) but in the opinion of the leader of the Roma Minority Government, this percentage is 8 per cent today – again consistent with the national average.

The history of the village has run parallel to the history of the country. During the forced industrialisation under socialism, 50 per cent of the local residents worked in industry and many people worked in the capital. This was the period when the local Roma had jobs and did not have to worry about income and living. However, after 1989, industrial workers had to face unemployment. These changes affected the Roma minority as well: 'Roma used to travel to work. They had beautiful, clean houses. They were working together with the Hungarians … there was no problem at all. The year 1989 was the beginning of the hard slump for them.' Nowadays even the non-Roma villagers have limited opportunities; they work mainly at institutes of local government, or travel to the capital to work and have a job in the surrounding villages or with the few local companies. Roma residents are often unemployed or work exclusively within the public work system.[3]

Social exclusion of the local Roma

Local residents usually considered their settlement as a 'peaceful island' where the relationship between the Roma and non-Roma inhabitants was calm. Although some of the villagers mentioned smaller conflicts in the past few years, and sometimes tensions were also observable, as they often emphasised, in comparison with other settlements, the situation was fine. However, when Foresee members were talking to some of the local Roma during the action research, the Roma told them different stories, according to which they had felt excluded.[4]

The case of the 'Civil Guard'

First, conflicts related to the local 'Civil Guard' should be mentioned. As one of the Roma residents, Tibor, the leader of the Roma Minority Government[5] and at the same time a representative of the City Council, shared with us, members of a local non-governmental organisation initiated the establishment of a civil guard in 2009. Dissent emerged at that time because members of that 'Civil Guard' were clearly against involving Roma residents in their work. Some members of the organisation invited Tibor to join the civil guard, but

> no other Roma from the village were welcome. I resented that for the local Roma local security was as important as for the non-Roma. It would have been great if the village had believed that the local Roma had been also for the local security, tranquillity and peace.

Finally, the conflict and harm that arose due to the Roma's exclusion from the 'Civil Guard' were not discussed. Neither Tibor nor other local Roma joined the initiative.

As the number of burglaries increased in Kisváros at the end of 2013, Tibor was motivated to do something for the local security. He initiated the establishment of a new 'Civil Guard'. He was not alone in this attempt; Henrik, another local resident, also supported the initiative. They agreed to set up the new organisation in order to 'make the sense of security of the local residents stronger'. Tibor and Henrik informed the members of their informal network about their intention, and advertised the plan on Facebook and in one of the local newspapers. Tibor tried to mobilise some Roma residents as well.

As Tibor and Henrik emphasised, they had several problems with the current 'Civil Guard', because the number of burglaries increased in 2013. As only two civil guards were on the street at nights and as their technical equipment was poor, they were not able catch 'criminals'. In addition, some members of the civil guard were not dedicated to their work. Despite the discontent, Tibor and Henrik wanted to avoid conflicts with the current 'Civil Guard'. As Tibor underlined, 'I would like to work not against but for them.' He got in contact with the facilitators of the Foresee Research Group, as he was afraid of the emergence of new dissent. As Tibor thought, members of the current 'Civil Guard' who were working in the village anyway would probably have resented the new initiative. As he put it,

> I knew that tension would have increased because of our plan. They would have considered our initiative as a criticism. [...] Mediation would have been important in order to get them to understand that we did not want to take away anything from them.

In the end, mediation was not possible because the organisers did not manage to involve enough volunteers. As there was no real reaction on the part of the villagers, Tibor and Henrik gave up organising the initiative.

Researchers were hardly able to detect and analyse the way social exclusion worked in this case, because only a very few villagers openly revealed their aversion regarding the involvement of the Roma in the work of the local 'Civil Guard'. Instead, most of the time, local residents avoided taking part in discussions where the issues of 'Roma', 'local security' and 'Civil Guard' together emerged.

Despite this avoidance, researchers managed to find some people pointing at 'problems with the Roma'. Somebody emphasised that 'if Roma go on patrol they will just check where to break in later on'. This opinion usually originated in the idea of the local Roma being contributors to several burglaries. According to this opinion, Roma commit crimes because they need money, they are lazy and they just live on social benefits. Some of the villagers even declared that committing crime 'somehow it is a kind of code … it is in their blood'. This is the reason why '90 per cent of the Roma are in prisons'. These negative stereotypes were part of the reason why the Roma people's potential activity in the 'Civil Guard' even decreased the chance that non-Roma would also contribute. As a villager put it, 'It also exists … that … Tibor is a … you know his colour. I know a guy who will not join the initiative because Tibor is a Roma.'

All in all, social exclusion of the Roma from the 'Civil Guard' was all too 'successful'. Furthermore, the organisers of the new 'Civil Guard' did not manage to involve enough volunteers partly because of the aversion towards the Roma.

It is worthwhile to emphasise that social exclusion went hand in hand with the lack of open communication. Nobody uttered explicitly why Roma should not have been involved in a local initiative that aimed at improving local security. Similarly, none of the Roma initiated open discussion about the harm that arose due to their exclusion from the 'Civil Guard'. 'Silence' was so prevailing that issues regarding local security were also not discussed. The local residents did not talk about the way they – even Roma and non-Roma together – could decrease the burglaries and thefts in the village. They did not have open communication about the way the work of the current 'Civil Guard' could be improved by all of them together.

The case of the 'Butcher Festival'

The conflict around the 'Butcher Festival'[6] emerged in 2013. As our interviewees informed us, visitors of the festival had to pay an entrance fee. Therefore, most Roma did not take part in the event. Some of the Roma referred to the Butcher Festival as the 'festival of the rich people'. Poor inhabitants – mainly Roma but non-Roma as well – were standing outside the fence. After these antecedents, some local actors fought for free entrance to the festival for all people in the name of (social) justice. These actors – the local government, the mayor and the leader of the Roma Minority Government – wanted to ensure this opportunity, mostly for those with poor living conditions. However, the organiser opposed the idea of free entrance because he wanted to avoid the participation of poor inhabitants. As he declared during a meeting with the local government, there were solely economic reasons behind his argumentation, because poor visitors 'will not buy anything and thus decrease our income'. In addition, he wanted to avoid offences committed by those participants 'who are not able to behave'. On the contrary, representatives of the city council and the mayor assumed that when the organiser spoke about disadvantaged people who might cause turmoil, he was actually referring to the Roma.

Even today it is not definitely known why the idea of free entrance was opposed: due to the poor residents (as the organiser emphasised) or due to the Roma (as the city council supposed)? However, at this point it should be mentioned that at the beginning of the action research, an interview was conducted with the organiser of the festival. He was one of those few residents who openly talked about thefts, which were presumably committed by the local Roma. In addition, as he reported, he had once been the victim of a crime, also assumed to be perpetrated by Roma. Unfortunately, his damage was not restored by the police, the court, or the local community – which intensified his negative attitudes. Moreover, during that interview he said:

> the local government wants me to ensure tickets for free for the disadvantaged.... In this case, I would not like to organise the festival. It is a huge investment and Roma are not able to behave. I do not want it to be free. I want all of the participants to have a good time.

Taking his opinion into consideration, one can conclude that he may really have wanted to hinder the free entrance of the Roma residents. However, silence and talking about doubts and problems regarding the participation of the Roma minority at the event did not come to the surface. The organiser of the festival probably avoided open communication and remained in silence; he did not reveal his opinion, and he did not explicitly express his problems with the Roma.

Soccer Conflict

'Silence' was the fundamental characteristic of the 'Soccer Conflict' as well. Men of Kisváros are members of the local soccer association from their childhood. As the leader of the local soccer association summed up, 'Out of ten only two did not play soccer as the member of our association. Everybody participated since the war.' Soccer gives all of the people in Kisváros the chance to meet, to have common experiences, to take part in an activity. Moreover, playing soccer is free – and almost the only opportunity to do some sports. Both Roma and non-Roma are welcome:

> Roma and Hungarians come to play soccer. It is very important that they know each other, they can see that the others do not eat human flesh, they are the same human being.... This is very significant in order not to have struggles.

One of the local Roma residents was also an active soccer player. As he shared with us, he had started to play soccer in a new team, which had been set up by the inhabitants outside the soccer association. 'After the matches we went out for a beer. And while we were drinking our beers we could have a talk about the problems of the village.' More and more people – altogether 25 players – joined the initiative. After a while, the group started to collect membership fees.

After these antecedents, it was a bolt from the blue when some of the players decided not to play with Roma. The decision was really a shock for the whole Roma community. Roma players and their relatives, cousins and friends felt humiliated because of the intention of exclusion. However, this conflict has also not been discussed until today. None of the soccer players – either the non-Roma or the Roma – have asked questions of each other in order to clarify the dissent. It is still an open question why some of the non-Roma wanted to play without the Roma. On the contrary, the Roma villagers' exasperation has not been resolved yet. To date, the teams of the Roma and non-Roma residents play football – separately.

Lessons from the action research

Knowledge about the different aspects of social exclusion undeniably supports the understanding of the reasons and the way disadvantaged people are excluded. One can recognise that victims of exclusion probably identify several realms of everyday life where inequalities arise. Furthermore, it becomes clear that it is impossible to decide whether a person is socially excluded by looking only at his/her circumstances themselves in isolation. However, it may be most crucial to understand and analyse the process through which people become excluded. Without this information, it is very difficult to interrupt the mechanism that results in further deprivations and thereby further decreases living opportunities.

As the action research revealed, the phenomenon of exclusion coexisted with the lack of open communication that emerged between the Roma and the non-Roma. Some of the non-Roma villagers have no doubts about how to describe the Roma, while a lot of Roma people in Kisváros have clear ideas about the non-Roma. According to our experience, participants of these groups have vivid and intense discussions about the 'others'. However, hardly any of them share their opinions – or feelings, harms or criticism – with members of the 'other group'. Instead, most of them voice their ideas, feelings, harms or criticism only within their own group.

It is difficult to guess why the Roma and non-Roma local residents do not communicate with each other openly. Probably, lack of trust in each other and negative experiences about unsolved debates are among the main reasons. In addition, villagers may fear to reveal their feelings honestly, as they do not want to become vulnerable. Moreover, they may interpret lack of communication towards the 'others' as a manifestation of loyalty towards their own group. Although the reasons are not certain, the consequences are. Lack of open communication results in lack of information, which only makes stereotypes, assumptions and suspicions about the 'others' stronger. This is the way local groups become homogeneous entities, which consist only of the same kind of people without any exceptions. This is the way local residents create stereotypes about the Roma and non-Roma villagers.

I agree with the scholars and practitioners who emphasise that the approach and techniques of restorative justice can lead us towards constructive conflict resolution and relationship building. Restorative response is not only able to involve those affected by the conflict and to remedy harms; its central aspect is open communication and conversations (Zehr, 2002; Törzs, 2013). It can lead to common norms being set up for the community, and the interconnectedness (Pranis, 2005; Fellegi and Szegő, 2013) of the people taking part in the process makes relationships stronger. It can overcome prejudice, and especially the transformative conception of restorative justice (Johnstone and Van Ness, 2011) could 'create a non-adversarial, inclusive dialogue on common issues, harms or conflicts. This facilitates open communication process, puts emphasis on empowering affected participants and improves relationships' (Törzs, 2013, p. 10) – the elements that would be crucial if vulnerable and disadvantaged groups were involved. It can allow people to tell their stories and listen to the others' stories, defining common themes, seeking for joint agreements. Thereby, the approach of restorative justice is able to solve conflicts emerging because of incidents in small communities and is therefore able to prevent conflict escalating and end the process of polarisation of communities and the exclusion of individuals and groups.

However, practitioners should take some special factors into consideration when applying restorative justice approaches to disagreements where Roma or other oppressed, vulnerable and disadvantaged groups are involved. Without being exhaustive, I would like to point to some of the lessons our facilitators have learned within the frameworks of the action research:

1 While understanding the conflict and the motivations of the actors, one should know that conflict at the local level may be a symptom that emerges due to the widespread prejudice towards the Roma in Hungarian society at the broader societal level. Therefore, the restorative justice process needs time to 'undo years of learnt prejudice, change any of the socio-economic, socio-structural and other cultural factors with give rise to individuals' prejudiced behaviours' (Pali, 2014).
2 Time is also necessary in order to build mutual trust with the local residents. People will not be honest and open overnight; they will not be brave enough to share their fears, feelings and problems with 'strangers' within a few days, or a few weeks, or even a few months.
3 Therefore, it would be important to build upon local 'resources'; to involve the inhabitants who are interested in restorative justice and could be the facilitators of local dissents in the future. Members of the local community would probably trust in these people – in the inhabitants who are of their own kind.
4 While gathering information about a conflict where Roma are also involved, one should be aware of the phenomenon of the 'culture of silence': community members may avoid open discussion about their conflicts. According to our impression, not only is 'conflict' itself a sensitive issue. Talking about 'Roma', 'minority', 'race' and 'racism' may also be difficult.
5 Therefore, it would be important to focus on the informal and proactive restorative practices with which building and maintaining relationships within the community can be a daily practice, an ongoing experience.

6 Participants in a restorative justice process personally and directly communicate with each other. Therefore, facilitators should pay specific attention to the different communication skills of members of different social classes. Roma are often undereducated, and this can push them into an unfavourable position when meeting representatives of the middle class.
7 Places of local settlements have their own meanings. The building of the local government may represent 'power'. The local residents may consider the local library the place of the educated, middle-class people. People living at the edge of the village often belong to the lower classes in Hungary, while the elite own the houses in the centre. Entrance to the territory of the others may be difficult for disadvantaged people. Facilitators of restorative justice programmes should be aware of these special issues while preparing a process and organising meetings with the locals.

Following these pieces of advice will not guarantee the implementation of a successful restorative justice programme. However, by taking this information into consideration, practitioners will have more chance of supporting those who are affected by a conflict, live on the periphery of the local society and are threatened by social exclusion. Thereby, the chance for communities to prevent escalation of conflicts will increase, and thereby, there will be more chance that the vicious circle of social exclusion will be interrupted.

Notes

1 The traditional Hungarian name for this ethnic group is 'Gypsy', but the politically correct one is 'Roma'. However, partly because of the historical perspective of my investigation, I use both of the terms and consider them as synonyms.
2 Within this study, all of the names are fictitious in order to protect confidentiality and anonymity.
3 The scheme of public work was introduced by the government in order to offer work to the long-term unemployed in exchange for social benefits. Public work is not obligatory, but those who refuse to participate become ineligible for social aid for up to a year.
4 The programme was primarily aimed at describing conflicts and conflict management strategies of the community under investigation. Our approach was simple: people were asked about the fragmented environment of the community (Hydle and Seeberg, 2013, p. 9), and we tried to understand the dynamic, relation-based context from the stories of our interviewees. These stories helped to categorise the kinds of groups which existed in the village. These groups could be named 'ordering groups' with different cultures and defined as groups with different feelings, unmet needs, 'incompatible interests or goals or in competition for control over scarce resources' (Avruch, 1998, p. 25). These groups showed the multiplicity of local subcultures (Kremmel and Pelikan, 2013, p. 17). During the action research programme, the researchers recognised that the local Roma were only one of the many groups of the village and were not the only victims of social exclusion. Almost all of the groups of the community used exclusionary practices in order to reject 'outsiders' and thereby to control their boundaries. As the exclusion of these various groups has already been discussed (Hera, 2013; Hera *et al.*, 2015), it is not one of the focal points of the present study.

5 The 'Act on the rights of national and ethnic minorities' offers a broad set of specific rights for minorities. The most important innovation of the law was the establishment of minority self-governments, which are organisations that offer a form of cultural autonomy for minorities.
6 The so-called Butcher Festival, whose purpose is to make a local tradition out of an old-new Hungarian custom: killing a pig at the end of winter and making different types of food from it (pudding, sausage, aspic, etc.).

Bibliography

Atkinson, A. B. and Hills, J., eds, 1998. *Exclusion, Employment and Opportunity*. London: Centre for Analysis of Social Exclusion.

Avruch, K., 1998. *Culture and Conflict Resolution*. Washington DC: United States Institute of Peace Press.

Babusik, F., 2004. *A szegénység csapdájában*. Budapest: Delphoi Consulting.

Babusik, F., 2007. Magyarországi cigányság – struktúrális csapda és kirekesztés. *Esély*, 19(1), pp. 3–23. Available at: www.esely.org/kiadvanyok/2007_1/babusik.pdf (accessed 2 May 2016).

Bársony, J. and Daróczi, Á., eds, 2007. *Pharrajimos: The Fate of the Roma during the Holocaust*. New York: The International Debate Education Association.

Bernáth, G. and Messing V., 2011. Szélre tolva. Kutatási zárójelentés a roma közösségek többségi médiaképéről, 2011. Available at: www.amenca.hu/uploads/pdf/szelre_tolva.pdf (accessed 2 May 2016).

Bradbury-Huang, H., 2010. What is good action research? *Action Research* 8(1), pp. 93–109.

de Haan, A., 1999. *Social Exclusion: Towards an Holistic Understanding of Deprivation*. London: Department for International Development. Retrieved from: http://webarchive.nationalarchives.gov.uk/+/http:/www.dfid.gov.uk/pubs/files/sdd9socex.pdf (accessed 2 May 2016).

Dupcsik, Cs., 2009. *The History of the Hungarian Gypsies*. Budapest: Osiris.

Estivill, J., 2003. *Concepts and Strategies for Combating Social Exclusion*. Geneva: International Labour Organization.

European Network against Racism (ENAR), 2011. ENAR Shadow Report. Racism and related discriminatory practices in Hungary. Available at. http://cms.horus.be/files/99935/MediaArchive/publications/shadow%20report%202010-11/12.%20Hungary.pdf (accessed 2 May 2016).

Fellegi, B. and Szegő, D., 2013. *Handbook for Facilitating Peacemaking Circles*. Budapest: Foresee Research Group.

Ferge, Zs., 2002. Az EU és a kirekesztés. *Esély*, 14(6), pp. 3–13. Available at: www.esely.org/kiadvanyok/2002_6/FERGE.pdf (accessed 2 May 2016).

Ferge, Zs., Tausz, K. and Darvas, Á., 2002. *Combating Poverty and Social Exclusion. Volume 1. A Case Study of Hungary*. Budapest: International Labour Office.

Foss, E. M., Hassan, S. C., Hydle, I., Seeberg, M. L. and Uhrig, B., 2012. *Deliverable 2.1: Report on Conflicts in Intercultural Settings*. Oslo: NOVA.

Fundamental Rights Agency of the European Union (FRA), 2012. *The Situation of Roma in 11 EU Member States – Survey Results at a Glance*. Luxembourg: Publications Office of the European Union. Available at: http://fra.europa.eu/sites/default/files/fra_uploads/2099-FRA-2012-Roma-at-a-glance_EN.pdf (accessed 2 May 2016).

Gábos, A., Szívós, P. and Tátrai, A., 2013. Szegénység és társadalmi kirekesztettség Magyarországon, 2000–2012. In: P. Szívós and Gy. Tóth István, eds, *Egyenlőtlenség és polarizálódás a magyar társadalomban. Tárki monitoring jelentések 2012*. Budapest: TÁRKI, pp. 37–61. Available at: www.tarki.hu/hu/research/hm/monitor2012_teljes.pdf (accessed 2 May 2016).

Gimes, G., Juhász, A., Kiss, K. and Krekó, P., 2009. *Látlelet 2009. Kutatási összefoglaló a magyar szélsőjobboldal megerősödésének okairól*. Budapest: Political Capital. Available at: http://hu.scribd.com/doc/31261194/Latlelet-2009-Copyright-Political-Capital (accessed 2 May 2016).

Gimes, G., Juhász, A., Kiss, K., Krekó, P. and Somogyi, Z., 2008. *Látlelet 2008. Kutatási összefoglaló az előítéletesség és intolerancia hazai helyzetéről*. Budapest: Political Capital. Available at: www.euroastra.info/files/20081016_eloiteletesseg_tanulmany_081016.pdf (accessed 2 May 2016).

Hancock, I., 2004. Romanies and the Holocaust: a reevaluation and an overview. In: S. Dan, ed. *The Historiography of the Holocaust*. New York: Palgrave Macmillan, pp. 383–396.

Hera, G., 2013. Roma and non-Roma conflicts in the light of power relationships. *Temida* 16(3–4), pp. 95–115.

Hera, G., Benedek, G., Szegő, D. and Balla, L., 2015. *Comprehensive Final Report on RJ in Intercultural Communities. Deliverable 5.5*. Budapest: Foresee Research Group.

Human Rights First, 2010. Combating Violence against Roma in Hungary. Human Rights First. Available at: www.humanrightsfirst.org/wp-content/uploads/pdf/HungaryBlueprint.pdf (accessed 2 May 2016).

Hydle, I. and Seeberg, M. L., 2013. *Deliverable 2.2.: Report on Conflict Transformation and Security*. Oslo: NOVA.

Jehoel-Gijsbers, G. and Vrooman, C., 2007. *Explaining Social Exclusion. A Theoretical Model Tested in The Netherlands*. The Hague: The Netherlands Institute for Social Research.

Johnstone, G. and Van Ness, D. W., 2007. The meaning of restorative justice. In: G. Johnstone and D. W. Van Ness, eds, *Handbook of Restorative Justice*. Cullompton: Willan, pp. 5–23.

Juhász, A., 2010a. *A Jobbik politikájának szerepe a pártrendszer átalakulásában – különös tekintettel a cigánybűnözés kampányra. Magyarország Politikai Évkönyve 2009*. Budapest: Demokrácia Kutatások Magyarországi Központja Közhasznú Alapítvány.

Juhász, A., 2010b. A 'cigánybűnözés', mint az igazság szimbóluma. *anBlokk*, 4(1), pp. 12–19.

Kemény, I., ed., 2005. *Roma of Hungary*. Boulder, CO: Columbia University Press.

Kemény, I., Janky, B. and Lengyel, G., 2004. *Roma of Hungary 1971–2003*. Budapest: Gondolat Kiadó.

Kertesi, G., 2005. Roma foglalkoztatás az ezredfordulón. *Szociológiai Szemle*, 15(2), pp. 57–87.

Kocsis, K. and Kocsis, Z., 1999. A cigány népesség társadalomföldrajza. In: F. Glatz, ed. *A cigányok Magyarországon. MAgyarország az ezredfordulón*. Budapest: Magyar Tudományos Akadémia, pp. 17–20.

Központi Statisztikai Hivatal (KSH), 2012. Magyarország Helységnévtára. Available at: www.ksh.hu/Helysegnevtar (accessed 2 May 2016).

Kremmel, K. and Pelikan, C., 2013. *Deliverable 4.1: Theoretical Research Report on Activating Civil Society*. Vienna: IRKS.

Ladányi, J. and Szelényi, I., 2002. Cigányok és szegények Magyarországon, Romániában és Bulgáriában. *Szociológiai Szemle*, 12(4), pp. 72–94. Available at: www.szociologia.hu/dynamic/0204ladanyi.htm (accessed 2 May 2016).

Letenyei, L. and Varga, A., eds, 2011. 'Roma Társadalom' TÁMOP – 5.4.1–8/1 'B' komponens. Unpublished manuscript.

Levitas, R., Pantazis, C., Fahmy, E., Gordon, D, Lloyd, E. and Patsios, D., 2007. The multi-dimensional analysis of social exclusion. Department of Sociology and School for Social Policy Townsend Centre for the International Study of Poverty and Bristol Institute for Public Affairs University of Bristol. Available at: www.bristol.ac.uk/poverty/socialexclusion.html (accessed 2 May 2016).

Marketing Centrum (MC), 2010. Roma society 2010. Unpublished manuscript. Available at: http://uccuprojekt.files.wordpress.com/2010/04/romak-marketing-centrum.pdf (accessed 2 May 2016).

Mathieso, J., Popay, J., Enoch, E., Escorel, S., Hernandez, M., Johnston, H. and Rispel, L., 2008. Social exclusion. Meaning, measurement and experience and links to health inequalities. A review of literature. World Health Organization. Available at: www.who.int/social_determinants/publications/socialexclusion/en/ (accessed 2 May 2016).

Mezey, B., 1998. A magyarországi cigányok rövid története. In: Z. Ács, ed. *Nemzeti és etnikai kisebbségek Magyarországon*. Budapest: Auktor Kiadó, pp. 45–79.

Miliband, D., 2006. Social exclusion: The next steps forward. London: ODPM Publication.

Murard, N., 2002. Guilty victims: Social exclusion in contemporary France. In: P. Chamberlayne, M. Rustin and T. Wengraf, eds, *Biography and Social Exclusion in Europe. Experiences and Life Journeys*. Bristol: Policy.

Nagy, P., 2004. A magyarországi cigányok korai története (14–17. század). Manuscript. Pécs. Available at: www.tte.hu/_public/ttorszkonf/korai.rtf (accessed 2 May 2016).

National Social Inclusion Strategy – Extreme Poverty, Child Poverty, the Roma (2011–2020), 2010. Budapest: Ministry of Public Administration and Justice State Secretariat for Social Inclusion. Available at: http://romagov.kormany.hu/download/5/58/20000/Strategy%20-%20HU%20-%20EN.PDF (accessed 2 May 2016).

NOL (Népszabadság On-Line), 2011. Még az LMP-szimpatizánsok fele is előítéletes [online]. Available at: http://nol.hu/belfold/20111205-a_rejtett_ketharmad (accessed 2 May 2016).

Oyen, E., 1997. The contradictory concepts of social exclusion and social inclusion. In: G. Rodgers, C. Gore and J.B. Figueiredo, eds, *Social Exclusion and Anti-Poverty Policy*. Geneva: International Institute of Labour Studies.

Pali, B., 2014. Intercultural RJ between justice and security. Manuscript.

Peace, R., 2001. Social exclusion: a concept in need of definition? *Social Policy Journal of New Zealand*, 16. Available at: www.msd.govt.nz/documents/about-msd-and-our-work/publications-resources/journals-and-magazines/social-policy-journal/spj16/16-pages17-36.pdf (accessed 2 May 2016).

Pranis, K. 2005. *The Little Book of Circle Processes. A New/Old Approach to Peacemaking*. Intercourse: Good Books.

Pytlas, B., 2013. Radical-right narratives in Slovakia and Hungary: historical legacies, mythic overlaying and contemporary politics. *Patterns of Prejudice*, 47(2), pp. 162–183.

Room, G., 1995. Poverty and social exclusion: the new European agenda for policy and research. In: G. Room, ed. *Beyond the Threshold. The Measurement and Analysis of Social Exclusion*. Bristol: Policy.

Saraceno, C., 2001. Social exclusion: cultural roots and diversities of a popular concept. Conference on Social Exclusion of Children, Institute on Child and Family Policy, Columbia University, 3–4 May 2001.

Sen, A., 2000. *Social Exclusion: Concept, Application, and Scrutiny*. Manila: Asian Development Bank. Available at: www.adb.org/sites/default/files/publication/29778/social-exclusion.pdf (accessed 2 May 2016).

Shaaban, S., 2011. A conceptual framework review of social exclusion, and its relation with social cohesion and poverty in Europe. *The International Journal of Diversity in Organisations, Communities and Nations*, 11(1), pp. 117–132.

Sibley, D., 1998. The problematic nature of exclusion. *Geoforum*, 29(2), pp. 119–216.

Silver, H., 1994. Social exclusion and social solidarity: three paradigms. *International Labour Review*, 133(5–6), pp. 531–578.

Silver, H., 1995. Reconceptualizing social disadvantage: Three paradigms of social exclusion. In: G. Rodgers, C. Gore, and J. B. Figueiredo, eds, *Social Exclusion: Rhetoric, Reality, Responses*. Geneva: International Labour Organization.

Silver, H., 2006. The process of social exclusion: the dynamics of an evolving concept. Working paper. Providence: Chronic Poverty Research Centre. Available at: www.chronicpoverty.org/uploads/publication_files/CP_2006_Silver.pdf (accessed 2 May 2016).

Smith, L., Bratini, L., Chambers, D. A., Jensen, R. V. and Romero L., 2010. Between idealism and reality: meeting the challenges of participatory action research. *Action Research*, 8(4), pp. 407–425.

Strausz, L., 2014. Producing prejudice: the rhetoric of discourses in and around current films on Roma–Hungarian interethnic relations. *Romani Studies*, 24(1), pp. 1–24.

Törzs, E., 2013. *Developing Alternative Understandings of Security and Justice through Restorative Justice Approaches in Intercultural Settings within Democratic Societies. Deliverable 3.1: Report on Restorative Justice Models*. Leuven: European Forum for Restorative Justice.

Van Ness, W.D., 2013. Restorative justice as a world view. In: E. Sellman, H. Cremin and G. McCluskey, eds, *Restorative Approaches to Conflict in Schools*. New York: Routledge, pp. 32–40.

Zehr, H., 2002. *The Little Book of Restorative Justice*. Intercourse: Good Books.

7 Reimagining security and justice in post-conflict societies through restorative lenses

Vesna Nikolić-Ristanović, Sanja Ćopić, Nikola Petrović and Bejan Šaćiri

Introduction

This chapter aims to explore and reimagine the concepts of security and justice in post-conflict societies through restorative lenses. We start with problematising and contextualising the concept of post-conflict society. This is followed by trying to look into what security and justice mean in such a context and in which way they are considered and understood. Our particular focus is on challenges in developing justice in the post-conflict society in terms of establishing the rule of law and other democratic values, and its move towards democratic society, understood as the final end of the process of transition or political change from 'military dictatorship and totalitarian regimes into freedom and democracy' (Teitel, 2000, p. 3). Therefore, we analyse the use of both retributive and restorative justice approaches in post-conflict societies for dealing with conflicts and the position and treatment of victims. All these issues are analysed and discussed using the example of Serbia as a post-conflict society, which is also 'undergoing a painful transition from communism to neo-liberal capitalism' (Nikolić-Ristanović and Ćopić, 2016, p. 144).

Post-conflict society as a context

The first step in contextualising the notion of post-conflict society is to try to define it. In the literature, the notion of 'post-conflict society' is usually not explained or defined precisely; but different authors use it, as it is understandable in itself. Additionally, in the literature one cannot see a clear difference in the use of the term 'post-conflict society' in works dominated by the security discourse, on the one side, and the restorative justice discourse, on the other. The terms 'post-conflict' and 'post-war society' are usually used interchangeably and considered to be synonyms. Therefore, the research into the existing literature suggests that it is rather hard to contextualise this concept, since conflict is often ongoing and it is hard to determine the length of time that needs to have passed after the war or violence to speak about 'post'. Thus, there are two main problems faced in trying to provide an accurate and comprehensive definition of the concept of post-conflict society. The first refers to its etymological meaning, while the second relates to the time frame, that is, the inability to determine precisely how long it takes for a society to be considered 'post-conflict'.

The root of the word post-conflict is 'post', which is a temporal signifier that implies a period after a conflict. Consequently, many authors contextualise post-conflict society as a society in which open warfare has come to an end (Licklider, 1995, according to Lambach, 2007); 'the period when a conflict is either interrupted or (temporarily) stopped by means of a peace agreement, the victory or defeat of a conflict party or the intervention of an external actor', for example the international community (Smith-Höhn, 2010, p. 13), or when the conflict parties are removed from the scene (Lambach according to Smith-Höhn, 2010, p. 15).

Another approach to contextualising the concept of post-conflict society is used, for example, by Lambach, who tries to make a distinction between 'conflict' and 'post-conflict' depending on the dominant narrative (2007). According to him, 'the central aspect of a definition of "post-conflict" must be a narrative of peace. A conflict can be considered over when violence is no longer explained in terms of the dominant narrative of conflict' (Lambach, 2007, p. 10). Therefore, as he puts it, 'the whole idea of "post-conflict" invites a mental dichotomy that transforms "conflict" and "post-conflict" into synonyms of "war" and "peace"' (Lambach, 2007, p. 9). On the other hand, some authors contextualise the concept of post-conflict society as a transitional period, for example as a period after the formal peace agreement has been signed when the 'journey of transition from war to peace' begins (Riesenfeld, 2008, p. 4). It is a society in the phase of peace-building, which 'involves glancing backwards at a history of violence while at the same time moving peacefully into the future' (Riesenfeld, 2008, p. 48).

Even though this is a transition from one stage to another, it is correctly noted by Lambach that post-conflict societies are more than a transitory phase from war to peace and they should not be understood only as an 'in-between phase' (Lambach, 2007, p. 5). Namely, it is rather hard to put a clear demarcation line between what can be perceived as a 'conflict' and as a 'post-conflict' society, because even after the formal ending of a conflict, unresolved problems, tensions, human rights violations and conflicts remain (Domonji, 2008; Nikolić-Ristanović and Ćopić, 2013; Fischer, 2016a). As pointed out by Smith-Höhn, 'post-conflict phases are often marked by high levels of violence, social injustices and structural inequalities'; thus, 'a simplified concept of conflict versus post-conflict fails to describe adequately the context' (2010, pp. 13–14). In post-conflict societies, the legacies of the past wars/violence are very much alive (Fischer, 2016a, p. 13). Some groups often persist in abusing civilians 'to reinforce conflict gains, shape the post-conflict environment, exact revenge for wartime grievances or spoil peace processes' (Kathman and Wood, 2016, p. 149). Many citizens (both civilians and ex-combatants) have to cope with the memories of the past violence (Fischer, 2016a, p. 13). Apart from coping with burdens of the past, victims have to face the discomforts of daily life, many of which are also a legacy of the past conflict(s). For example, some rape victims must live with post-traumatic stress disorder (PTSD), sexually transmitted diseases, stigma and shame (Zeigler and Gunderson, 2006). Some people are refugees or internally displaced, so many challenges need to be addressed in respect to return and reintegration. Children lost their parents, families lost their breadwinners, people lost their limbs, communities were fractured, and dialogue between different social groups was almost non-existent. Not all victims in the times of conflict were victims of war; they could also be victims of economic sanctions, political oppression, discrimination, social injustice and so on. Life in a shattered post-conflict society aggravates these daily concerns (Rombouts, 2002).

The results of the empirical research on conflicts, security and justice in the intercultural context of Serbia conducted by the Victimology Society of Serbia within the ALTERNATIVE project confirmed the above-mentioned points (Nikolić-Ristanović *et al.*, 2014, 2015a). In three multi-ethnic communities encompassed by the research, which are situated in the border regions of Serbia and which were more directly affected by the wars in the former Yugoslavia, the timing of conflicts and victimisations experienced by the respondents during the 1990s coincided with armed conflicts in Croatia, Bosnia and Herzegovina, and Kosovo. After 2000, the bulk of victimisations were also related to the armed conflicts, suggesting a continuity of the conflicts from the war to the post-war period. Apart from that, new conflicts emerged as well. These new conflicts, particularly those occurring in the period 2010–2012, mainly related to the political situation in these communities and political transition in Serbia in general.

Therefore, as correctly observed by Rohne, Arsovska and Aertsen, post-conflict society is usually seen as an unstable environment characterised by 'continuous eruption of violence' (2008, p. 12). How fragile the line is between what is perceived as a conflict and what as a post-conflict (situation, society, environment) is visible in the way the neologism 'post-conflict' is sometimes written – '(post)-conflict' (Rohne *et al.*, 2008, p. 11).

Another point to be made when contextualising the notion of post-conflict society refers to the fact that it is almost impossible to determine precisely how long a society is to be treated as post-conflict. Practice suggests that a society can be considered to be post-conflict for decades (e.g. Serbia and Northern Ireland). Some authors propose criteria or conditions through which one can determine the beginning and the end of 'post-conflict' societies. Brown *et al.* (2011, p. 4) suggest that post-conflict society should be viewed as a process of continuous movement from conflict to peace, which is assessed on the basis of the achievements made in implementing the following key tasks: cessation of hostilities and violence; signing of political/peace agreements; demobilisation, disarmament and reintegration; refugee repatriation; establishing a functioning state; achieving reconciliation and societal integration; and economic recovery. In this process, it is desirable that the society moves forward and implements these tasks, but sometimes there is a regression that reverses the process (Brown *et al.*, 2011). However, there are differences between various post-conflict societies, which go through different tasks at a different pace. Each post-conflict society is unique and has its own peculiarities. Post-conflict societies differ in the level of economic and social development, security situation, bureaucratic capacity, natural resources, political situation and the scope of social (in)equalities (Brown *et al.*, 2011). Each of these criteria determines the time frame in which a society is to be treated as a post-conflict society.

Keeping this in mind, for the purpose of this chapter we contextualise conflict and post-conflict society as parts of a continuum with a continuity of conflicts from the war to the post-war period, but with new conflicts that are emerging as well. All conflicts (both past and present) should be dealt with as part of a continuum, in an inclusive way and taking care of their inter-connection. However, as suggested by some authors and confirmed by the research conducted in Serbia within ALTERNATIVE, 'post-conflict societies often lack mechanisms and institutions for upholding the rule of law' and for dealing with both past and present conflicts in a constructive and inclusive way, presenting a 'vacuum' (Rohne *et al.*, pp. 12–13), which provides a fertile soil for further violence, discrimination, crime, insecurity and social injustice. Consequently, in fragile post-conflict settings, justice, reconciliation, peace-building, security and democracy are emerging as mutually reinforcing imperatives for further development, which may impact the reduction of existing tensions and lower the risk for relapse into new conflicts and new victimisations (Riesenfeld, 2008). This leads us to re-examining and reimagining concepts of security and justice in the post-conflict society setting through restorative lenses, putting an emphasis on the position of victims.

The notion of security in a post-conflict context

Security issues are central to the process of reconstruction and reconciliation in the post-conflict context (Ní Aoláin *et al.*, 2011). In such a context, security is primarily linked to freedom from fear from new violence, internal conflicts, serious crime and human rights violations. Therefore, in the early phase of a post-conflict society the focus is on disarmament, demobilisation and reintegration of ex-combatants, which is considered to be a key component of peace processes and post-conflict reconstruction (Brinkerhoff, 2005; Theidon, 2007). Sometimes even external peacekeeping troops are engaged in re-establishing security. In such situations, as pointed out by some authors, 'internal and external actors must cooperate in mutually reinforcing socio-economic, governance and security dimensions of a highly fragile environment' (Schnabel and Ehrhart, 2006, p. 7). In re-establishing security in a post-conflict society, the focus is very much on reforming the security sector (Schnabel and Ehrhart, 2005, according to Smith-Höhn, 2010, p. 2). Additionally, most resources are directed towards retributive and repressive mechanisms and instruments for dealing with the past, while no or little attention is paid to reconciliation and peace-building, and agency is often denied to both local political actors and citizens, including victims.

Notwithstanding the importance of the security sector reform, it is obvious that this does not provide a basis for creating socio-economic security (True,

2012), while socio-economic insecurity can ignite the conflict again and endanger the whole process of peace-building. Therefore, security sector transformation can only be accomplished if it reaches far beyond the military and police security context (in terms of providing physical safety for citizens) and if it encompasses economic, social, legal and political issues as well (Schnabel and Ehrhart, 2006). It seems that only when socio-economic development goes hand in hand with increasing security in terms of freedom from fear (from war, crime and violence) can the process of transforming a post-conflict society into a 'normal' society be completed. Therefore, we may conclude that in post-conflict societies the focus needs to be moved from the 'state' to 'human' security as a people-centred concept, which focuses on the protection of individuals. The human security concept shifts the focus 'from political concerns to the importance of economic and social issues' (Shinoda, 2004, p. 12). According to the United Nations Development Programme (1994, p. 23), the concept of human security refers to the protection of the vital core of all human lives in ways that enhance human freedoms and human fulfilment. It is identified as the protection of individuals from risks to their physical and psychological safety, dignity and well-being in a broader sense; thus, it has two main components: 'freedom from fear' and 'freedom from want'. Consequently, the concept of human security refers to seven main categories/forms of security: economic, environmental, personal, political, food, health and community security. Therefore, human rights and needs could be, at least to some extent, considered as indicators of the achieved human security.

The findings of the above-mentioned empirical research conducted by the Victimology Society of Serbia within ALTERNATIVE suggested that the large majority of the respondents felt safe living in their communities at the time of the research (2012) (Nikolić-Ristanović *et al.*, 2014, 2015b). Most of them feel safer today than during the 1990s, while a third feel the same. For a fifth of respondents, the period before the 1990s and the wars in the former Yugoslavia was safer, while for about a quarter of them it was less safe. However, problems, such as discrimination, hate crime and insecurity, still exist. In addition to the negative influences of armed conflicts, new factors that negatively impact the security of citizens of all ethnic groups have emerged, such as economic transition and related crisis, ruined institutions and the lack of rule of law, widespread corruption and the prevailing influence of political parties in all spheres of life. Therefore, the inefficiency of the state in solving problems and economic factors appeared to be the greatest contributors to respondents' personal feelings of insecurity (Nikolić-Ristanović *et al.*, 2014, 2015b). Ethnicity and political affiliation, as well as relationships with members of the same and different ethnic groups, seem to have a smaller, but still important, impact. Additionally, survey findings suggested that the state is not seen as a guarantor of the safety/security of its citizens, but is, rather, perceived by the respondents as one of the main sources of unsafety/insecurity. Consequently, economic measures (creating job opportunities for citizens), more communication between people about problems they have, and different measures aimed at raising the efficiency of the state have been recognised as the best means to increase safety. Therefore, a strong link with the concept of 'human security' has been noted (United Nations Development Programme, 1994).

Keeping this in mind, we may conclude that in post-conflict settings it would be more appropriate to speak about the concept of safety rather than security. In other words, security should be understood as a 'sense of safety people experience' in different fields of social life (Vanfraechem, 2012, p. 6). Consequently, apart from feeling safe in the physical sense in terms of freedom from crime, war or violence, the concept of safety also encompasses economic safety (e.g. having jobs, regular payments), legal safety (the laws exist, supremacy of the law, equality before the law, equal access to justice, fairness in application of the law, etc.), social safety and political safety, which are all relevant in the process of transition towards democracy.

Re-examining the concept of justice in the context of a post-conflict society

Justice is another important component of peace-building, the reconstruction and (re-)establishing of democracy, rule of law and security in the post-conflict context (Lambourne, 2004). Over the past decades, in the context of post-conflict societies, justice has been conceptualised as a transitional justice, which involves prosecuting perpetrators, revealing the truth about past crimes, providing victims with reparation and promoting reconciliation (Fischer, 2016a). Nevertheless, justice in post-conflict settings (transitional justice), as is the case in Serbia, is primarily identified with legal approaches (legal justice), very much relying on retributive instruments (Fischer, 2016b, 2016c; Nikolić-Ristanović and Ćopić, 2016). In such a context, the institutional mechanisms for achieving justice include prosecution and sentencing before national and/or international courts, special courts and tribunals, or in foreign courts (Lie *et al.*, 2007, p. 6). Legal (criminal) justice is quite often seen as the best and necessary means to 'undo past state justice and to advance the normative transformation of these times to a rule-of-law system' (Teitel, 2000, p. 28). But, as correctly noticed by some authors, it suffers from retroactivity, politicisation and selectivity (Minow, 1998, pp. 30–31), while 'the work of the courts has not been complemented by programmes that provide compensation for victims' (Fischer, 2016c, p. 248). Trials conducted within this framework may sometimes be described as winners' justice (Gloppen, 2005) or political justice (Elster, 2004), directed at the conflict's losing party, with the intention of repression and deterrence rather than forgiveness and reconciliation. Still, trials should not be viewed only as expressions of a societal desire for retribution (a desire of victims, their families or a broader society); they also play an important role in reaffirming essential norms and values among the public and also contribute to the increase of people's trust in institutions. Therefore, repressive/retributive justice undoubtedly has an important role to play in post-conflict societies, in preventing future hostilities and as a starting point in peace-building. But, as correctly observed by Stover and Weinstein (according to Clark, 2009) or Fischer (2016c), the key point is that there is no direct link between legal justice, that is, criminal trials (international, national and local/traditional), and reconciliation, at least in the short term.

Increased use of repressive mechanisms and focusing on legal justice in dealing with past conflicts/violence fits well into the global policy of penal populism (Garland, 2001), which is visible in Serbia as well (Soković, 2012).[1] It pursues the politics of repression and increases the severity of punishments in the name of protecting victims. However, trials do not give enough space for victims to be heard; their needs, feelings and preferences are usually not taken into account. As they were manipulated and used as numbers to fuel the propaganda machine and justify violence during the war (Nikolić-Ristanović, 2000; Raković, 2005), victims are sometimes not treated as individuals in need of assistance, protection and support in the post-conflict environment as well. They are often not actively involved in conflict transformation but are, rather, passive observers of the processes, particularly of the criminal justice procedures, as confirmed by the research conducted in Serbia within ALTERNATIVE (Nikolić-Ristanović and Ćopić, 2013).

It is also visible that in a post-conflict society only some victims achieve a 'victim status' and receive compensation. The bare fact that someone was hurt or suffered is usually not sufficient for them to be recognised as a victim (Nikolić-Ristanović *et al.*, 2012). Thus, the crucial condition for becoming recognised as a victim is being seen as a victim by others and adopting a victim role with certain rights and obligations (Strobl, 2010), especially if one does not meet the requirements to be regarded as a completely innocent 'ideal victim' (Christie, 1986).[2] In such a context, taking care of victims amounts to supporting only those among them who are undergoing criminal proceedings (who are willing to testify), and the rights of victims are primarily concerned with punishing the perpetrators. Additionally, in a post-conflict society, victim competition sometimes creates a hierarchy of victims.[3] For example, in Serbia, the state has not yet recognised the status of civilians as victims of war; consequently, they are excluded from the reparation mechanisms (Nikolić-Ristanović and Ćopić, 2013). The same goes for members of the Liberation Army of Presevo, Medvedja and Bujanovac who fought against the government forces. We may conclude that in a post-conflict society an instrumentalist and retribution-oriented ideology towards victims is visible, which sees care for victims only as an instrument in the battle against the crime or, in this context, in dealing with the past violence (Elias, 1993; Goodey, 2005; Spalek, 2006). Additionally, in a post-conflict society some groups exploit their victimisation for economic or political gains, and it is often a subject of politicisation (Rombouts, 2002). Finally, in the post-conflict context, victim–offender binarism is visible. This usually relates to the two sides that participated in armed conflicts in such a way that each side is emphasising its own victimisation while minimising or denying victimisation on the enemy's side (the or–or approach). So, the innocent victims are usually from 'our' community, not 'theirs'. This binarism also implicates that the blame should be put on the 'other' (McEvoy and McConnachie, 2012). In general, this all negatively impacts on how people, particularly victims, perceive and experience justice in a post-conflict society.

The findings of the empirical research conducted in Serbia proved that in the post-conflict society the notion of victim and perpetrator is the broader one, including both those directly and indirectly injured and those responsible for the interethnic and other related conflicts (Nikolić-Ristanović *et al.*, 2014). Moreover, respondents' understanding of victimisation included physical, material, psychological, emotional and social impact of victimisation on a victim (Dignan, 2005, p. 24; Vanfraechem, 2012, p. 35), including primary, secondary and tertiary victims (Spalek, 2006, p. 12; Condry, 2010; Vanfraechem, 2012; Wemmers and Manirabona, 2014). Additionally, victims in the post-conflict settings are not only individuals, but groups and entire communities as well (Shaw, 2001). Many people are multiple victims, even with memories of victimisation in previous wars, or with war trauma passed to them by their parents or other relatives (Nikolić-Ristanović and Ćopić, 2013). Sometimes perpetrators blame the ideological indoctrination they were subjected to, and consider themselves victims of the 'system' or 'regime'. In cases of prolonged conflicts, large sections of the population become victimised, even those who are perpetrators of violence themselves. This is especially true for child soldiers and female combatants (Duthie and Specht, 2009). They should be dealt with according to what has been endured and what they need, instead of according to the role that is assigned to them in the criminal procedure, by the media, politicians and so on. This is particularly important in societies undergoing transition from violent conflicts. As Luc Huyse observed, arguing for a similar approach, 'the alternation of roles between victims and offenders is an important consideration in preparing and implementing reconciliation programs' (2003, p. 64). Thus, a feeling of general victimisation opens the space for an inclusive approach in dealing with conflicts and in 'doing justice' (Walgrave, 2008). It enables recognition of all those who feel victimised, avoidance of binarism and allowing overlaps of victims and perpetrators/responsible parties (Fattah, 1993, according to Vanfraechem, 2012).

The findings of a qualitative survey of how civil society and the state dealt with interethnic and related political and intercultural conflicts in Serbia in the period 1990–2012, conducted by the Victimology Society of Serbia within ALTERNATIVE, suggested that in dealing with past and present interethnic conflicts by the state institutions in Serbia, the security discourse prevailed, and state institutions focused primarily on judicial mechanisms (Ćopić, 2013; Nikolić-Ristanović and Ćopić, 2013, 2016; Nikolić-Ristanović and Šaćiri, 2013). However, the effects of such a policy are not visible: conflicts still exist, and they become even deeper. Additionally, the security discourse of civil society organisations, being the most visible, provokes resistance and hostile attitudes rather than contributing to dialogue and conflict transformation. The research confirmed how inefficient and even counterproductive the use of retributive justice and security discourse could be as the only means in one post-conflict society.

Therefore, notwithstanding the importance of legal justice as a component of transitional justice and a necessary precondition for reconciliation (Fischer, 2016b), we may argue that it may also contribute to deepening the conflicts and may not bring justice either to victims or to offenders and communities. Some authors correctly argue that legal justice is in a way a 'symbolic justice' (Liebmann, 2007, p. 362), and it needs to be complemented with non-judicial means that would be more victim-oriented, oriented towards conflict transformation and closing cycles of violence and to prevent the deepening of existing conflicts. Transitional justice strategies should be as holistic and comprehensive as possible and not focused exclusively on only one component of transitional justice. These strategies should also include restorative approaches.

To sum up, justice is a complex concept, which has different meanings, such as substantive and symbolic, economic and social (distributive justice), legal and psychological; thus, justice could be retributive, restitutive or restorative (Lambourne, 2004). Sometimes traditional justice in some form of ritual can be a part of transitional justice processes (Allen and MacDonald, 2013). Even socio-economic justice, as pointed out by Lederach, is critical to peace. Lederach identifies what he calls the 'justice gap' in peace-building, emphasising that no one has 'adequately developed a peace-building framework that reduces direct violence and produces social and economic justice' (Lederach, 1999, p. 32, according to Lambourne, 2004, p. 7). As Moghalu puts it, justice can be a catharsis for those who have been psychologically or physically injured during the conflict, which removes the old resentments and produces a clean slate (Moghalu, 2004, p. 216, according to Clark, 2008, p. 332). This is relevant for reconciliation, which, as argued by Mobekk, 'is the ultimate objective in all post-conflict societies and post-conflict reconstruction processes' (Mobekk, 2005, p. 262). Reconciliation in a post-conflict society presents a whole strategy that involves understanding, dialogue, joint operations of conflict parties, storytelling, and developing grass-roots structures for peace (Kumhar, 1999). This approach, which stems from the restorative justice discourse, is inclusive (taking into consideration all conflicting parties) and allows two-way communication and trust-building at the same time.

In place of conclusion: potential of restorative approaches in post-conflict societies

In a post-conflict society, the emphasis should be on peace-building and reconciliation, a process that has to be as inclusive as possible, fostering active participation. This can be achieved by applying restorative approaches. The findings of empirical research on conflicts, security and justice in the intercultural context of Serbia suggested that although punishment is still seen as an important mechanism for achieving justice in a post-conflict society, respondents gave high relevance to restorative approaches and mechanisms as well, including restorative processes (dialogue, mediation or community meeting/conference) and restorative outcomes (apology and compensation) (Nikolić-Ristanović *et al.*,

2014, 2015a). For example, survey findings showed that knowing why what happened had happened, which requires some form of encounter and dialogue, is seen as an important mechanism that may bring justice in concrete cases of victimisation. This suggests the need for those victimised to actively participate in the process of conflict transformation and not to be left on the edge of the social reaction. The survey findings also suggested that respondents use different restorative approaches for solving everyday problems, particularly dialogue and informal mediation. Respondents' answers are also proven to open the space for a broader use of restorative approaches even in cases of victimisation where a power imbalance exists (Nikolić-Ristanović *et al.*, 2014, 2015a).

Restorative approaches should enable participation and support to all people in any way affected by conflict, with the final aim of reintegrating them into society and closing the cycles of violence. Restorative approaches may help overcome negative consequences of selective recognition and hierarchies of victimhood in a post-conflict society. They may also help avoid any kind of binarism and should work towards empowering all those who suffer and help them finally abandon the role of a victim. Moreover, people should be trusted and treated accordingly both when they claim to be victims and when they refuse to be treated like that.

The essence of restorative approaches is interactive communication and dialogue (Foss *et al.*, 2012). In this context, dialogue is seen as an inclusive, open-ended process of constructive, two-way communication that puts the participants into interaction: dialogue participants are cooperating, working towards common understanding. Dialogue is primarily a relationship-oriented process: it tries to transform the relationship by promoting empathy and enlarging possibilities for participants to change their views and to understand the other side. It is an interactive process, which creates a space for the parties 'to become aware of implicit assumptions', gives space to the parties to express their reactions and gives an opportunity to others to reflect on them (Tschudi, 2008, p. 56). Nevertheless, it provides a framework for exploring and trying to find a solution that would be acceptable to all parties. Dialogue is based on mutual respect for diversity and acknowledgement of equality of all parties involved, fostering active listening and empathy, temporarily suspending one's own assumptions, ideas, emotions and opinions, and allowing new impulses to emerge (Berghof Foundation, 2012, p. 30). However, for the dialogue process to be successful, some prerequisites need to be met, including power balance, refraining from mutual blaming, respectful active listening, and mutual understanding and respect for diversity (Nikolić-Ristanović and Srna, 2010, p. 51). It provides a basis for cooperation, trust-building and moving conflicting parties closer to each other, preventing estrangement.

An example of such an approach is the 'third way' model of communication about past and present conflicts, developed by the Victimology Society of Serbia within the initiative called *Joint Action for Truth and Reconciliation* (also known as ZAIP) (Nikolić-Ristanović and Ćopić, 2013; Nikolić-Ristanović, 2015). The goals of this initiative are, *inter alia*, to find out the truth about the past conflicts from various perspectives, to empower and reintegrate all persons affected by the conflict, and to reconcile ethnic groups that were in conflict. Members of ZAIP, people from various backgrounds and views, often victims, join together to discuss difficult topics and speak about personal experiences in a space which they perceive as safe and without being exposed to an outside public, to blaming and judgement. The 'third way' model was tested and further, both practically and theoretically, upgraded through the action research conducted by the Victimology Society of Serbia within ALTERNATIVE (Nikolić-Ristanović *et al.*, 2015c). The research confirmed that the 'third way' model of communication, which has been recognised by some authors as a possible way of applying restorative justice in post-conflict societies (Liebmann, 2007; Aertsen *et al.*, 2008), is an applicable and appropriate approach to conflict prevention and transformation in multi-ethnic communities in Serbia as a post-conflict society.

To conclude, in a post-conflict society, restorative justice is an important social force that contributes to the revival of participatory democracy, which needs to be more inclusive, responsive and just, and to promoting active participation, active responsibility, mutual respect and solidarity (Walgrave, 2008, pp. 194–195). Restorative justice is about active participation in reflecting (on one's own and the others), restoring trust and relationship building, which are 'crucial in advancing conflict transformation and reconciliation in war-torn societies' (Fischer, 2016b, p. 25). As pointed out by Bloomfield, democracy and reconciliation are 'intertwined, indeed, interdependent' (2003, p. 11), while in line with Bloomfield's idea of democracy, it should be understood as a system for managing conflict with win–win, instead of either–or or win–lose solutions as a result. This assumes the coexistence of different truths, beliefs and values, the possibility of dialogue and dissent, and the active search for lines of difference between the conflicting parties that can be resolved and overcome. This enables renewal, conflict resolution and inclusion of all members of the society or the community, opening the space for different restorative approaches to both past and present conflicts, tensions and problems in post-conflict societies.

Notes

1 Already in the first decades of the development of victims' rights, in the 1960s, selective recognition of victims was criticised for serving political interests (Nikolić-Ristanović, 2013). This trend was particularly emphasised in connection with conservative ideology and increased punitiveness in the 1980s, and even more after 2001, when the security discourse became the dominant approach to crime. Elias stressed that the central motive for this kind of approach is scoring political points in the battle against crime and through tightening penal politics, and not providing social and humanitarian response to the needs of people who suffer (Elias, 1986).

2 Victims who do not fulfil the criteria to be called an 'ideal' (right, good) victim are considered as victims who deserve to be victimised and therefore not worthy of victim status and support. Such victims are considered as 'bad', 'worthless', 'guilty' or in other ways inadequate victims. It is therefore thought that they are less qualified to be victims than the 'ideal' victims, or their victim status is completely denied. For

example, victim status is usually not granted to immigrants, minorities, victims of the enemy side in war, or victims of war who belong to the nation that is considered by those outside the conflict to be more responsible for committed crimes then the other side (for example, German victims in World Wars I and II, or Serbian victims of wars in the former Yugoslavia in the 1990s).

3 Christie (1986) insightfully noted that, in order for a person who fulfils the criteria to become actually recognised as a victim and receive adequate support, it is necessary that he/she has a certain position within the system of power which enables them to speak and put pressure on society. Victims often gain this power indirectly, through the attention of the media, politicians and organisations dealing with victims' rights. In fact, those actors claim their rights for them. However, efforts to protect the rights of ideal victims are often limited to raising their public visibility; they still rarely get legal victim status and efficient support and protection.

Bibliography

Aertsen, I., Arsovska, J., Rohne, H. C., Valiñas, M. and Vanspauwen, K., eds, 2008. *Restoring Justice after Large-Scale Violent Conflicts: Kosovo, DR Congo and the Israeli-Palestinian Case*. Cullompton: Willan.

Allen, T. and Macdonald, A., 2013. *Post-Conflict Traditional Justice: A Critical Overview*. JSRP Paper, 3. London: Justice and Security Research Programme. [pdf]. Available at: http://eprints.lse.ac.uk/56357/1/JSRP_Paper3_Post-conflict_traditional_justice_Allen_Macdonald_2013.pdf (accessed 3 April 2016).

Berghof Foundation, 2012. *Berghof Glossary on Conflict Transformation – 20 Notions for Theory and Practice*. Berlin: Berghof Foundation Operations GmbH.

Bloomfield, D., 2003. Reconciliation: an introduction. In: D. Bloomfield, T. Barnes, and L. Huyse, eds, *Reconciliation after Violent Conflict: A Handbook*. Stockholm: International IDEA, pp. 10–18.

Brinkerhoff, R. O., 2005. The success case method: a strategic evaluation approach to increasing the value and effect of training. *Advances in Developing Human Resources*, 7(1), pp. 86–101.

Brown, G., Langer, A. and Stewart, F., 2011. *A Typology of Post-Conflict Environments*. Centre for Research on Peace and Development. Working Paper no. 1. [pdf]. Available at: https://lirias.kuleuven.be/bitstream/123456789/330374/1/wp01.pdf (accessed 3 April 2016).

Christie, N., 1986. The ideal victim. In: F. A. Ezzat, ed., *From Crime Policy to Victim Policy: Reorienting Justice*. Basingstoke: Macmillan, pp. 17–30.

Clark, J. N., 2008. The three Rs: retributive justice, restorative justice, and reconciliation. *Contemporary Justice Review*, 11(4), pp. 331–350.

Clark, J. N., 2009. Learning from the past: three lessons from the Rwandan genocide. *African Studies*, 68(1), pp. 1–28.

Condry, R., 2010. Secondary victims and secondary victimization. In: S. G. Shoham, P. Knepper, and M. Kett, eds, *International Handbook of Victimology*. London/New York: CRC, pp. 219–249.

Ćopić, S., 2013. Aktivnosti i diskurs državnih organa i institucija u Srbiji u bavljenju međuetničkim sukobim (Activities and the discourse of the state agencies and institutions in Serbia in dealing with interethnic conflicts). *Temida*, 16(3–4), pp. 61–94.

Dignan, J., 2005. *Understanding Victims and Restorative Justice*. Berkshire: Open University Press.

Domonji, P., ed., 2008. *Vojvodina's Multiethnic Identity: Challenges in 2007–08. Helsinki Files No 27.* Belgrade: Helsinki Committee for Human Rights in Serbia.

Duthie, R. and Specht, I., 2009. DDR, transitional justice and the reintegration of former child combatants. In: A. Cutter Patel, P. de Greiff and L. Waldorf, eds, *Disarming the Past: Transitional Justice and Ex Combatants.* New York: International Centre for Transitional Justice – Advanced Series, pp. 190–227.

Elias, R. 1986. *The Politics of Victimisation: Victims, Victimology and Human Rights.* New York: Oxford University Press.

Elias, R., 1993. *Victims Still: The Political Manipulation of Crime Victims.* Newbury Park: Sage.

Elster, J., 2004. *Closing the Books: Transitional Justice in Historical Perspective.* Cambridge: Cambridge University Press.

Fischer, M., 2016a. Struggling with the legacy of war – Croatia, Serbia and Bosnia-Herzegovina, 1995–2015. In: M. Fischer and O. Simić, eds, *Transitional Justice and Reconciliation – Lessons from the Balkans.* Oxford: Routledge, pp. 3–22.

Fischer, M., 2016b. Dealing with the past from the top down and bottom up – challenges for state and non-state actors. In: M. Fischer and O. Simić, eds, *Transitional Justice and Reconciliation – Lessons from the Balkans.* Oxford: Routledge, pp. 25–60.

Fischer, M., 2016c. Dealing with past violence as a long-term challenge – lessons from the Balkans. In: M. Fischer and O. Simić, eds, *Transitional Justice and Reconciliation – Lessons from the Balkans.* Oxford: Routledge, pp. 245–262.

Foss, E. M., Hassan, S. C., Hydle, I., Seeberg, M. L. and Uhrig, B., 2012. *Deliverable 2.1.: Report on Conflicts in Intercultural Settings.* Oslo: NOVA. (Deliverable 2.1. of FP7 project ALTERNATIVE – Developing alternative understandings of security and justice through restorative justice approaches in intercultural settings within democratic societies). [pdf] Available at: www.alternativeproject.eu/assets/upload/Deliverable_6.2_Research_report_on_interethnic_conflicts_and_citizens_security_perceptions_.pdf (accessed 21 June 2017).

Garland, D., 2001. *The Culture of Control – Crime and Social Order in Contemporary Society.* Oxford: Oxford University Press.

Gloppen, S., 2005. Roads to reconciliation: a conceptual framework. In: E. Skar, S. Gloppen and A. Suhrke, eds, *Roads to Reconciliation.* Lanham: Lexington Books, pp. 17–50.

Goodey, J., 2005. *Victims and Victimology: Research, Policy and Practice.* Essex: Pearson.

Huyse, L., 2003. Victims. In: T. Barnes and L. Huyse, eds, *Reconciliation after Violent Conflict: a Handbook.* Stockholm: International IDEA, pp. 19–32.

Kathman, J. and Wood, R., 2016. Stopping the killing during the 'peace': peacekeeping and the severity of postconflict civilian victimization. *Foreign Policy Analysis*, 12(2), pp. 149–169.

Kumhar, K., 1999. *Promoting Social Reconciliation in Postconflict Society: Selected Lessons from USAID's Experience.* USAID Program and Operations, Assessment Report No. 24. [pdf]. Available at: www.oecd.org/derec/unitedstates/35112635.pdf (accessed 15 September 2015).

Lambach, D., 2007. *Oligopolies of Violence in Post-Conflict Societies.* Hamburg: GIGA Working Paper Series. [pdf]. Available at: http://repec.giga-hamburg.de/pdf/giga_07_wp62_lambach.pdf (accessed 15 September 2015).

Lambourne, W., 2004. Post-conflict peacebuilding: meeting human needs for justice and reconciliation. *Peace, Conflict and Development*, 4, pp. 1–24.

Lie, T. G., Binningsbø, H. M. and Gates, S., 2007. *Post-Conflict Justice and Sustainable Peace*. Post-conflict transitions working paper No. 5. [pdf]. Available at: http://siteresources.worldbank.org/INTLAWJUSTINST/Resources/PostConflict.pdf (accessed 10 September 2015).

Liebmann, M., 2007. *Restorative Justice: How It Works*. London: Jessica Kingsley.

McEvoy, K. and McConnachie, K., 2012. Victimology in transitional justice: victimhood, innocence and hierarchy. *European Journal of Criminology*, 9(5), pp. 527–538.

Minow, M., 1998. *Between Vengeance and Forgiveness – Facing History after Genocide and Mass Violence*. Boston: Beacon.

Mobekk, E., 2005. Transitional justice in post-conflict societies – approaches to reconciliation. In: A. Ebnother and P. Fluri, eds, *After Intervention: Public Security Management in Post-Conflict Societies – from Intervention to Sustainable Local Ownership*. Geneva: Geneva Centre for the Democratic Control of Armed Forces (DCAF), pp. 261–292.

Ní Aoláin, F., Cahn, N. and Haynes, D., 2011. *Linking Gender Security with the Armed Conflict to Peace Continuum*. Transitional Justice Institute Research Paper No. 11–08.

Nikolić-Ristanović, V., 2000. Žrtve ratova u bivšoj Jugoslaviji: obim, struktura i obrasci viktimizacije (Victims of war in the former Yugoslavia: prevalence, structure and forms of victimisation). *Temida*, 3(2), pp. 11–21.

Nikolić-Ristanović, V. 2013. Different understanding of the notion of victim and their consequences on social attitude towards victimization. In: M. Vmbrož, K. Filipčić and A. Završnik, eds, *Zbornik za Alenko Šelih*, Ljubljana: Slovenska akademija nauka, Pravni fakultet i Institut za kriminologiju Pravnog fakulteta, pp. 383–399.

Nikolić-Ristanović, V., 2015. Communication about the past and reconciliation: lessons from the Western Balkan. *Restorative Justice*, 3(2), pp. 188–211.

Nikolić-Ristanović, V. and Ćopić, S., 2013. Dealing with interethnic conflicts in Serbia and the place of restorative justice and victims. Belgrade: Victimology Society of Serbia. [pdf]. Available at: www.alternativeproject.eu/assets/upload/Deliverable 6.1_Research_report_on dealing_with_conflicts_by_NGOs_and_the_state.pdf> (accessed 15 September 2015).

Nikolić-Ristanović, V. and Ćopić, S., 2016. Dealing with the past in Serbia: achievements in the past 20 years. In: M. Fischer and O. Simić, eds, *Transitional Justice and Reconciliation – Lessons from the Balkans*. Oxford: Routledge, pp. 141–168.

Nikolić-Ristanović, V. and Šaćiri, B., 2013. Bavljenje međuetničkim konfliktima od strane organizacija civilnog društva u Srbiji: aktivnosti i diskurs (Dealing with interethnic conflicts by civil society in Serbia: activities and discourse). *Temida*, 16(3–4), pp. 27–60.

Nikolić-Ristanović, V. and Srna, J., 2010. Pomirenje sa sobom i drugima: od pristupa ka modelu (Reconciliation with ourselves and others: from approach to model). *Temida*, 13(1), pp. 43–58.

Nikolić-Ristanović, V., Ćopić, S., Petrović, N. and Šaćiri, B., 2012. Draft research report 6.1. Belgrade: Victimology Society of Serbia. [pdf] unpublished.

Nikolić-Ristanović, V., Ćopić, S., Petrović, N. and Šaćiri, B., 2014. Conflicts, security and justice in intercultural context of Serbia. Belgrade: Victimology Society of Serbia. (Deliverable 6.2. of FP7 project ALTERNATIVE – Developing alternative understandings of security and justice through restorative justice approaches in intercultural settings within democratic societies). [pdf] Available at: www.alternativeproject.eu/assets/upload/Deliverable_6.2_Research_report_on_interethnic_conflicts_and_citizens_security_perceptions.pdf (accessed 15 September 2015).

Nikolić-Ristanović, V., Ćopić, S., Petrović, N. and Šaćiri, B., 2015a. Viktimizacija i pravda u interkulturalnom kontekstu Srbije (Victimisation and justice in intercultural context in Serbia). *Temida*, 18(2), pp. 31–58.

Nikolić-Ristanović, V., Ćopić, S., Petrović, N. and Šaćiri, B. 2015b. Security and justice in the multi-ethnic communities in Serbia. In: D. Kolarić, ed., *Međunarodni naučni skup 'Dani Arčibalda Rajsa'-Tematski zbornik radova međunarodnog značaja/International Scientific Conference 'Archibald Reiss Days' – Thematic Conference Proceedings of International Significance*. Beograd: Kriminalističko-policijska akademija/ Belgrade: Academy of Police and Criminalistic Studies, tom/vol. II: pp. 27–36.

Nikolić-Ristanović, V., Srna, J. and Ćopić, S., 2015c. Primena restorativnih pristupa u interkulturalnim sredinama u Srbiji: Teorijska polazišta i metodološki pristup akcionog istraživanja VDS u tri multietničke sredine (Applying restorative approaches in intercultural settings in Serbia: theoretical departures and methodological approach of the VDS' action research in three multiethnic communities). *Temida*, 18(3–4), pp. 81–102.

Raković, S., 2005. We are not like them: denial of the Other in Serbia, Croatia and Bosnia-Herzegovina. In: M. Pajnik and T. Kuzmanić, eds, *Nation-States and Xenophobia: in the ruins of Ex-Yugoslavia*. Ljubljana: Peace Institute, pp. 63–74.

Riesenfeld, C., 2008. *Instruments of Reconciliation? Potentials and Risks of Reparation Measures in Post-Conflict Guatemala*. Department of Peace and Conflict Research, Uppsala: Uppsala University. [pdf] Available at: www.pcr.uu.se/digitalAssets/67/c_67531-l_1-k_mfs_riesenfeld.pdf (accessed 15 September 2015).

Rohne, H. C., Arsovska, J. and Aertsen, I., 2008. Challenging restorative justice – state based conflict, mass victimisation and the changing nature of warfare. In: I. Aertsen, J. Arsovska, H. C., Rohne, M. Valinas and K. Vanspauwen, eds, *Restoring Justice after Large-Scale Violent Conflicts*. Cullompton: Willan, pp. 3–46.

Rombouts, H., 2002. Importance and difficulties of victim-based research in post-conflict societies. *European Journal of Crime, Criminal Law and Criminal Justice*, 10(2–3), pp. 216–232.

Schnabel, A. and Ehrhart, H. G., 2006. Post-conflict societies and the military: challenges and problems of security sector reform. In: A. Schnabel and H. G. Ehrhart, eds, *Security Sector Reform and Post-Conflict Peacebuilding*. New York: United Nations University Press, pp. 1–16.

Shaw, M., 2001. The historical transition of our times: the question of globality in historical sociology. *Cambridge Review of International Affairs*, 14(2), pp. 273–289.

Shinoda, H., 2004. *The Concept of Human Security: Historical and Theoretical Implications. Conflict and Human Security: A Search for New Approaches of Peace-Building*. IPSHU English Research Report Series, 19, pp. 5–22. [pdf]. Available at: http://home.hiroshima-u.ac.jp/heiwa/Pub/E19/chap1.pdf (accessed 10 September 2015).

Smith-Höhn, J., 2010. *Rebuilding the Security Sector in Post-Conflict Societies: Perceptions from Urban Liberia and Sierra Leone*. New Jersey: Transaction.

Soković, S., 2012. Penitersijarne statistike: mera kriminaliteta i/ili više od toga? (Penitentiary statistics: a measure of crime and/or more than that?) In: V. Nikolić-Ristanović, ed., *Evidentiranje kriminaliteta: iskustva iz sveta i Srbije (Crime Recording: Experiences from the World and from Serbia)*. Beograd: Prometej, pp. 83–104.

Spalek, B., 2006. *Crime Victims: Theory, Policy and Practice*. New York: Palgrave Macmillan.

Strobl, R., 2010. Becoming a victim. In: S. G. Shoham, P. Knepper and M. Kett, eds, 2010. *International Handbook of Victimology*. Boca Raton: CRC, pp. 3–25.

Teitel, R., 2000. *Transitional Justice*. Oxford: Oxford University Press.

Theidon, K., 2007. Transitional subjects: the disarmament, demobilization and reintegration of former combatants in Colombia. *Transitional Justice*, 1(1), pp. 66–90.

True, J., 2012. *The Political Economy of Violence against Women*. New York: Oxford University Press.

Tschudi, F., 2008. Dealing with violent conflicts and mass victimisation. A human dignity approach. In: I. Aertsen, J. Arsovska, H.-C. Rohne, M. Valiñas and K. Vanspauwen, eds, *Restoring Justice after Large-Scale Conflicts*. Cullompton: Willan, pp. 46–69.

United Nations Development Programme, 1994. *Human Development Report 1994*. New York, Oxford: Oxford University Press.

Vanfraechem, I., 2012. Deliverable 8.1: Work document on operationalisation of theoretical concepts. Leuven: KU Leuven (Deliverable 8.1. of FP7 project ALTERNATIVE – Developing alternative understandings of security and justice through restorative justice approaches in intercultural settings within democratic societies).

Walgrave, L., 2008. *Restorative Justice, Self-Interest and Responsible Citizenship*. Cullompton: Willan.

Wemmers, J. A. and Manirabona, A., 2014. Regaining trust: the importance of justice for victims of crimes against humanity. *International Review of Victimology*, 20(1), pp. 101–109.

Zeigler, S. and Gunderson, G., 2006. The gendered dimensions of conflict's aftermath: a victim-centered approach to compensation. *Ethics and International Affairs*, 20(2), pp. 171–192.

8 Security and justice in transition

Restorative justice and the politics of hope in Northern Ireland

Derick Wilson and Hugh Campbell

Introduction

This chapter from Northern Ireland explores the possibilities, and limitations, of those wishing to promote restorative justice practices that underpin security and justice for all and that assist this society to transform itself, moving beyond our recent history of violent conflict. In the ethnic frontier society of Northern Ireland (Wright, 1987), pro-British and pro-Irish identities have competed in a space where the cosmopolitan powers, represented by London and Dublin, were at best benign and never prepared to go to war. In many other ethnic frontiers, external cosmopolitan powers have often not been so benign. Also, Northern Ireland, or the North of Ireland as a region – the very use of dual terms denotes different political aspirations – and its conflict threatened the wider European project, belonging to a wider European Union structure associated with resolving regional conflicts.

After a violent conflict in which about 3585 people were killed from 1969, peace in Northern Ireland is based on the premise that there is no ethnically pure peace. Each person, from opposed historical traditions, still has to live in the midst of others. This has proved very difficult to operationalise, as each group finds it very difficult to own its own aggression as anything but the *righteous retaliation* of having once been a victim.

In Northern Ireland, the signing of the Good Friday Agreement (GFA) in April 1998, and its subsequent endorsement by referendum in Northern Ireland and in the Irish Republic, delivered a political solution to the previously intractable problems that had blighted the province (Monaghan, 2008). This political agreement released all politically motivated prisoners; promoted an inclusive government with those associated with opposed political positions involved in a local Assembly and administration; established legislation on equality, good relations and human rights; and provided for a Commission for Victims and Survivors, although the later comprehensive report on Acknowledging the Past was not unanimously embraced.

The opportunities afforded to promote restorative practice approaches are examined within what Braithwaite and Rashed (2014, p. 201) identify as a 'politics of hope' approach against an admittedly slender, but pre-existing, background history of reconciliation practice since at least 1965; an internationally mediated political settlement of 1998 that was overwhelmingly supported by all the people on the island of Ireland and which established restorative justice as one of the transitional mechanisms within the criminal justice system; extensive resources and political support from the governments of the USA, Canada, Australia and New Zealand and the International Fund for Ireland; the UK and Republic of Ireland governments with the extensive and long-term European Union Peace Programmes; and significant philanthropic foundations.

Against the background of addressing historical asymmetries of access to the state and the law and order systems before the conflict,[1] this chapter examines the importance of restorative practices being embedded in wider societal institutions and societal transformation and not restricted, or confined, to the criminal justice system alone.

Restorative justice and the politics of hope

Braithwaite and Rashed (2014) argue that in contested societies there is often a political narrative of how peace came that ignores *the politics of hope* developed by many reconciliation groups, and so it is important to consider the contribution of the spectrum of civic reconciling actions that are restorative in character. In Northern Ireland, this reconciling narrative predates the explicit emergence of restorative justice (RJ) and enhances it. This chapter examines this earlier reconciliation base of practice, and the emerging range of more explicit restorative practices that have developed from it, because such a fragile, yet fertile, practice base nurtured some hope through very dark times.

RJ in Northern Ireland, as a concept and as a way of working (see Payne *et al.*, 2010), has contributed to the inclusion of a wider range of citizens and identities in the peace process in Northern Ireland[2] than could previously have been imagined. As such, it had, and continues to have, an important potential in developing an agreed sense of equal citizenship for many Nationalists and Republicans, who previously experienced themselves as being treated in a second-class manner. Additionally, in the aftermath of the GFA and the subsequent failure of Loyalists to secure continuing representation in the locally elected Legislative Assembly, RJ has offered some people and organisations representing these communities a way back into mainstream civil society activity.

RJ, through being mandated as a part of the Northern Ireland juvenile justice system, offers possibilities for young people to take responsibility for their actions and the possibility for those offended against to have their fears lessened through participating in restorative conferences. This inclusive and demanding approach has an additional important role for many citizens, young and old, coming to these meetings. The conferences, potentially, offer additional significant and new learning processes of meeting *different others* in a society seeking to move beyond conflict. Such restorative processes can build deeper relationships between people from historically opposed traditions who share a society together; enable previously silent voices to be heard, especially those who have been victimised, denied or locked out; offer new experiences of moving beyond fear and conflict where the victims establish new ways forward; and offer a structure (Zehr, 2002, pp. 21–22) that brings diverse local people into a new order where people may feel safer, where the talents of all are pooled, where vulnerability is held, and where talents and gifts are released.

This chapter locates the specific gifts the RJ developments have, conclusively, made to the peace process in Northern Ireland, drawing on future-oriented definitions of 'restorative', such as giving '*new strength and vigour*' (Jenkins, 2006, p. 153, italics in original) to all aspects of societal life together. This interpretation points to something new, something better and healthier. It associates restoration explicitly with the reinvigorating of relationships and the revitalisation of structures.

Restorative processes are supportive of a more restorative society culture

The systems associated with how community and civic institutions resolve their internal difficulties with staff and model new organisational forms of governance that restore and nurture relationships between diverse, and sometimes conflicted, human beings are, potentially, transformative. They can also contribute to wider societal healing and understanding. It is a common temptation, commented on by many (for example Cunneen, 2007; Green, 2007; Daly, 2008), that RJ activists often romanticise and uncritically promote RJ. There is local evidence (e.g. from critical reflective practice with Ulster's Restorative Society Module) that when RJ fieldwork practitioners develop conferences and work to their best, the experience of victims, offenders and their various supporters is that a level of mutual engagement can develop a new and diverse form of community meeting that, in essence, contributes to experiencing that the wider society needs to move on politically.

When many have been made anxious and afraid from wider threat and intimidation historically, some people who experience meeting in a new manner can gain space for difficult experiences to be voiced. When such restorative skills and experiences are multiplied within a wider set of civil society practices, people move forward and are, potentially, more open to one another (Wilson, 1994). These various restorative actions, some in the heat of much emotion, fear, violence and death, were, and are, part of a wider family of restorative actions that make the emergence of RJ more challenging to promote on a wider societal front, nudging this society to become more whole. Embedding the principles of 'justly engaging' with one another; 'accepting responsibility' with and for one another; and 'causing us to engage' again with our distant other in this place is a new reality[3] that locates restorative techniques, values and processes within Johnstone's wider societal and systemic change agenda (Johnstone, 2008).

Against this background of reconciling actions, it is clear that, although often not explicitly stated as being restorative, restorative processes and restorative structures have been promoted through the relational and structural history of previous strategic reconciliation practice since at least 1965. Restorative processes have been important in enabling some excluded people and traditions to begin to experience equal citizenship, although until the recent meeting of the UK queen and the Irish president(s), the enmity historically associated with the competing traditions of metropolitan identity, centred on London and Dublin, could often dilute that movement.

Participation in civil society through more robust dialogue and encounter, and the development of new meetings between people previously very estranged from and at enmity with one another, has also become a new restorative reality. The reconciling history has accumulated some models of victims and those associated with groups who took violent action meeting together, and this has offered a challenging contrast culture. Dialogue and engagement between people from very different sides of the fear/force line have modelled intercultural dialogue and healing being possible (Wilson, 1994).

Post-conflict (Lederach, 2011, p. 17) small and local reconciling actions have been future oriented and inclusive. As contrasts to the fascination of the media with violence, such inclusive ways establish restorative steps that become restorative processes between people. In some cases, such as with bereaved parents who established integrated schools[4] or with previous combatants who agreed to meet together over time, new restorative agreements and developing structures have developed between people who were previously opposed.

Post-conflict, partisan feelings are still understandably deep and draw some people to separate themselves from their historic *dangerous others*. However, as the diversity of societies changes, community leaders have to face into greater local diversity, including those who have had no part of local historical enmities and who have come to live in Northern Ireland for reasons of seeking sanctuary, asylum or new opportunities for work in a more globalised world. The restorative challenges in such settings often place community leaders in difficult 'pushes forward' towards embracing diversity and heterogeneity and 'pulls back' to partisanship and homogeneity. As such, people and groups face challenges around whether community is understood as something that is narrow, homogeneous, potentially excluding and judgemental or whether it is open, invitational, hospitable and inclusive (see Pavlich, 2001).

The journey to securing RJ as a credible approach in Northern Ireland was undertaken by a range of independent actors, often working apart, yet influencing one another. The embracing of RJ within the criminal justice system (CJS) was promoted by critical civil society non-governmental organisations (NGOs) such as the Quakers and the Mennonites for many years prior to the 1990s. It was then promoted as a new and a more community-focused way to develop a renewed CJS by community-based organisations[5] prior to the GFA of 1998. The practice of these community-based groups was often initially contested by the state;[6] however, this resistance was dissolved through Section 6 of the 1998

Agreement.[7] Since then, the evidence emerging from the youth conferencing programme of the Youth Justice Agency (see Youth Justice Agency Report, 2006) and the accumulated practice and independent assessments evolving from different community-based programmes became important new base lines from which to engage the wider society about its value (Payne *et al.*, 2010, p. 18). The devolution of an agreed Justice System to the NI Assembly, and Department of Justice (established in April 2010) support for RJ programmes across the Youth Justice System, Prisons, Policing and in local communities, have been further supports.

The explicit engagement of former combatants has been significant, as many former combatants have told their story and heard the stories of different others. The Junction and its related projects in Derry have been to the fore in this. The reality of opposed former combatants agreeing to meet together about the past and to consider ways beyond conflict now open to them has been a most positive contribution to the wider peace process. Sometimes initially facilitated by third parties, but often now taken on by the participants themselves, these engagements have been important restorative signals.

It is important to note that there also have been a number of small but significant RJ-informed projects beyond the CJS. Examples are creative work with anti-bullying approaches in primary schools (Tyrell, 1995; Tyrell *et al.*, 1998),[8] work with cared for children and young people, Barnardo's restorative school approaches (Healy *et al.*, 2002), family group conferences, the Northern Ireland Association for the Care and Resettlement of Offenders (NIACRO) community-based programmes, and Ulster University's Restorative Practices team working with schools, prisoners and prison officers in the Republic of Ireland and Northern Ireland (Wilson, 2012; Campbell *et al.*, 2013), as well as some developmental youth work approaches incorporating restorative principles.

Working towards a restorative society in Northern Ireland – reconciliation practice

Wright (1987, 1996) insists that a history of only conflict, although dominant in the North of Ireland, needs to be tempered by an acknowledgement of slender reconciling strands of healing practice that have always existed too. His studies of political history in Ireland, the former Yugoslavia, ethnic frontiers in Europe and the southern states of the USA give further historical underpinning to the suggestion of Braithwaite and his 'politics of hope' reconciliation strand as well as his argument that the RJ movement needs to be transformational around the holistic nature of living and the 'way we do justice in the world' (2003, pp. 1–20).

A number of political and inter-community reconciliation practices have been a reality since the early 1960s and have challenged narrowly generated understandings of homogeneous communities and ethnocentric or cultural identities. These groups are identified as being a lasting element in the Peace Monitoring Report of 2014 (Nolan, 2014) and act as points of contrast to a political reconciliation project that has often been stalled. Nolan, when reviewing the progress made since 1998, has highlighted among ten key themes:

> Theme 9. At grassroots level the reconciliation impulse remains strong. The people of Northern Ireland escape sectarian identities as often as they are trapped by them. Much of what takes place in neighbourhoods defies stereotyped notions.... Reconciliation continues to be stronger at the grass roots than at the top of society.

This strand of reconciliation practice, now considerable in terms of its relational and structural work (Morrow *et al.*, 2013), took one institutional form in 1964–1965 with the establishment of the Corrymeela Community. Its emergence was due to people variously involved in the wider ecumenical movement; the response to the World War II challenges in creating a diverse and unified Europe; the challenges emerging from poverty; the return of students from overseas development assignments; and the need to address the failure of Northern Ireland to treat all equally.

Systemic change challenges

Over the years, people seeking a more open and shared society, while developing reconciliation practices and programmes, argued for the emergence of public policy, institutional and legal responses to act as a bed of compliance underpinning new, more restorative and human ways of living with one another.

In terms of public policy, the initial NI Community Relations Commission, established by the Community Relations Act (Northern Ireland) 1969, had diverse foci on empowering local community development groups formed in areas of conflict. It also housed a pilot project for Schools Community Relations Programmes and developed a range of Cultural Awareness initiatives. In each of these programme initiatives, the task of relationship building across cultural, religious and political divides was central and essentially, when they worked, restorative. However, the word 'restorative' would not normally have been part of the language used at that time.

Institutional responses to the conflict were varied in quality and longevity and often not core funded. Many were primarily supported by local and international philanthropy and the European Union. The institutional legacy of this practice has been that numerous local programmes, initiated and developed by youth workers and school teachers from diverse cultural traditions, have continued for years to bring children, young people, parents and staff together from diverse traditions, but have had difficulties in embedding this work centrally within core public budgets. The institutional emergence of integrated schools underpinned by the GFA, the moves to develop a *sharing in education*[9] approach between schools with different political/religious governance structures, and the civil society development of some cross-community institutions have been important in terms of building institutional models of contrast.

In this work, the focus has been on the triple interconnected challenges of addressing 'societal separation', 'dissolving inequality' and 'promoting good relations'. Legally, the re-establishing of the NI Community Relations Council in 1989, the establishment of the Equality Commission for NI and the NI Human Rights Commission from the Equality and Good Relations legislation, 1998 (Sect 75 (i) and (ii)) have all been important foundation blocks for underpinning restorative actions on the above trio of themes.

The strand of non-violence

The focus on violence is an important theme. The emergence of the non-violent Civil Rights Association campaign, in 1967, was a restorative challenge, seeking 'the end to seven "injustices", ranging from council house allocations to the "weighted" voting system.'[10] This call, to have inequalities of treatment in voting, housing allocation and employment addressed, highlighted fundamental institutional and systemic restorative tasks.

In a contested society, homogeneous identity groups tend to move people towards those they think they are like and away from different others. Identity groups, associated with fears and uncertainty, are often ambivalent about violence, espousing our violence is justified, yours is not!

Non-violence and the struggle for justice have been, and are still, important themes in the actions of individuals and small groups connected with small yet distinct voices associated with the Quaker Peace Service tradition (Le Mare and McCartney, 2009), the Mennonites and the Peace People. Programmes such as the Quaker House Programmes (1982–2010) in localities in Belfast and Derry; the Quaker Centre for Neighbourhood Development Programmes; the Quaker Family Centre at the Maze Prison; the work of the Quaker Peace Education Project based in Derry and its development of peer mediation and anti-bullying approaches; and early youth initiatives such as Extern, VSB and Youth Action have been important restorative impulses, as well as the development of the Restorative Justice Working Group in 1994, later the RJ Forum in 2005.

The Peace People emerged in 1976 and harnessed the energies of many people from diverse backgrounds as well as developing international youth camps. Along with the Quaker contribution and International Voluntary Service (SCI), there was a space for non-violent approaches to be reflected on and developed, a theme developed in civil society by, among others, the Women Together (1970) and Witness for Peace (1972) initiatives.

These initiatives were central to the 'politics of hope' tradition. Even though some of the above no longer exist, they left a restorative trace and modelled that meeting the different other was possible, and that a way of living and working together was, and still is, restorative. In essence, such a non-violent tradition is restorative in intent, committed to finding new ways for previous enemies to meet and structure their power relations differently, without the use of violence. It is important that these non-violent approaches were, and still are, promoted, even though, in terms of the wider escalating conflict, many remain dismissive of them, or, worse still, are unaware of them. Standing, as they did, for restorative ways of living and working together within and between communities, the non-violent civil society groups challenged partisan identities, and, in restorative process-value terms, brought people from very opposed traditions into a shared and interdependent experience of being part of a wider civil society tradition through the practice of inclusion and the central building block of offering simple hospitality.

There were also non-violent strands in political life that need to be acknowledged: John Hume's non-violent Social and Democratic Labour Party (the SDLP), the formation of the Women's Coalition and the Alliance Party, all of whom were party to the GFA, with the SDLP becoming one of the two major governing parties, having the position of deputy first minister. Currently, the Women's Coalition has no political representation. Formed in the specific period leading up to and following the GFA, the contribution of the Women's Coalition political party to the Belfast Agreement, 1998 is important to remember.[11]

Inclusive second chance adult education and community development

Sustained UK, Irish and international charitable philanthropic and governmental and European Union support[12] enabled the enduring growth of civil society groups as strands of community work and adult education. From 1972 onwards, the emergence of highly innovative community education programmes offered a welcoming and hospitable learning environment, nurturing personal confidence and a critical community perspective within many adults previously excluded from adult education opportunities.[13]

Various locality-based community development, and what would now be termed 'social economy', initiatives, such as in Ballymurphy, West Belfast; the Bogside Residents Association, Derry; the Shankill; and the Ulster Political Research Group, as well as smaller rural initiatives such as those developed by the Rural Community Network, laid down seeds of wider across-tradition initiatives associated with area and regional Economic Development Initiatives. An important impulse of this community development practice was the potential and willingness of some to promote a non-sectarian and 'cross-community' vision. There were periods and instances when government either was suspicious of it or sought to co-opt it (Rolston, 1984). Sometimes government and local activists co-worked, and sometimes each found it useful to also distance themselves (see Craig *et al.*, 2011).

Some victims' experiences

The need to find ways to acknowledge the past and honour victims and their families is a restorative challenge in the peace process and is still paramount and unfinished. The place of victims is contained in the second paragraph of the Declaration of Support in The Belfast Agreement, 1998. There is a restorative intent, stated as:

> 2. The tragedies of the past have left a deep and profoundly regrettable legacy of suffering. We must never forget those who have died or been injured, and their families. But we can best honour them through a fresh start, in which we firmly dedicate ourselves to the achievement of reconciliation, tolerance, and mutual trust, and to the protection and vindication of the human rights of all.

A variety of programmes that made space for victims' stories to be told and different historical narratives to be heard evolved in many areas. Although this is not the experience of every victim and their family, it is a fact that some victims and their families have engaged with those associated with the killing or injury of their relatives. There have been some statements of families wishing to be associated with finding restorative ways forward beyond lasting hurt and grievance. This theme is still work in progress and, for many, still an unresolved issue, even though there is a Commission for Victims and Survivors and a Victims and Survivors Forum. One major restorative failure was the failure by governments, and the uncritical and too hasty rejection by some involved in the victims sector, to embrace the comprehensive set of proposals of the Consultative Group on the Past (Eames and Bradley, 2009). After eight-plus years of rejection, it has re-emerged as a possible template of restorative ways forward in the current impasse around the past, where government, security services, and policing and former paramilitary groups have real difficulties with acknowledging their past involvements.

The emergence of mediation approaches as a systemic civil society response

The establishment of the Northern Ireland Mediation Network, hereafter Mediation Network NI, and its contribution to resolving a number of major conflicts (McAllister, 2003), contributed to some institutions, political groups and communities being more open to mediation attempts (Morrow *et al.*, 2014). The reality has been that many people in the business and civil society sectors have become involved in mediation initiatives, and some resolutions to seemingly intractable conflicts have been developed through such third-party restorative mediations.

In 1990, Counteract, an Irish Congress of Trade Unions (ICTU)-supported anti-sectarian initiative, and later Trademark promoted major restorative workplace programmes that directly resolved disputes and promoted new organisational cultures that addressed inequities of treatment on issues including, but not limited to, sectarian and racist acts. These projects also challenged the trade union organisations to look at their own corporate cultures and align themselves internally with the larger, inclusive, external shared societal values and practices they were promoting.

Joint and comprehensive institutional church actions in support of reconciliation have been conspicuous by their absence since 1965, yet some leading Protestant Church leaders did lead the way by meeting the IRA at Feakle in 1974, and small groups of clergy, such as those led by Fr Alex Reid of Clonard Monastery, were important in assisting movements to the 1998 agreement. There have been courageous individuals, small groups and local models of inter-church co-working and joint inter-faith action, and, at different times, some individual courageous church leaders used their position to stand and confront sectarian and ethnocentric behaviours or to mediate (Liechty and Clegg, 2001). Some of the sustaining and principled thinking about reconciliation challenges and faith work has been that of the Faith and Politics Group, who, over the course of many years, developed bold joint statements and reflections in response to local incidents or in anticipation of major societal issues. The Northern Ireland Inter-Faith organisation (NIFF) currently undertakes important educational and cultural diversity awareness-raising work as well as the work of the Irish School of Ecumenics.

However, the major Christian Churches in Ireland, for many years, tended to be more bound to pastoring their traditions than promoting reconciliation as a primary action. There has been a tendency for each to be more a hostage to the fears of their co-religionists than a promoter of good relations with different others.

Future challenges to becoming a more restorative society

Restoring hope in politics

In light of the above and many other organisations, there is a body of historic reconciliation practice that comes into the 'politics of hope' category. Although not often explicitly using the language of restoration, the impulse of the bulk of this activity has been restorative of relationships and structures to better serve a more open, diverse, just and secure society. One area of concern currently is that, in a time of austerity, many civil society groups and organisations are under immense financial pressures, and a number of significant players in the adult education field have recently closed down, while the role of civil society actors in mutual understanding education has been sharply cut back by a reduction in government support.

Using the earlier Jenkins definition of restoring as nurturing and developing, there are major restorative challenges for the NI Executive and politicians working to promote a shared society. *A Shared Future* (Northern Ireland Office, 2005) was an earlier comprehensive public policy platform set out before the current power-sharing NI Executive was established. The new local Executive developed its own *Together Building a United Community* (2013) policy. While this new locally driven policy is to be welcomed, the programme lacks the underpinning critical analysis of the 2005 policy and the comprehensive equality, good relations and race relations targets and attainment measures established across all government departments that accompanied it then.

Implicit within the recent Third Peace Monitoring (2014) report is the view that the vision of working to a shared society is politically weak and compromised.

> Twenty years on from the first ceasefires the terms of trade have been set by deals and side-deals. These have prevented the return of large-scale violence but the model on offer from the top is peace without reconciliation. A culture of endless negotiation has become embedded and, without a vision of a shared society to sustain it, the peace process has lost the power to inspire.
>
> (Nolan, 2014)

Among ten key summary points in this report worth highlighting are large restorative challenges. The research identified the challenge of nurturing hope in political processes and in civic culture, and the need to develop trust and halt increased segregation. It argued that

> The moral basis of the 1998 peace accord has evaporated (Key Theme 1);
> The absence of trust has resulted in an absence of progress (Key Theme 2);
> There has been some increase in polarisation (Key Theme 3).

As mentioned earlier, the argument that 'reconciliation continues to be stronger at the grass roots than at the top of society' poses a major challenge for all the political parties and the power-sharing executive.

The Nolan report highlighted that there still remain huge educational disparities that leave a large number of young males from both Catholic and Protestant backgrounds fundamentally impoverished educationally. While, currently, some young working-class Protestant males are lowest in this order, some years ago this applied to young Catholic males. In short, Northern Ireland has among the highest levels of pupil attainment educationally in the UK sitting alongside some of the lowest levels of non-attaining male pupils. This is a restorative challenge (Nolan, 2014, p. 97).

It might well be that 'common work' on commonly agreed problems such as the massive educational underachievement levels of young males across traditions could comprise incremental restorative steps.

Promoting agreed law and order and societal compliance measures

Even though there is now an agreed policing order, there have been events where the different political traditions have acted in a partisan manner rather than working to support the agreed, overarching, law and order systems and structures. This has meant that 'front line police have been the human shock absorbers for failures elsewhere' (Third Peace Monitoring Report Key Theme 7). As long as resources associated with developing good day-to-day community policing practices are hostage to unresolved political identity arguments, the wider restoration of good policing is truncated, and justice and security are impacted.

The 1998 Equality and Good Relations legislation established new standards of compliance. Even though currently 'the rebalancing of inequalities unbalances unionism' (Nolan, 2014, Key Theme 8), Catholics still experience more economic and social disadvantage than Protestants. In addition, the society has experienced racial abuse incidents that have often not been immediately and comprehensively challenged by all in political and civil society. It is only very recently that the details of a race relations policy have emerged. Such established legal compliance measures underpin the securing of an equality, good relations and human rights culture.

Promoting a commitment within public and civil society cultures that promote a shared society and the primacy of citizenship

George Pavlich (2001) questions fixed or absolute images of community that, for him, can hide totalitarian hints and fail to question accepted divisions of insiders and outsiders. He warns about too readily accepting the uncritical use of community as an immutable, fixed reality that privileges insiders and disenfranchises outsiders. Without this critical interrogation of the term, the boundaries of ethnocentric and partisan identities still too readily dominate political, public and civic life in Northern Ireland, and there are only small spaces of contrasting actions.

Promoting more just, inclusive and welcoming expressions of community is a major challenge now, because the umbrella terms of 'community' or 'communities' are still used in public policy as well as in service delivery, and they can be too quickly equated with the historically competing identity communities here. As such, they are limited as transcendent or overarching concepts; are not usually associated with developing a 'shared society'; and limit momentum gathering around the more challenging theme of creating an inclusive future society of diverse individual citizens.

Allied to challenging narrow notions of community that feed oppositional identities, an additional restorative task is to establish a transcendent overarching vision of citizenship. It is important to bring public and civic leadership together in creating the conditions where people engage with one another primarily as citizens, and not as members of identity groups or communities. To settle for anything less is to avoid the transformative and restorative challenges facing us. Restoring citizenship as a primary goal, therefore (Wilson, 2013), is a central restorative task, and all public policy, all visions, working practices and governance cultures for public and charitable NGOs could be usefully measured against such a 'shared future' backdrop.

Promoting opportunities for schools, trade unions and employers, community organisations, and faith and inter-faith organisations to embrace restorative practices

Even in the absence of a dynamic forward momentum around an agreed political 'shared future' society here, there is still much that can be done to cradle and nurture contrasting models of restorative practices that have societal significance.

There is a local evidence base of a small number of schools embracing restorative practices holistically. This practice is linked to best international practice of creating community experiences of association[14] and school cultures where underachievement levels are cut, levels of safety increase, and partnership working between pupils, parents and staff is enhanced.[15] Such local practice could be grown further and developed as a future-oriented strand of practice promoting a shared society, at ease with difference.

Initiatives exist locally where trade union engagement with employers is seeking to establish less confrontational and more restorative organisation/ employee relations. These open up the potential of establishing a wider restorative societal culture. Examples exist internationally and locally where local councils, trade union members and staff work in restorative ways with citizens, and evidence improvements in local authority–citizen relations as well as substantial savings in legal and other costs that rely on a more adversarial approach.

There is a vast base of energetic and diverse community organisations existing in Northern Ireland. However, a culture of 'silence' or 'politeness' around the 'shared future society' still pervades many organisations in this sector. Whatever the discrete and valuable focus of their services and advocacy activities, it is now important that all organisations in this sector revisit their aims and are encouraged to locate their work within an explicit commitment to a 'shared and mutually respectful society' explicitly in their governance, staffing and volunteer structures.

With the exception of many notable individual local faith-based initiatives for reconciliation and healing, the map of institutional Christian churches working for restoration and healing in this society is by no means overflowing. By comparison, it is a growing area of activity in many other societies.

The emergence of diverse faith tradition members living in Northern Ireland is a new reality that may still be too readily dominated by majority–minority dynamics that are not helpful and work against a mutually respectful restorative learning culture between members as equals.

There is a local knowledge base and best practice internationally that can be drawn on. The potential of this institutional faith base, were it to embrace restorative principles within its internal relationships, between institutions as well as in new listening relationships with the communities in which they are located, is vast, and potentially restorative of their vision and practice.

Inter-church and inter-faith linkages evidenced through organisations such as the Irish Council of Churches, NIFF and the Irish School of Ecumenics are important. The collaboration potential of development charities such as Christian Aid, Concern, Habitat, Tear Fund, Islamic Relief, the Islamic Family Centre, the Indian Centre and the Sikh Community is also large because so much of their practice is restorative in intent.

There are many international development programmes drawing energy and support from local support groups in Northern Ireland. Such projects could take critical learning and experience about the poverty and conflict they are seeking to address internationally back into critical questions about how people live often separate and conflicted lives in Northern Ireland. However, these learning insights can often be made peripheral within the life of our major local institutions.

Conclusion

There is considerable work that is restorative in nature across diverse civic and public sector organisations, although it is not often conceptualised in that way. 'Restorative practices' is one umbrella that sustains creative actions in this society across a range of settings; however, a more expanded learning community around this theme needs to be established.

A variety of regional political, civic, business, trade union, faith, inter-faith, educational and professional forums could be encouraged to explore how they could promote a more restorative way of working in their diverse practices and establish civic, public, business and professional arguments in support of these activities.

The recent withdrawal of funding to many civil society groups makes *active participation*, a key ingredient in this movement, more difficult. This also impacts on the strength and vitality of civil society organisations. The voluntary energy traditionally associated with civil society groups needs attention and nurturing.

Central to citizen safety and state security is the experience of diverse people feeling they are equal citizens. However, a major dynamic coming out of conflict is that partisan identities can so readily trump citizenship (Wilson, 2013). A major restorative challenge is the establishment of citizenship as a primary, fundamental experience in a post-conflict society.

Community is a contested concept, with its romantic history offering comfort and security to those from homogeneous identities and its, mostly unacknowledged, aspects of exclusion, judgement and homogeneity at a time of increasing diversity that brings the challenge of being open to intercultural engagement and trust. Working to promote a restorative society demands critical thinking on the part of community actors, organisations and the state about the concepts associated with the more open and welcoming communities they wish to support and develop. Certainly, Pavlich's notions of communities that welcome, expand to accommodate all who come, are inclusive, just and future oriented need continued attention (2001).

Working to promote a restorative society demands – from each of us – that we understand security and justice as more than just formal laws, policies and conventions between diverse people. We need to come to understand them as both relational experiences and in the essential cultures of the institutions we belong to, or go to, in daily life.

We benefit from having fundamental inalienable standards laid down as compliance standards that save us from our worst impulses and our willingness to act violently, but to have only these means that society is so vulnerable.

Beyond compliance, we need a transformative approach that supports the creation of commitment cultures, commitments to treat the different other respectfully and justly, commitments to secure her or his place because 'I look out for them and they, in turn, look out for me.' The real alternative is that we come to see how our security and sense of being justly treated is deeply, and reciprocally, tied up with whether we are committed to securing the rights and place of the different others in our midst. This is the practical transformative outworking of a *politics of hope* approach.

Notes

1 The asymmetrical experiences of the state were to a major extent initially dealt with through the responses to the demands of the Civil Rights Movement (1967). The full programme of rights, agreed representation, law, and public institutions and safeguards was agreed in the peace-building agenda, and the establishment of a devolved Assembly anchored in the Belfast Agreement (1998) and an Ireland-wide plebiscite vote, the St Andrews Agreement (2006) and the Hillsborough Agreement (2010). The asymmetries in experiences of the law, while still critically examined by many human rights activists, have been mainly attended to with the devolution of criminal justice to the NI Assembly in May 2010.
2 Central to these problems had been the contested nature of the criminal justice system, in particular the police, who at this point were unable to effectively police certain communities (McEvoy and Mika, 2001).
3 Adapted from Zehr's three principles of RJ (Zehr, 2002, Ch. 2, pp. 21–32).
4 In May 2015, the visit of Prince Charles to Mullaghmore, Co. Sligo, to the site of Lord Mountbatten's assassination in 1979 also highlighted the loss of several children in that IRA bombing. The Maxwell family, who lost their son in that incident, went on to establish an integrated school in Enniskillen as an expression of their desire to create a transformed society in Northern Ireland.
5 Organisations such as Community Restorative Justice Ireland (CRJI), with its roots in the Republican movement and community activism, itself outside the existing CJ system, and later Alternatives, with its roots in the Loyalist tradition and local community activism and, at that time, due to its pro-British history, positioning itself in an often uneasy proximity to the existing policing and the CJ system. Other Loyalist and Republican groups later explored this practice in varying degrees, based on the experiences of the groups above.
6 Wilson, with colleagues, hosted meetings between state officials and community organisations during a 'Policing Our Divided Society' Programme, 1996–2003. See http://eprints.ulster.ac.uk/27681/ and http://kennedyinstitute.nuim.ie/ (accessed April 2015).
7 Central to the (1998) Agreement, as specifically detailed in Section 6, was a commitment to bridge the gap between the state and communities in Northern Ireland. Measures included supporting 'the development of special community-based initiatives based on international best practice', and recognising the need to give support to both community and statutory-based programmes (Good Friday Agreement 1998: 7.12) (McEvoy and Eriksson, 2008). From Payne *et al.* (2010).
8 This chapter discusses how education will help lead to the success of the Multi-Party Negotiations, which attempt to resolve the conflict in Ireland. Citizenship development can teach values such as tolerance, care and respect for others as equals. Education can promote movement from the rhetoric to the practice of collaboration and encourage participative democracy. Education can also be a foundation for social harmony.

9 See Sharing Works – A Policy for Shared Education, www.deni.gov.uk/a_policy_for_shared_education_jan_2015.pdf (accessed April 2015).
10 The Northern Ireland Civil Rights Association (NICRA) called for wide-ranging reforms: it demanded equal voting rights in local government elections; a fairer system for the allocation of public housing; an end to 'gerrymandering' (the manipulation of electoral boundaries to give one community an electoral advantage); an end to discrimination in employment; the disbandment of the 'B-Specials' (an all-Protestant auxiliary police force); and the repeal of the Special Powers Act (which allowed internment of suspects without trial). See www.bbc.co.uk/history/events/day_troubles_began (accessed April 2015).
11 The story of the Northern Ireland Women's Coalition is one of do-it-yourself politics. Founded in 1996 as a result of frustration with the sterility of local politics, the NIWC had a broad cross-community base, attracting women (and men) from the nationalist and unionist communities, and from both Republican and Loyalist traditions (see Fearon, 1999).
12 Philanthropic charities represented by The UK Charitable Trust Administrators Group; The Ireland Funds and Atlantic Philanthropies; The International Fund for Ireland and The European Union Peace Programmes.
13 Examples of this work were the Community Education Courses in West and North Belfast through QUB and St Mary's College (Rowlands and Rowlands, 2001); the Rupert Stanley College initiatives in east Belfast; community development programmes such as Chadolly Street and, throughout Northern Ireland, the work of the Ulster People's College and the Workers Educational Association. The above voluntary initiatives no longer exist!
14 See Michael Sandel's discussion on 'communities of association and communities of entanglement'. Sandel argues that modern society has become more a space 'associated with entanglement than association', where the absence of a lived and experienced vision and aspiration together, in a very commodified world, potentially sets many people more and more apart and against. When the 'familiar turns strange' (Sandel), tensions emerge that are essential to engage and embrace. To engage with and meet those different from us by culture and belief, and so build a more open and challenging discussion, is how, eventually, the common good might be developed.
15 As examples, refer to: Braithwaite (2003); Cameron and Thorsborne (1999); Cremin *et al.* (2013); Drewery (2004); Flanagan (2010); Hendry (2009); Hopkins (2004); Kecskemeti (2011); McCluskey *et al.* (2008); Campbell *et al.* (2013). See also resources at: www.educ.cam.ac.uk/research/projects/restorativeapproaches/ (accessed April 2015).

References

Braithwaite, J., 2003. Principle of restorative justice. In: A. Von Hirsch, J. Roberts, A. Bottoms, K. Roach and M. Schiff (eds), *Restorative Justice and Criminal Justice: Competing or Reconcilable Paradigms*. Oxford: Hart.

Braithwaite, J. and Rashed, T., 2014. 'Non violence and reconciliation among the violence in Libya', *Restorative Justice* Vol. 2, Issue 2, pp. 185–204.

Campbell, H., McCord, J., Chapman, T. and Wilson, D., 2013. *Developing a Whole System Approach to Embedding Restorative Practices in YouthReach Youth Work and Schools in County Donegal*. County Donegal Vocational Education Committee. University of Ulster and Co. Donegal ETB Restorative Practices Project.

Cunneen, C., 2002. Restorative justice and the politics of decolonization. In: Elmar G. M. Weitekamp and Han-Jurgen Kerner, *Restorative Justice: Theoretical Foundations*, Cullompton: Willan, pp. 32–49.

Daly, K., 2008. Seeking justice in the 21st century: Towards an intersectional politics of justice. In: Holly Ventura Miller (ed.), *Restorative Justice: From Theory to Practice (Sociology of Crime, Law and Deviance, Volume 11)*, Bingley: Emerald, pp. 3–30.

Eames, R. and Bradley, D. (co-chairs), 2009. *Report of the Consultative Group on the Past*, Presented to the Secretary of State for Northern Ireland, 23 January 2009. www.cain.ulst.ac.uk/victims/docs/consultative_group/cgp_230109_report.pdf(accessed April 2015).

Green, S., 2007. The victims movement and restorative justice, in G. Johnstone and D.W. Van Ness (eds), *Handbook of Restorative Justice*, Cullompton: Willan, pp. 171–191.

Healy, J., Gribben, M. and McCann, C., 2002. *School Restorative Conferencing*, Barnardos, Belfast. www.barnardos.org.uk/pp_no_4_school_restorative_conferencing.pdf (accessed April 2015).

Jenkins, A., 2006. 'Shame, realisation and restitution: The ethics of restorative practice', *ANZJFT* Vol. 27, No. 3, p. 153.

Johnstone, G., 2008. The agendas of the restorative justice movement. In: Holly Ventura Miller (ed.), *Restorative Justice: From Theory to Practice (Sociology of Crime, Law and Deviance, Volume 11)*, Bingley: Emerald, pp. 59–79. ISBN: 978-0-7623-1455-3.

Le Mare, A. and McCartney, F., 2009. *Coming from the Silence: Quaker Peacebuilding Initiatives in Northern Ireland 1969–2007*. York, UK: William Sessions Ltd.

Lederach, J.P., 2011. *The Poetic Unfolding of the Human Spirit*. Kalamazoo: Fetzer Institute.

Liechty, J. and Clegg, C., 2001. *Moving beyond Sectarianism: Religion, Conflict, and Reconciliation in Northern Ireland.* Dublin: Columba Press.

McAllister, B., 2003. 'Unearthing the strange: Mediation and the journey towards other', *Conflict Resolution Notes* Vol. 20, No. 4, p. 3. www.mediate.com//articles/mcAllisterB.cfm (accessed April 2015).

McEvoy, K. and Eriksson, A., 2008. Who owns justice?: Community, state, and the Northern Ireland transition. In: J. Shapland, (ed.), *Justice, Community and Civil Society: A Contested Terrain across Europe*. Cullompton: Willan.

McEvoy, K. and Mika, H., 2001. 'Punishment, politics and praxis: Restorative justice and non-violent alternatives to paramilitary punishment', *Policing and Society* Vol. 11, Issue 1, pp. 359–382.

Mika, H. and McEvoy, K., 2001. 'Restorative justice in conflict: Paramilitarism, community and the construction of legitimacy in Northern Ireland', *Contemporary Justice Review* Vol. 3, Issue 4, pp. 291–319.

Monaghan, R., 2008. 'Community-based justice in Northern Ireland and South Africa', *International Criminal Justice Review* Vol. 18, Issue 1, pp. 83–105.

Morrow, D., McAllister, B., Campbell, J. and Wilson, D., 2014. *Mediated Dialogues and Systemic Change in Northern Ireland – Policing Our Divided Society 1996–2003.* Dublin: Kennedy Institute; National University of Ireland, Maynooth. www.eprints.ulster.ac.uk/27681/ (accessed April 2015).

Morrow, D., Robinson, G. and Dowds, L., 2013. *The Long View of Community Relations in Northern Ireland: 1989–2012*, Research Update, 87, ESRC and OFMDFMNI. www.ark.ac.uk/publications/updates/update87.pdf (accessed April 2015).

Northern Ireland Office, 2005. *'A Shared Future' 2005. The Framework for Good Relations in Northern Ireland.* www.ofmdfmni.gov.uk/asharedfuturepolicy2005.pdf (accessed April 2015).

Nolan, P., 2014 March. *Northern Ireland, Third Peace Monitoring Report*, NICRC, Belfast. www.nicrc.org.uk, search for 'Peace Monitoring Report' (accessed 19 June 2017).

Pavlich, G., 2001. The force of community. In: H. Strang and J. Braithwaite (eds), *Restorative Justice and Civil Society*. Cambridge: CUP, pp. 56–68.

Payne, B., Conway, V., Bell, C., Falk, A., Flynn, H., McNeil, C. and Rice, F. *Restorative Practices in Northern Ireland: A Mapping Exercise*. Belfast: School of Law, Queen's University Belfast, 2010.

Rolston, B., 1984. Education, conflict and community development. In: G. Craig, M. Mayo, K. Popple, M. Shaw and M. Taylor (eds), *The Community Development Reader*. Bristol: Policy, 2011.

Rowlands, D. and Rowlands, B., 2001. *'Carry on Learning': Report of an Experimental Project in Community Education*. Belfast: QUB.

Tyrell, J., 1995. *The Quaker Peace Education Project 1988–1994: Developing Untried Strategies*. University of Ulster, Coleraine, p. 122. ISBN 1 85923 007 5.

Tyrrell, J., Hartop, B. and Farrell, S., 1998. *Schools: Lessons from the Agreement*, 22 Fordham Int'l L.J. 1680. At FILE: /main/production/doc/data/journals/ir.lawnet.fordham.edu/ilj/assets/ir_citation.inc Available at: http://ir.lawnet.fordham.edu/ilj/vol22/iss4/24/ (accessed 19 June 2017).

Wilson, D., 2013. A restorative challenge: Can citizenship trump identity in Northern Ireland? In: G. McCluskey, E. Sellman and H. Cremin (eds), *Restorative Approaches to Conflict in Schools*. London: Routledge, pp. 59–74. ISBN 978-0-415-65611-5.

Wilson, D. A., 1994. Learning Together for a Change, D.Phil. Thesis (Unpublished), Ulster University.

Wilson, D. A., 2012a. *Platforms for a Restorative Society in Northern Ireland: A Concept Paper Underpinning the Restorative Practices Programme*. Coleraine; Ulster University.

Wilson, D. A., 2012b. Dún Laoghaire/Rathdown Comenius Regio 'Restorative Approaches' Programme 2010–2011 – A Formative Evaluation, in Dún Laoghaire/Rathdown Comenius Regio 'Restorative Approaches' Programme, University of Ulster, p. 81.

Wright, F., 1987. *Northern Ireland: A Comparative Analysis*. Dublin: Gill and Macmillan.

Wright, F., 1996. *Two Lands on One Soil: Ulster Politics before Home Rule*. Dublin: Gill and Macmillan.

Youth Justice Agency Report, 2006. www.youthjusticeagencyni.gov.uk/document_uploads/NI_Youth_Reoffending_Stats_from_the_2006_Cohort.pdf (accessed April 2015).

Zehr, H., 2002. Journey to belonging. In: Elmar G. M. Weitekamp and Han-Jurgen Kerner, *Restorative Justice: Theoretical Foundations*. Cullompton: Willan, pp. 21–31.

9 Community in conflict in intercultural contexts and how restorative justice can respond

Tim Chapman and Katrin Kremmel

Introduction

This chapter focuses on a concept that is relevant both to understanding conflict in intercultural settings and to the practice of restorative justice – *community*. For restorative justice, community has been seen in terms of a community of care that supports each party and is a vehicle for reintegrative shaming (Braithwaite, 1989; Zehr and Mika, 2003), or as a separate party affected by harm in a restorative process (Johnstone, 2001; Van Ness and Strong, 2010; Umbreit and Armour, 2011; Zinsstag and Chapman, 2012), or as a goal implicit in healing relationships (Sullivan and Tifft, 2001; Pranis *et al.*, 2003). In spite of this definitional confusion, it is generally viewed in a positive light, though for some writers (Walgrave, 2002; Pavlich, 2004) it is a contentious concept, which has limited validity or usefulness in restorative justice. Interestingly, very few writers have understood community as responsible for harm, as Harbin and Llewellyn (2016) have. Conflicts in intercultural settings are usually between communities that threaten or actually harm each other.

Community for each of these writers was understood in the context of mainstream restorative justice addressing crime and the harm it causes. But what if restorative justice is not addressing a conflict processed within criminal justice but is addressing a conflict in an intercultural setting, beyond the remit of the criminal justice system? How, then, is community understood, and what significance does the concept have to approaches to restoring security and justice when conflict between groups of people has caused harm?

These questions have not received much attention in the restorative justice literature. We will thus draw on the work of broader disciplines, sociology and social and political theory. We ground our analysis in two research fields in which the ALTERNATIVE project has undertaken action research, working-class areas of south and east Belfast in Northern Ireland and social housing estates of Vienna, Austria. In these two very different historical and societal contexts, we studied conflicts within intercultural settings.

The violent conflict of Northern Ireland's recent past (and to some extent present) has meant that a very particular understanding and appreciation of 'the community' has been part of the discourse of the daily life of people and the particular form of politics that has emerged from the peace process, whereas the notion of community is notable for its absence in the discourse of local residents of social housing estates in Vienna. If at all, community is referred to as it was in the past.

We rely on these differences between the settings to extend and differentiate our thinking about community. We begin with some theoretical considerations on community. We are especially interested in using the contributions of Habermas and Esposito to develop new understandings of community and its impact on the transformation of conflicts in intercultural settings. We apply their analysis to the localities in which we conducted our action research and to the conflicts which we observed and examined. We then apply these new understandings to actual restorative responses with a view to identifying how the positive aspects of community can be activated to transform conflict.

The idea of community

Community as a concept has been notoriously difficult to define (Hillery, 1955; Willis, 1977; Lee and Newby, 1983). Is it a place, a network of relationships, a commitment to shared values, a perception of connectedness (Walgrave, 2002)? Nevertheless, there seems to be a prevalent intuitive understanding that whatever community is, 'Community, we feel, is always a good thing' (Bauman, 2001, p. 1). Its attractiveness, which we see as caused by its blurred conceptual boundaries and its consequent flexibility, has resulted in community being a popular component in a variety of often conflicting cultural and political discourses.

There is an old Irish proverb '*Ar scáth a chéile a mhaireas na daoine*', which captures the ambivalence inherent in the function of human communities. Since the Gaelic word '*scáth*' can be translated into 'shelter' or 'shadow', the proverb can mean 'It is in the shelter of each other that the people live' or 'We live in each other's shadow.' This ambiguity reflects the tension within the idea of community, the offer of not only protection but also intrusion and constraint.

Habermas's (1987) concept of the lifeworld encompasses the idea of community in the sense of the informal and largely taken-for-granted norms and personal obligations, the networks of relationships, and the shared meanings of people's everyday world. Following Parsons (1951), Habermas analysed the lifeworld as being made up of 'culture', through which meaning is generated and reproduced, 'society', or the relationships and identities that sustain social cohesion or solidarity, and 'personality', the narratives, beliefs, values and capabilities that members of the community have internalised so as to function effectively in society. A community is nourished through open and dynamic cultural transmission, through social inclusion and integration, and through the effective socialisation of individuals. These levels of community are interconnected and interact through communicative action (Habermas, 1987).

According to Habermas, these important resources to community life are under threat in modern society. Habermas (1984) maintains that the lifeworld is being colonised by the state and the market through their strategic actions. He states that 'in modern societies, economic and bureaucratic spheres emerge in which social relations are regulated only via money and power. Norm-conformative attitudes and identity-forming social memberships are neither necessary nor possible in these spheres; they are made peripheral instead' (Habermas, 1987, p. 189).

Bauman similarly observes that bureaucratic regulation increasingly takes the place of personal commitments and social bonds or obligations: 'Modern power was first and foremost about the entitlement to manage people, to command, to set the rules of conduct and extort obedience to the rules' (Bauman, 2001, p. 40). Systems are designed to control processes and people so as to achieve predetermined political or economic outcomes. The lifeworld, on the other hand, relies upon people acting voluntarily and informally to achieve understanding and consensus through communicating freely with each other. Agamben (1993) has argued that the values of the capitalist market infiltrate language and, as a result, communication between people. This interferes with people's capacity to communicate to each other what they have in common and thus restricts the development of community. While acknowledging that democratic political systems enable citizens to gain liberties and rights, Agamben (1998) observes that the same system can politicise everyday life to the extent that private lives become subordinated to state order.

While increased bureaucratic regulation has reduced people's motivation and ability to interact and address problems in community, the global market has increased inequality and social distance between people and reduced opportunities for social engagement and participation in civic and community life (Marmot, 2004). Wilkinson and Pickett (2009) have provided substantial empirical evidence of the difference between societies in which there are huge disparities of income and power and societies where gaps in income are not so large and where there is a culture of mutual interdependence. The former societies perform least well according to a wide range of indicators of well-being. They are also characterised by high levels of conflict and crime. Sennett (2012) believes that economic inequality weakens the desire and capacity to cooperate with those who are different. He observes that the skills of paying attention to detail and listening, of empathy, of tentativeness so as to respect the other, of distinguishing between information sharing and communication, of understanding context and meaning are being eroded in modern society.

To compensate for the consequent lack of social cohesion, states develop a culture of control (Garland, 2001) through both private security organisations and the criminal justice system. Public services become industries that sell products. As McKnight and Block (2010, p. 30) write, 'All that is uncertain, organic, spontaneous and flowing in personal, family and neighbourhood space is viewed in system space, and in science, as a problem to be solved.' These problems must be allocated to professional experts, and 'Professionalization is the market replacement for a community that has lost or outsourced its capacity to care' (McKnight and Block, 2010, p. 36). How do these concepts and ideas materialise in our research sites?

Vienna

About one-third of the population of Vienna live in flats built, owned and subsidised by the city. This substantial public share of the housing market, the specific architectural language of its buildings and the political visions these embody make social housing in Vienna a unique phenomenon. Vienna's public housing can be understood as having developed through three important phases, between the World Wars, the post-war phase of reconstruction and the formation of the corporate Fordist welfare state (Kremmel and Pelikan, 2014).

The first phase of housing policy was a reaction to the squalor of living circumstances, to improve the living conditions of the working class (Novy, 1981; Förster, 1998). The public housing estates were supposed to anticipate a new socialist society by instilling in their inhabitants the qualities required for this new society, a certain '*Gemeinschaftsgefühl*' ('community feeling') and solidarity as the basis of a proletarian class-consciousness (Novy, 2011, p. 241). Haller and Karazman-Morawetz (2004) found that this *Gemeinschaftsgefühl* did not last beyond the 1980s.

In the second phase, social housing estates became part of the project of a corporatist welfare arrangement resting on the consensus-oriented labour relations of a 'social partnership' (*Sozialpartnerschaft*).[1] Within this welfare arrangement, housing constituted a third column of institutionalised social entitlements, which also included secure employment and social assistance. Social housing was no longer targeted exclusively at the working class but increasingly at the middle classes, for their advancement and defence against economic and social risks. Architecturally, the estates became more standardised and 'industrialised'. Communal facilities (except the common laundry rooms) were no longer part of the building. The access criteria were defined by occupational status, family status and citizenship (in the narrow sense of having Austrian citizenship), excluding the working migrants (guest-workers) who had lived in Vienna since the early 1960s.

The third phase is characterised as an individualisation and fragmentation in the post-corporatist welfare state. The overall global tendencies became manifest in public housing policies through higher rents, but also through the construction of more flats for singles and so-called emergency flats for individuals and families in difficult and disadvantaged circumstances, that is, with very special urgent needs. Overall, the social composition of the tenants changed from the 1970s onwards; the proportion of socio-economically disadvantaged households increased. Compared with inhabitants living in other types of housing, the residents of social housing estates have lower educational attainment, lower per capita income and higher unemployment rates (IFES, 2007). In 2008, almost 30 per cent of the tenants lived below the poverty line. The ethnic and cultural background of the residents of the public housing estates has also changed. The decisive pressure to change the access policies came from the European Union through the Council Directive 2003/109/EC of 25 November 2003 'concerning the status of third-country nationals who are long-term residents'. Social housing estates have become populated by the disadvantaged and by diverse ethnic groups segregated from the mainstream of society.

These developments can be interpreted as a reorganisation of the welfare state in response to global pressures and as a redefinition of what it means to be an Austrian citizen. The government promotes an 'integration-oriented diversity', which means making use of the potential and the capacities of immigrants and their social and cultural diversity. As a consequence, the general public suspect the authorities of unjustly favouring persons and families with a migration background in the allocation of accommodation.

The ALTERNATIVE research confirmed findings (Hanak, 1996; Reiter and Reppé, 1997) that conflict lines in the social housing estates included problems of noise, problems around pets, problems regarding the behaviour of children and youngsters (the way they occupy and behave in public space), problems around alcohol and drugs, problems around dirt, garbage and smells, and car-related problems (parking, etc.). Hanak (1996) and Reiter and Reppé (1997) identified an ethnicisation or culturalisation of conflicts, whereby issues relating to noise, garbage and the use of public space by children became increasingly framed along the division lines of old-time residents (*Alt-Eingesessene*), on the one hand, and newcomers, foreigners (*Ausländer*), on the other hand.

Hanak compared aspects of the Austrian national culture (high control of affects, strong separation of private and public space, individualisation) with aspects of '*Einwandererkulturen*' (cultures of immigrants). The usage of public spaces (pavements, etc.) for purposes other than established in Austria (traffic vs. playground) by migrants (also depending on these spaces because of small flats) is experienced as the 'occupation' of 'territory' and the 'expulsion' of natives from these spaces (Hanak, 1996, p. 68). Hanak had also reported that problem solving through direct encounter was hindered and happened less frequently due to uncertainty regarding language, norms and expectations. The tendency to turn to the authorities for solution is more pronounced, and consequently conflicts between Old-Viennese and Newcomers tend to remain, smouldering and sustaining uneasiness, frustration and fears. The ALTERNATIVE action research process was designed to discover whether the activation and democratic participation of tenants in restorative processes addressing conflict can improve relationships within the community (Haller and Karazman-Morawetz, 2004).

Northern Ireland

Northern Ireland is a divided society, which has experienced 30 years of intercommunal violence. There has been a conflict over the legitimacy of the state of Northern Ireland since it was partitioned from the rest of the island of Ireland in 1922. This has been a conflict between the unionist and predominantly Protestant population, who wish to be part of the UK, and the nationalist and predominantly Catholic population, who wish to be part of a united Ireland.

After 30 years of violent conflict, there is now a peace process, which has substantially reduced the level of violence and has created a devolved government through which unionists and nationalists share power. The peace agreement created a form of power-sharing government, which guaranteed that the parties representing the two main identities in Northern Ireland are always represented in government. This arrangement has institutionalised a politics based upon protecting the interests of separate identities. Community and politico-religious identity became almost co-terminous, and 'pessimistic common sense readily pervaded relationships' (Wright, 1996, p. 7). Out of such insecurity emerged a politics of identity, which Favell (1999) refers to as the dirty work of community boundary maintenance and their contestation by others. In Northern Ireland, community linked to identity in many places is literally defined by walls, ironically called 'peace walls'. This reality is close to what Esposito (2013, p. 43) sees as 'the perversion of the idea of community into its opposite, into one that erects walls rather than breaking them down'.

After many years of violent sectarian conflict, individuals seek security by living in neighbourhoods with people who share their religion and culture. They experience community as a source of security from the perceived threat of the other. This forms the bedrock for a politics based upon identity through which fear and hostility can be channelled strategically for political ends. Segregation and lack of contact with the other (Byrne *et al.*, 2015) strengthen community solidarity. Peace walls representing ethnic frontiers (Wright, 1987) are not only a product of ethnocentrism but also reproduce and sustain ethnocentrism. Ethnocentrism, the belief that one's own culture and ways of being are the norm and as such are a means of judging other cultures, lies at the core of identity politics. The ethnic frontier analysis by Wright (1996) locates Northern Ireland as a country where relationships between communities of different identities are dominated by antagonism. As Caldeira (2000, p. 334) writes of another city, Sao Paulo,

> Among the conditions necessary for democracy is that people acknowledge those from different social groups to be co-citizens, having similar rights despite their differences. However, cities segregated by walls and enclaves foster the sense that different groups belong to separate universes and have irreconcilable claims. Cities of walls do not strengthen citizenship but rather contribute to its corrosion.

Meanwhile, the state adopts a technical approach to managing and limiting the damage due to the conflicts that result from its politics. This strategic approach to maintaining order can take the form of law enforcement or of services and resources to divert protagonists from conflict. Very little effort is made to transform conflict through addressing and restoring relationships.

Northern Ireland thus remains a deeply divided society. Data from the 2001 Census demonstrates that over 90 per cent of social housing estates have more than 80 per cent of residents from either the Protestant or the Catholic community.

Ninety per cent of children attend schools that are predominantly Protestant or Catholic. The many years of violence have left a legacy of issues that continue to be contentious, sustain sectarianism and cause disorder on the streets from time to time. These issues are largely cultural, as each of the two national traditions struggles to have its own culture recognised while often seeming to disrespect the other culture.

Northern Ireland's politics is primarily a form of identity politics, and this is reflected in segregated local communities, which identify themselves through their cultural and national identity. This situation sustains a level of conflict which, while rarely violent, is disruptive of social and economic life and prevents society from moving on from the past. Vienna's social-democratic politics has followed a social integration approach to migrants. However, this strategy has not transformed the underlying tensions between longstanding residents and newcomers in local social housing estates. This, combined with other global political and economic issues, may be providing a climate conducive to the politics of identity in Austria represented by the rise of the Freedom Party.

The right in politics has proved more adept at activating this sense of communal identity (Haidt, 2012), while liberal and progressive politics have been drawn towards the advancement of human rights and the recognition of those groups who have been most oppressed (Bauman, 2001). Sandel (2009) has argued that progressive politics has neglected moral discourse and as a result has allowed conservatives to exploit people's needs for core values to give their civic life meaning. As Sandel (2009, p. 28) states, 'Fundamentalists rush in where liberals fear to tread.'

Staub (2001) has observed the conditions that lead to violent conflict. A community experiences deteriorating economic, political and social conditions. People threatened by the insecurity caused by these conditions seek protection with people with whom they identify. In doing so, they may be encouraged by leaders to blame another group for their plight. This polarisation may result in scapegoating, thus justifying a disregard for the others' rights and perspectives. Scapegoating (Girard, 1986) relieves people from the obligations of personal responsibility for the needs of others and of respect for their culture and rights. This scapegoating will often be obscured by a political ideology, which generally claims a legacy of historic harm and unresolved victimisation and trauma. The violence tends to be committed by a relatively small group, who are supported tacitly by a silent majority or passive bystanders.

So far, we have identified some key difficulties with the concept of community in relation to both conflicts in intercultural settings and to restorative justice responses. The politics and the global economy of the modern world undermine the culture and relationships on which community depends. This creates a problem in both definition and operationalisation for restorative justice. We have argued that the concept of community has been incorporated into identity politics and can form the basis of conflict in intercultural settings, which may escalate into violence. Does this mean that the idea of community is both untenable and undesirable in the field of conflict in intercultural contexts, or can alternative understandings of community, conflict and restorative justice inform the development of restorative responses to such conflict?

The complexity of community, identity and conflict: the case of the flags dispute in Belfast

On 3 December 2012, Belfast City Council voted to restrict flying the British flag on the City Hall to 18 designated days each year. This decision was followed by four months of street protests, many of which became serious riots. This period of disorder was generally perceived by the media as another example of Loyalist sectarianism and propensity for violence. This thin description obscures the complexity of what Loyalists regard as an intercultural conflict. It also fails to take into account the class tensions within the Unionist community and, indeed, the divisions within Loyalism. Further, the focus on the incidents of disorder and violence does not represent the work that community activists, many of whom are committed to restorative principles and values, did to mediate and keep the peace. Politically, the Democratic Unionist Party (DUP) used the flags protests to discredit the Alliance Party, who had won the east Belfast seat at the last general election from the leader of the DUP and Northern Ireland's first minister. The Alliance party, a moderate non-sectarian party, had brokered a compromise between Sinn Fein's wish to have no flag flying and the Unionist wish that the flag would fly every day of the year.

Working-class Loyalist fears of more concessions to Republicans were mobilised for political ends. Researchers found a number of key themes underpinning the protests, including the protesters' sense of loss, political apathy, disillusionment with the peace process and the notion of a shared future, and disengagement with the police:

> From the outset the participants were keen to stress much more than an acknowledgement of anger about the decision to remove the flag from City Hall. The protests were about telling those in power and wider society that the Protestant, Unionist and Loyalist people were not going to let their sense of identity, which they defined as 'Britishness', be airbrushed from the 'new' Northern Ireland.
>
> (Byrne, 2013, p. 8)

This perception among Loyalist communities that there is no place for them within the 'new' Northern Ireland was reinforced by the condemnation and righteous indignation rained upon them from the police, politicians, media and wider society in general. The lack of revenue suffered by retailers and the hospitality industry in the run-up to Christmas 2012 was attributed to the Loyalist protests and became a critical turning point in political attitudes.

This case study from the ALTERNATIVE research resonates with Staub's (2001) model for explaining violent ethnocentric conflict. The threat to basic human needs such as security, positive identity, effectiveness and control, connection to other people, and meaningful understanding of reality and one's place in the world is a critical factor in the escalation of inter-group conflict. It is important to note that these are the same needs that are addressed on a daily basis through the lifeworld. When these basic needs are not met, people feel a sense of injustice and grievance. The causes of the injustice in many cases may be global and beyond the control of the group. However, usually another group, which is perceived as competing for scarce resources, becomes the object of resentment. The politics of identity constructs the very threat from which it functions to protect its community.

During the flags protests, there were community activists trained in restorative practices attempting to maintain peace. The ALTERNATIVE research studied two areas, south Belfast and east Belfast. In both areas activists attempted to reduce the violence restoratively, but with very different results. In south Belfast, the protests did not descend into violence and rioting. A leading community activist stated:

> The one good thing is that people within this area have been able to maintain their protests in a dignified and productive manner against the backdrop of those social elements that would want to portray those expressing their cultural identity as a way of destroying cultural expression.

In south Belfast, relationships between the community and the police had been built over many years. As the activist said,

> I can only speak for the area around here and there was a conscious movement to ensure there would be no violence because of the fact that community relations with the police had been quite good for a number of years and there was regular liaison with the police.

This was due in part to the efforts of community leaders who mediated between the protesters and the police. The primary mediator reported:

> We were hearing from the police that technically the people who were protesting were breaking the law; we advised that if that was the case that any movement made against these people would destroy community relations for the next number of years and have adverse effects relating to further protests in and around this area.... The inspector on the ground made a conscious decision when he was under pressure from his bosses and decided to take a chance and hold off on deploying TSGs.[2]

South Belfast experienced the period of protests over the flying of the flags without any serious damage to property or community life. By using the basic restorative practice of mediation, people could protest without causing violence. In this way, local people experienced both enhanced justice and security. The same could not be said in the case of east Belfast, which was the site of the most disorder, the most violence, the most conflict with the police and the most arrests. Yet in the area there were also community activists trained in restorative practices striving to reduce the violence and arguing for democratic values. What was different? The short answer is – politics.

East Belfast was the constituency that the DUP desperately wanted to regain from the Alliance Party. It was in its interest to blame Alliance rather than the traditional enemy, Sinn Fein, for the flags being taken down from the City Hall. So the party supported the protests, at least until they became unpopular with the business community. Yet, it was more complex than that. It was clear that some community activists had an interest in supporting, if not escalating, the protests, while others adopted a more reconciliatory approach. Activists who had been trained in restorative processes participated in round table dialogues whose ostensible purpose was to find a peaceful solution. But it was clear to them that other community representatives, while they seemed to subscribe to the same purpose, could not be trusted in their commitments. They had another political agenda that depended upon sustaining the conflict.

This can be understood in the context of Habermas's (1987) validity claims. The purpose of communicative action is to reach a mutual understanding. For this process to be effective, the speech must be subject to three claims to validity: truth, normative rightness and sincerity. So each party must give a commitment to speaking the truth, to interact with each other according to what is right and to be sincere in expressing intentions to act in the future. In south Belfast, the mediations between the protesters and the police were truthful, undertaken in the right way and commitments to action were sincere and fulfilled. In other words, they were based upon communicative action. In east Belfast, the meetings may have been set up with the right intention and conducted in a reasonable way. But the participants were not committed to speaking the truth or to being sincere in their future actions. In other words, some parties were acting strategically to achieve their own political ends.

It was clear from the ALTERNATIVE research that communicative action maintained peace in south Belfast during the flags protests while strategic action in east Belfast escalated the disorder and violence. It was not the dispute over national culture that caused harm, but its politicisation.

Esposito's distinction between immunity and community

The Italian philosopher Roberto Esposito has written extensively about the double bind of community as shelter and shadow. Analysing the etymology of the word from a different perspective than that of others, who have tended to focus on the *com* of community, concluding that its meaning is what we have in common, Esposito focused on the second half of the word, derived from the Latin *munus*. This word means debt, duty, obligation or gift, leading him to conceive of community as founded upon its members' obligations to each other. He sees community as both a necessity and an impossibility. 'What we have in common is precisely this lack of community. As I have stated elsewhere, we are a community made up of those who do not have community' (2013, p. 15).

However, people also huddle together for safety. They believe that living in community will protect them like a body's immune system. Originating in the same word, *munus*, immunity is the internalisation of community. Rather than living by the obligation to care for and protect one's neighbour, individuals are only concerned for themselves.

> If the members of the *communitas* are bound by the same law, by the same duty, or gift to give (the meanings of munus), *immunis* is he or she who has no obligations toward the other and can therefore conserve his or her own essence intact as a subject and owner of himself or herself.
>
> (2013, p. 39)

In law, immunity represents exemption from liability or obligation to others.

Immunity also has a biological meaning, the ability of an organism to resist disease, either through the activities of antibodies or by a vaccine. The risk of contact is associated with contagion, infection and contamination. Esposito (2013, p. 40) sees this as engendering strategies that 'allow men and women to live next to each other without touching, and therefore to enlarge the sphere of individual self-sufficiency by using "masks" or "armour" that defend them from undesired and insidious contact with the other'. This echoes Luhmann's (1995, p. 403) understanding of immunity: 'The immune system disposes over the use of "no", of communicative rejection. It operates *without communication with the environment*' (italics in original). Later in this chapter we will return to the importance of communicative action. So, while community takes us outside of ourselves into a world of solidarity and obligation, immunity returns us to ourselves detached from the others.

If the need for community is based upon fear rather than the social obligations owed to others, Esposito maintains that we turn community 'into its exact opposite – a community of death and the death of community' (2013, p. 15). He argues that such a community restricts liberty and ultimately explains the emergence of totalitarianism as the illusion of community characterised by the fear, stigmatisation and exclusion of the other.

In Vienna, conflict between longstanding residents and so-called foreign newcomers was usually provoked by noise, pets, the way children behave in public space, dirt, garbage and smells. These problems can be seen as concrete manifestations of cultural contamination from which people seek immunisation. In Belfast, community has become a sanctuary, often protected by high walls from the other community. On a macro scale, immunity may be represented by the actual or virtual walls being proposed on the frontiers of European countries to exclude refugees and by the rise of right-wing, ethnocentric politics promising protection from the foreign. Such politics, combined with neoliberal global economic policies, are, as Habermas suggests, colonising the world in which people live their daily lives, thus weakening a sense of solidarity that embraces diversity and a sense of responsibility that leads to active participation in solving problems. This need for immunity reinforces a belief that different groups defined by identity are competing for resources and cultural recognition (Martin, 1996). This was exemplified by the attitude of the Loyalist communities in Belfast during their protests over the threat to their British culture as represented by the reduction in flying the Union flag.

For Esposito (2013, p. 55), the concept of community needs to be revitalised by separating it from identity:

> Here, I intend community not as a locus of identity, belonging, or appropriation but, on the contrary, as a locus of plurality, difference and alterity. It is an option that is both political and philosophical, and one in which I believe the very task of contemporary political philosophy lies: liberating freedom from liberalism and community from communitarianism.

Several other writers are striving to redefine what we mean by community. Agamben (1993) wishes to conceive of community as not requiring a commonality or identity as a precondition of membership. He seems to seek a solidarity in humanity rather than in politics. Sennett (2012, p. 39) distinguishes two versions of solidarity. Politics emphasises the unity of the group, which is often solidarity *against*. A more social version values inclusion of difference or solidarity *with*. Nancy (1991, p. 33) proposes a concept of community that does not depend upon identity and belonging (being-in) but which continuously seeks more democratic, open and fluid relationships with others (being with). In south Belfast, the community activists perceived the police as part of the community, and as a consequence the protesters and the police recognised that they had obligations towards each other. This was not the case in the more politicised atmosphere in east Belfast.

Block (2008) perceives community as about the experience of belonging. However, his is not a passive belonging but an active membership. He points out that the word *belong* also relates to owning, which he connects with responsibility, commitment and accountability. For Sennett and Block, solidarity and belonging are not passive properties of community based upon tradition and a common identity, but qualities, which require activation. In such a frame, community becomes an activity, something people do rather than something people are in. The activity is communication and the struggle to establish connectedness. Community is thus conceived as a project on how to live equitably in interdependence with an increasingly diverse range of others.

Summarising the positions of these thinkers, in modern society community is not an abstract idea or a place but a set of relationships, which cannot be independent of social processes and communicative actions that can either sustain or weaken them. This suggests a dynamic rather than static phenomenon, transient rather than permanent, never perfect or complete but replete with possibilities. Does this way of conceiving community fit with restorative justice approaches, which seek to actively involve people in dialogic communication about their conflicts and needs, in order to transform relationships?

Restorative justice

Walgrave (2002) writes that community may not only have limited use as a concept in restorative justice but may also be a dangerous idea. He argues that community is not an ontological reality but a socio-ethical ideal. He suggests that we should unpack the social values of community and combine these with the principles of a democratic constitutional state. Walgrave asserts that, if community simply represents the values of responsibility, solidarity and respect, it can be replaced by the concept of dominion or a set of assured rights and freedoms. Through this formulation, restorative values can be incorporated into the criminal justice system and be subject to the rule of law. This argument assumes that restorative justice is positioned within the field of criminal justice. It also assumes that the restorative processes are engaging with individuals rather than groups or communities (cf. Harbin and Llewellyn, 2016). What if, as in the ALTERNATIVE research study, restorative justice is not addressing a conflict within criminal justice but is addressing a conflict in an intercultural setting?

We have seen how the idea of community can lead to narrow identity politics that can threaten democracy and result in violent conflict. What if active democratic processes became part of community life rather than being restricted to political institutions? This would depend upon membership similar to what Benhabib (2004) calls political membership, the right and capacity to participate actively in the political life of a country as a citizen. Membership of a community not only confers individual rights to participate but also requires commitment to the reciprocal obligations that arise from the specific situation. In doing so, we are confronted by the tension between the politics of universalism and the politics of difference (Taylor, 1994).

The ALTERNATIVE research has found that many conflicts cannot be reduced and simplified to a clash of culture or political ideology. They are particular to a specific set of social, political and cultural conditions in a pluralist society. They cannot be resolved through the simple applications of universal principles such as the rule of law or rights, but must be mediated through dialogue or, as Benhabib (2004) puts it, through democratic iterations.

Agamben's (1993) approach to reconciling universal principles with the particular is through the concrete example. He asserts that specific events can exemplify the coming community. This view is supported by Ferrara (2008), who sees exemplarity as a key to the reconciliation of universalism and pluralism. He argues that a specific example of *what is as it should be* can serve

> to illuminate new ways of transcending the limitations of what is and expanding the reach of our normative understandings. Over and beyond providing us with a sense of our possibilities for transformation, the force of the example often provides us with anticipatory prefigurations of reconciliation – in the first place, a reconciliation of the tragic rift of necessity and freedom reverberated by a world shaped only by the force of what exists or

> the force of things, on the one hand, and the force of ideas or of what ought to be, on the other hand.
>
> (Ferrara, 2008, p. 3)

Restorative justice works most effectively when addressing a specific conflict and when engaging those individuals or groups most affected by the conflict in the process. Intercultural conflicts need to be addressed through a process that is recognised as valid across cultural frontiers. The process of effectively transforming such a conflict can be an example of how to be 'sensitive to the plurality of contexts but not hostage to it' (Ferrara, 2008, p. 23).

The restorative perspective locates the problem in the problem, the injustice or the harm that has occurred (White, 2007). The politics of intercultural conflict sees the problem as other people (Reisigl and Wodak, 2001). Conflicts that have caused real harm, hurt or violence may be the most productive in bringing people together. The experience of injustice and conflict creates a set of relationships, which have the potential to lead to contact, connectedness and transformation through an exemplary experience. Restorative justice is based upon the principle that when one harms another person, one takes on an obligation to make amends. 'When you commit a crime, you create a certain debt, an obligation, – to restore, to repair, to undo' (Zehr, 2003, p. 79). The critical importance of obligation resonates with Esposito's (2013) understanding of community. Restorative justice processes are designed not simply to consider how to restore justice and to repair what has been lost or damaged by an injustice but to consider what obligations the person responsible must fulfil to be accepted again as a member of the community (Braithwaite, 1989). In return for fulfilling these obligations, the community reintegrates the other, and through this process social inclusion is reconciled with social cohesion.

Following Benhabib (2004), we have found that processes addressing harmful conflict work best when based on the understandings that the people are interdependent, that conflicts between communities are normal, and that communities should be assumed to be made up of diverse people. Cultural integration should not be confused with social integration. The challenge is to enable a sense of belonging to a larger community while at the same time recognising the richness and variability of cultural identities.

We would argue that restorative justice is a product of the lifeworld and its mode of communication. Restorative justice should play its part in creating, occupying and defending spaces in civil society in which ordinary persons engage in democratic dialogue to resolve conflicts and harmful incidents in the family, in schools, in community life, and in the public spheres of identity and culture. Habermas (1996) develops a concept of discourse in which people address issues of common concern free of internal domination or external control. In doing so, they are clarifying, strengthening and sometimes revising the cultural meaning, social relations and socialisation processes of the lifeworld. Traditions, rituals and knowledge are transmitted and refreshed to meet modern conditions. Individual agency, social obligations and cultural identity are reconciled and strengthened in the lifeworld.

The location of the space where people meet must be consciously chosen so as to resist the domination by the power of the expert (Christie, 1977). As bell hooks puts it,

> I am located in the margin. I make a definite distinction between that marginality which is imposed by oppressive structures and that marginality one chooses as site of resistance – as location of radical openness and possibility. This site of resistance is continually formed in that segregated culture of opposition that is our critical response to domination.
>
> (1990, p. 153)

The ALTERNATIVE project chose research sites in communities away from the centres of power and studied processes that took place in these sites. The importance of this marginal location is that it provides a space for communication that is not dominated by political or economic power. It creates sites where people can resist imposed 'otherness' and assert and, if they choose, reconstruct their own identity, and where groups can create community, if only temporarily, and in so doing imagine new possibilities.

Restorative justice offers ordinary people the opportunity to cooperate in addressing issues that concern them. As Sennett writes,

> the good alternative is a demanding and difficult kind of cooperation; it tries to join people who have separate or conflicting interests, who do not feel good about each other, who are unequal, or simply do not understand one another. The challenge is to respond to others on their own terms.
>
> (2012, p. 6)

He says that such cooperation enables people to grasp the consequences of their own actions and gain self-awareness. Sennett states that 'people's capacities for cooperation are far greater and more complex than institutions allow them to be' (2012, p. 29).

Key to the analysis so far is the assumption that restorative practices are based upon dialogue or communicative action rather than the strategic action of political practice. Without referring to communicative action, Arendt (1958, p. 200) describes this distinction:

> Power is actualised only where words are not empty and deeds not brutal, where words are not used to veil intentions but to disclose realities, and deeds are not used to violate and destroy but to establish relations and create new realities.

The purpose of communicative action is to reach a mutual understanding about something. For this process to be effective, the speech must be subject to truth, normative rightness and sincerity (Habermas, 1987). When giving an account of what happened, the truth is very important. Can people rely on this account of what happened as a basis for further consideration? When speaking about what should be done about what happened, normative rightness is critical. Is the dialogue being conducted fairly and with respect according to the agreed rules? Is what is being suggested just and proportionate? Are people's commitments to act sincere? For the process to work, each party must give a commitment to speak the truth, to interact with each other according to what is right and to be sincere in expressing intentions to act in the future. During the dialogue, any party can challenge another on the basis of these validity claims, and in return, the other person must justify what they have said. This means that he or she must assert the conditions under which the other will accept the truth (factual evidence), normative rightness (the validity of the moral norms on which assumptions are being made) or sincerity (acting according to the commitment) of what has been said.

Through the requirements to justify (from *justificare*, to make just) one's words as true, to behave towards each other appropriately and to keep one's word, one's communicative action not only transmits information but also establishes a relationship with the other person, and through this practice meaning and understanding emerge. Language, for Habermas, has three principal functions: to represent the reality of the outer world, to establish relationships and to express the inner world of emotions, beliefs and values. Strategic action instrumentalises language, draining words of meaning. The dialogical processes of restorative justice enable people to express themselves in a language of their own choosing and to listen to and question others' narratives, thus enabling meanings to emerge that are thicker (Geertz, 1973) than any broad political discourse could muster. People can cross social frontiers through communicative action or dialogue: 'that flow of meaning, that encounter with existence outside of itself that I define with the word communitas, which refers the constitutively open character of existence' (Esposito, 2013, p. 61).

Gadamer (1989) states that to understand the other, one must be aware of one's own point of view or horizon. 'A person who has no horizon is a man who does not see far enough and hence overvalues what is nearest to him' (1989, p. 269). Acting and communicating as if one has a grasp of the true reality rather than being limited by one's vantage point severely limits one's ability to understand the *otherness* of the other, which, in turn, results in the unconscious assimilation of the other within one's own taken-for-granted understanding. One cannot acquire a new horizon; one can only extend one's horizon through the encounter and conversation with others. In this way, both parties find that they are connected in a new community.

> To reach an understanding with one's partner in a dialogue is not merely a matter of total self-expression and the successful assertion of one's own point of view, but a transformation into a communion, in which we do not remain what we were.
>
> (Gadamer, 1989, p. 341)

This does not mean that differences do not continue to be present, but that relations have changed.

Conclusions

We have argued that community, seen as providing immunity (Esposito, 2013) from the threat of the other, increases the risk of inter-group conflict and violence. Such a conceptualisation facilitates the factors that Staub (2001) identified as causing ethnic conflict: devaluing and dehumanising others, responding to a scapegoating ideology, and dependence upon political leadership. Choosing immunity rather than community based upon obligations to others is made more likely by the insecurity caused by the colonisation of the lifeworld by the political and market systems (Habermas, 1987). This means that any effective response to conflict in intercultural contexts should attempt to counter these factors.

Esposito (2013) offers a different vision of community, dependent not upon exclusive identity or common cultural values but upon obligations to others and solidarity. Such a community is activated by communicative action and dialogue typical of the lifeworld rather than the strategic action of the state. This supports the view of Van Ness and Strong (2010) that government's responsibility is to maintain a just order, whereas community is responsible for establishing a just peace.

For this reason, we believe that restorative justice processes can make a significant contribution to activating community to respond positively to conflicts in intercultural settings. A successful restorative process can become an example (Ferrara, 2008) of how conflict should be transformed and, thus, develop the confidence of ordinary people that they can live together at peace.

We have identified some key principles that increase the likelihood that the process will be exemplary:

1 Inter-group conflict within intercultural communities should be seen as normal and as opportunities to strengthen both social integration and social inclusion.
2 The process should address the harms or injustices that have arisen from the conflict, rather than the people, and focus on the obligations that the parties should commit to so that they can live at ease with each other in the future.
3 The location of the process should be where the parties feel most able to articulate their narratives and enter into dialogue.
4 The process should be communicative rather than strategic, aiming for mutual understanding and consensus through truth telling, normative rightness and sincerity of intent.
5 This process should be based upon sharing truth, a safe, fair and respectful process, and sincere commitments to act according to what has been agreed.

Through these principles, restorative processes can enable people to expand the horizons of their concept of community. The yearning for community lies within all people. To realise this yearning, people must act on the basis of mutual obligations. Of course, it is impossible to act in such a way permanently. Community as a constant state is impossible. But it can be activated to celebrate historical or current events, to respond to crises and to address conflict. Restorative justice is one means of activating community when people come together to find just resolutions to conflict.

'Care, rather than interest, lies at the basis of community. Community is determined by care, and care by community. One may not exist without the other: "care in common"' (Esposito, 2013, pp. 25–26).

Notes

1 Austria enjoys – or has enjoyed – a particularly well-developed system of cooperation between the major economic interest groups and between them and the government. Such cooperation was essential for the reconstruction of Austria after the Second World War and created the basis for further economic growth and social stability. The social partnership can be regarded as a very special brand of a political structure set upon the Fordist mode of social integration and of balancing the powers of work and capital/entrepreneurship, with an emphasis on corporatist negotiations and the achievement of compromise.
2 Tactical Support Group, police officers trained to manage public disorder.

References

Agamben, G., 1993. *The Coming Community*. Michael Hardt (trans.). Minneapolis: University of Minnesota Press.

Agamben, G., 1998. *Homo Sacer: Sovereign Power and Bare Life*. Stanford, CA: Stanford University Press.

Arendt, H., 1958. *The Human Condition*. Chicago: University of Chicago Press.

Bauman, Z., 2001. *Community: Seeking Safety in an Insecure World*. Cambridge: Polity.

Benhabib, S., 2004. *The Rights of Others: Aliens, Residents and Citizens*. Cambridge: Cambridge University Press.

Block, P., 2008. *Community: The Structure of Belonging*. San Francisco: Berrett-Koehler.

Braithwaite, J., 1989. *Crime, Shame and Reintegration*. Cambridge: Cambridge University Press.

Byrne, J., 2013. *Flags and Protests: Exploring the Views, Perceptions and Experiences of People Directly and Indirectly Affected by the Flag Protests*. Belfast: Intercomm.

Byrne, J., Gormley-Heenan, C., Morrow, D. and Sturgeon, B., 2015. *Public Attitudes to Peace Walls 2015 Survey Results*. Belfast: Ulster University.

Caldeira, T. P. R., 2000. *City of Walls: Crime, Segregation and Citizenship in Sao Paulo*. London: University of California Press.

Christie, N., 1977. 'Conflict as Property'. *British Journal of Criminology*, 17, 1–26.

Esposito, R., 2013. *Terms of the Political: Community, Immunity, Biopolitics*. New York: Fordham University Press.

Favell, A., 1999. To Belong or Not to Belong: The Postnational Question. In: A. Geddis and A. Favell, eds, *The Politics of Belonging: Migrants and Minorities in Contemporary Europe*. Aldershot: Ashgate.

Ferrara, A., 2008. *The Force of the Example: Explorations in the Paradigm of Judgment*. New York: Columbia University Press.

Förster, W., 1998. 80 Years of Social Housing in Vienna. Available at: www.wien.gv.at/english/housing/promotion/pdf/socialhous.pdf (accessed 6 February 2014).

Gadamer, H.-G., 1989. *Truth and Method*, 2nd edn. London: Sheed and Ward.

Geertz, C., 1973. *The Interpretation of Cultures*. New York: Basic Books.

Girard, R., 1986. *The Scapegoat*. Baltimore: Johns Hopkins University Press.

Habermas, J., 1984. *The Theory of Communicative Action: Lifeworld and System: A Critique of Functionalist Reason*. Boston: Beacon.

Habermas, J., 1987. *The Theory of Communicative Action, Vol. 2: Lifeworld and System: A Critique of Functionalist Reason*. Boston: Beacon.

Habermas, J., 1996. *Between Facts and Norms: Contributions to a Discourse Theory of Law and Democracy*. Cambridge: Polity.

Haidt, J., 2012. *The Righteous Mind: Why Good People Are Divided by Politics and Religion*. London: Allen Lane.

Haller, B. and Karazman-Morawetz, I., 2004. *Konfliktlösungsmodelle für Großwohnanlagen*. Vienna: Report of the Institute for Conflict Research.

Hanak, G., 1996. Finstere Gassen – dunkle Gestalten. In W. Hammerschick, I. Karazman-Morawetz and W. Stangl, eds, *Die Sichere Stadt, Jahrbuch für Rechts- und Kriminalsoziologie*. Baden-Baden: Nomos Verlagsgesellschaft, pp. 57–87.

Harbin, A. and Llewellyn, J. J., 2016. Restorative Justice in Transitions: The Problem of 'the Community' and Collective Responsibility. In: K. Clamp (ed.), *Restorative Justice in Transitional Settings*. London: Routledge.

Hillery, G. 1955. 'Definitions of Community: Areas of Agreement'. *Rural Society*, 20, 111–125.

hooks, b. Choosing the Margin as a Space of Radical Openness. In: *Yearning: Race, Gender, and Cultural Politics*. Boston: South End, 1990, pp. 145–153.

IFES (Institute for Empirical Social Studies). 2007. *Lebensqualität im Wiener Gemeindebau*. Wien: Stadt Wien – Wiener Wohnen.

Johnstone, G., 2001. *Restorative Justice: Ideas, Values, Debates*. Cullompton: Willan.

Kremmel, K. and Pelikan, C., 2014. Living Together in the Gemeindebau in Vienna: On Tensions, Conflicts, Fears and Hopes. ALTERNATIVE: deliverable 4.2. Available at: www.alternativeproject.eu/publications/public-deliverables/ (accessed 13 June 2016).

Lee, D. and Newby, H. (1983) *The Problem of Sociology*. London: Hutchinson.

Luhmann, N., 1995. *Social Systems*. Stanford: Stanford University Press.

McKnight, J. and Block, P., 2010. *The Abundant Community: Awakening the Power of Families and Neighbourhoods*. San Francisco: Berrett-Koehler.

Marmot, M., 2004. *The Status Syndrome: How Social Standing Affects Our Health and Longevity*. New York: Henry Holt.

Martin, I., 1996. Community Education: The Dialectics of Development. In: R. Fieldhouse and Associates, *A History of Modern British Adult Education*. Leicester: National Institute of Adult Continuing Education.

Nancy, J. L., 1991. *The Inoperative Community*. P. Connor, L. Garbus, M. Holland and S. Sawhney (trans.). Minneapolis: University of Minnesota Press.

Novy, A., 2011. 'Unequal Diversity – on the Political Economy of Social Cohesion in Vienna'. *European Urban and Regional Studies*, 18(3), 239–253.

Novy, K., 1981. Selbsthilfe als Reformbewegung. Der Kampf der Siedler nach dem 1. Weltkrieg. *Arch+ 55*, Kampf um Selbsthilfe: 27–40.

Parsons, T., 1951. *The Social System*. New York: The Free Press.

Pavlich, G., 2004. Restorative Justice's Community: Promise and Peril. In: B. Toews and H. Zehr, eds, *Critical Issues in Restorative Justice*. Monsey, NY: Criminal Justice Press.

Pranis, K., Stuart, B. and Wedge, M., 2003. *Peacemaking Circles: From Crime to Community*. St. Paul, MN: Living Justice.

Reisigl, M. and Wodak, R. (2001) *Discourse and Discrimination: Rhetorics of Racism and Anti-Semitism*. London: Routledge.

Reiter, C. and Reppé, S., 1997. *Vom Zusammenleben im Gemeindebau. Verbesserungsmöglichkeiten des Zusammenwohnens von ‚Alt-ÖsterreicherInnen' und Neu-ÖsterreicherInnen in Wohnhausanlagen der Gemeinde Wien. Studie im Auftrag des Wiener Integrationsfonds*. Wien: GSD-Gesellschaft für Stadt- und Dorferneuerung.

Sandel, M. J., 2009. *Justice: What's the Right Thing to Do?* London: Allen Lane.

Sennett, R., 2012. *Together: The Rituals, Pleasures and Politics of Cooperation*. London: Allen Lane.

Staub, E., 2001. Individual and Group Identities in Genocide and Mass Killing. In: R. D. Ashmore, L. Jussim and D. Wilder, eds, *Social Identity, Intergroup Conflict and Conflict Reduction*. Oxford: Oxford University Press.

Sullivan, D. and Tifft, L. 2001. *Restorative Justice: Healing the Foundations of Our Everyday Lives*. Monsey: Willow Tree.

Taylor, C., 1994. The Politics of Recognition. In: C. Taylor, ed., *Multiculturalism: Examining the Politics of Recognition*. Princeton: Princeton University Press.

Umbreit, M. S. and Armour, M. P., 2011. 'Restorative Justice and Dialogue: Impact, Opportunities, and Challenges in the Global Community', *Washington University Journal of Law and Policy*, 36, 65–88.

Van Ness, D. W. and Strong, K. H., 2010. *Restoring Justice: An Introduction to Restorative Justice*, 4th edn. New Providence, NJ: LexisNexis.

Walgrave, L., 2002. From Community to Dominion; in Search of Social Values for Restorative Justice. In E. G. M. Weitekamp and H. Kerner, eds, *Restorative Justice. Theoretical Foundations*. Cullompton: Willan.

White, M., 2007. *Maps of Narrative Practice*. New York, NY: Norton.

Wilkinson, R. and Pickett, K., 2009. *The Spirit Level: Why More Equal Societies Almost Always Do Better*. London: Allen Lane.

Willis, P. 1981. *Learning to Labor: How Working Class Kids Get Working Class Jobs*. New York, NY: Columbia University Press.

Wright, F., 1996. *Two Lands on One Soil*. Dublin: Gill and Macmillan and The Understanding Conflict Trust.

Zehr, H., 2003. Retributive Justice, Restorative Justice. In: G. Johnstone, ed., *A Restorative Justice Reader: Texts, Sources, Contexts*. Cullompton: Willan.

Zehr, H. and Mika, H., 2003. Fundamental Concepts of Restorative Justice. In: E. McLaughlin, R. Fergusson, G. Hughes and L. Westmarland, eds, *Restorative Justice: Critical Issues*. London: Sage.

Zinsstag, E. and Chapman, T., 2012. Restorative Youth Conferencing in Northern Ireland. In E. Zinsstag and I. Vanfraechem, eds, *Conferencing and Restorative Justice: Challenges, Developments and Debates*. Oxford: Oxford University Press.

10 Critical reflections on active participation under new governance models

Christa Pelikan and Mario Ragazzi

Introduction

This chapter is a comparative discussion of the meaning of 'active participation' in restorative practices, mainly as it relates to the specific settings in our project, and will illustrate its ambivalence. The project ALTERNATIVE has aimed to investigate the potential of active participation of citizens and civil society organisations in the handling of conflicts in intercultural contexts, in order to promote security and diminish feelings of insecurity.

The chapter will reflect on the ambivalence of participation and mobilisation, especially as it interplays with stakeholders in the four action research sites, achieved mainly through comparative research.

This research points to the potential role of restorative justice (RJ) in societies with diverse degrees of leadership, public institutions and socio-economic redistributive policies towards de-securitisation of conflicts, strengthening of social solidarity between stakeholders, and improving the perceptions of safety.

The relevance of 'participation' in restorative justice and the ALTERNATIVE project

RJ is a way of responding to crime, harm, conflict, injustice and wrongdoing. It has been articulated as a new approach to justice which challenges retributive justice mainly on three grounds: (a) it views crime as a harmful event for the people concerned rather than as breaking the law (*lifeworld* versus *system orientation*); (b) it gives back to those affected by a crime the power to participate rather than having the state deal with it (*participation* versus *delegation*); and (c) it emphasises restoration of the harm caused in terms of mending broken relations, offering reparations to the victims and restoring a sense of security, rather than applying punishment for the sake of inflicting pain (*restoration* versus *retribution*) (Pelikan, 2003, 2007).

Active participation – as opposed to delegation to institutionalised authority – is thus one of the defining features of RJ. As a normative stance that echoes seminal works in critical criminology (Christie, 1977) advocating for the restitution of conflicts to those who own them, issues of property and power will feature prominently in the characterisation of participation sketched here.

'Core' Restorative Justice versus ALTERNATIVE

The ALTERNATIVE research project aims at 'providing an alternative and deepened understanding based on empirical evidence of how to handle conflicts within intercultural contexts in democratic societies in order to set up security solutions for citizens and communities'. This was carried out over four years (2012–2016), developing a coherent theoretical framework for an alternative understanding of security and justice and developing empirically applicable knowledge on conflict and conflict transformation in intercultural settings. At the same time, teams of researchers in four European countries developed action research models in several settings characterised by various kinds of conflict on the micro–meso–macro scale and cultural diversity.

The action research in Vienna dealt with everyday conflicts at the micro level between local residents and residents with a migrant background in public/social housing estates (*Gemeindebau*). Researchers explored the potential of active participation of citizens and of civil society organisations, aiming at enhancing perceptions of safety.

The research program in Kisváros, a small town in rural Hungary, dealt with different – if mostly undercurrent – sources of tension among the inhabitants (e.g. between old residents and newcomers, Roma and non-Roma, etc.). The action research focused on finding out how and at what points restorative theory and practice can be integrated into the existing institutional structure, with special attention to the justice and law enforcement system.

The researchers in Serbia worked with a mixed method approach (e.g. quantitative survey and qualitative in-depth interviews) on the perceptions and involvement of citizens from multi-ethnic communities in three border towns – Bačka Palanka, Prijepolje, Medvedja – with an ethnically diverse population (Serbs, Albanians, Croats and Muslims). The researchers paid special attention to victims of past abuses and observed their roles in democratic processes for peace-building and conflict resolution.

The researchers in Northern Ireland focused on the relationship between the state system and local communities in three research sites (south Belfast, east Belfast, Derry/Londonderry) and the restorative potential of promoting active citizenship and community development. Local capacity to resolve intra- and inter-communal conflict is being evaluated in projects dealing with problems between local community and gangs of youths, and between long-term residents and recent immigrants, and inter-community sectarian conflict.

The findings from the four pilot settings have been analysed comparatively to advance knowledge by integrating the empirical results into theoretical insights and by adapting the latter where appropriate.

Overall, the ALTERNATIVE project has been prodding the boundaries of established RJ practices, trying to expand and test its field of application in several directions: the cultural context; the level of analysis; the scope of the action research; the participation model. The intercultural features of the societal context are problematised by design and brought to the methodological centre stage. Crucially, the scope of the research is widened to deal with more complex 'conflict' situations in society, where responsibilities and harm claims are more blurred than the 'crime' situations of established RJ, where the identification of a 'victim' and an 'offender' is normally a given. The level of analysis of these conflicts has been expanded from the mainly interpersonal focus of standard RJ approaches to the community and macro levels.

The question of active participation of the stakeholders concerned in a crime/ conflict situation, which is highly relevant for RJ in general and for the ALTERNATIVE project in particular, both normatively and methodologically, will be specifically explored here. This chapter contends that this task cannot eschew a critical appraisal of the current hegemonic discourse of new governance that constitutes the ideological and regulatory horizon of public policy making in Europe (Rhodes, 1996; Pishchikova *et al.*, 2010; Héritier and Rhodes, 2011). New governance models have embraced active participation and contribute to shaping its current meanings. Among different participatory institutional formats, multistakeholder partnerships (MSPs) are particularly apt at modelling RJ practices because they are modes of governance geared towards enhancing the participation, legitimacy and effectiveness of policy making. RJ stresses the importance of participation of all stakeholders affected by a crime or conflict, with great attention to processes, the 'how' of each action research. It is therefore necessary to analyse at some length the hegemonic conceptualisation of participation within the new governance discourse before taking a critical step away from it.

Participation in new governance models

Ideas of a community-based approach to policy design, a way of tackling poverty with the direct participation of poor people, emerged briefly in the 1930s and 1940s – together with the discovery of the 'group' in American social sciences and popular culture – as part of the response to the Great Depression and the suspicion of the unbridled individualism associated with the self-regulating market that had so spectacularly failed. The idea faded away, at least in the Western world, during the Second World War – requiring the ultimate top-down state-controlled policy making – and the post-war period, when most Western European countries built comprehensive welfare states. The 'participatory' approach nevertheless survived, and it was 'exported' to the Third World in the guise of development aid programmes in the 1950s, from the Philippines to Latin America (Immerwahr, 2015). Participation as community-based development resurfaced in the 'core' countries in the 1960s, in particular in the USA, where it was championed, among others, by Saul Alinski for inner-city, mostly African-American community organisation. With the general critique of hierarchies and big government programmes that marked the neoliberal turn between the end of the 1970s and the 1980s, the participatory focus became a staple of international development aid programmes in the 1990s.

There is a clear normative trend during the last three or four decades towards a shift from 'government' (hierarchy, principal–agent) to 'governance' (networks;

partnerships with the private and civic sector, participation): a non-hierarchical mode of coordination between public, private and civic actors and between different public actors themselves (Shearing and Wood, 2003; Wood *et al.*, 2011). This trend comprises the following central elements: first, *instrumental rationality*, whereby governance should increase quality and performance by processing more information and taking into account various perspectives, or is normatively posited to ensure this; second, *democratisation* as a devolution of responsibility for the definition of principles and of the means to achieve them. Participation, together with joint action and representation (putting issues of concern to stakeholders on the political agenda), becomes a procedural aim within an increased focus on both process and outcome. There is an inherent potential in the combination of instrumentalist rationality and democratising turn: 'transformative democratic strategies that can advance [...] egalitarian social justice, individual liberty combined with popular control over collective decisions' (Fung, 2001), even if sometimes presented in rather idealised ways.

Together with the vaunted benefits of the new approach, it is important to stress what the *preconditions of good governance* are, because many of them are also relevant for RJ programmes: namely, a strong, functionally differentiated, well-organised civil society; and a government that has a strong institutional capacity, is legitimised and ready to step in (safety net, provider of last resort, not only regulator), ultimately enabling governance to work 'in the shadow of hierarchy' (Héritier and Rhodes, 2011). These are rather strong assumptions, to put it mildly.

Public–private partnerships were introduced with the neoliberal turn of the 1970s–1980s, with the main aim of injecting investment and efficiency into the system while government retains ownership and ultimate responsibility. Beyond the initial focus on government and business, at some point these partnerships were extended to civic actors (third sector, non-governmental organisations etc.). All partnerships are based on cooperative working relationships between two or more organisations. The democratic character of the partnership may vary: whether partners have equal powers of decision making and implementation or the partnership is simply an extension of hierarchical authority whereby principal and agent are part of two different organisations. The partnership's power structure, organisational roles and accountability of partners are the key analytical dimensions to be investigated and, as we shall see, constitute the main criterion for the definition and assessment of participation.

An MSP is a governance arrangement that brings together several stakeholders to address a particular issue. Issues in our case are mainly about handling of conflicts in intercultural settings through RJ practices. The stakeholder is a social actor who has an interest in the outcome and demonstrates some degree of ownership with respect to a particular issue. Each stakeholder can affect and is affected by the issue, and has a shared interest with the others, but also a specific one; the partial misalignment of interests within the partnership is up to a point physiological, and it is relevant to the analysis. Ownership refers to the investment of resources (human, material, financial etc.) and the degree of participation in decision making.

The theory of public networks adds an important focus on the 'activation' of MSPs: which are the involved stakeholders? What resources are they committing? How and why did they decide to establish this common endeavour; which are the drivers and expectations, the risks taken? What is the level of trust in the coordination and governance mechanism? How does the partnership find goal consensus? How is coordination practically achieved? Is there an incentive/disincentive structure in place? Is there a network facilitator? Is it one of the internal stakeholders or external to the partnership?

Risks and limitations of MSPs

In MSPs there is a latent tension between efficiency and inclusiveness. Especially in post-conflict environments, inclusiveness is linked to the goal of reconciliation. However, the partnership should keep an ability to deliver concrete results (services, infrastructure, decisions) instrumental to the ultimate goal (e.g. human security).

The risks and limitations of MSPs in a post-conflict environment are particularly relevant for the case studies in Serbia and, up to a point, Northern Ireland. Effective new governance needs strong institutions to start with. But the absence of strong, democratically controlled institutions is often part of the legacy of civil strife, if not one of its causes. Even when new governance arrangements do provide solutions, these may be isolated and lead to a fragmentation of governance. The new governance arrangements, especially when introduced from the outside during an international post-conflict reconstruction mission, risk duplicating the efforts of existing democratic institutions, raising the costs of decision making at best, undermining institutional development at worst. Especially under forms of regulatory capture by organised private sector or organised interest groups, there is a risk of 'dubious complementarity' whereby the MSPs replace official decision making and ultimately weaken the state institutions they rely on as a precondition for their effectiveness. Martens (2007) presents a taxonomy of possible limits in MSP operations that offers useful analytical insights. It is important to assess the relative power positions of stakeholders and whether there are distortions of competition or pretences of representativeness. Are the partners exclusive towards non-partners with a legitimate stake in the issue? Do partners use the MSP to leverage resources – financial, symbolic, social – to enhance their position in wider social networks? Who nominates or selects stakeholders during the activation of the partnership?

Paradoxes of participation

This section will look at the new governance discourse on participation from the outside, leveraging its own key features – the analytics of ownership and decision-making powers – for a critical appraisal. Even in its heyday during the cultural revolutions of the late 1960s, participation's ambivalence was patent to observers, as famously engraved in this Paris May 1968 poster:

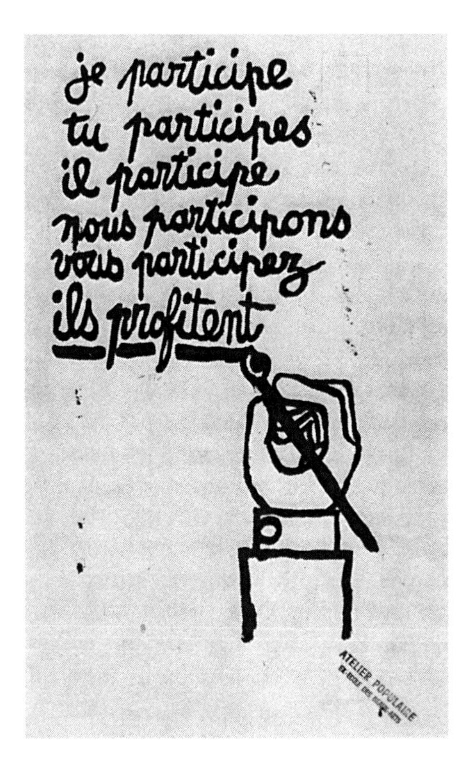

Figure 10.1 'Je participe, tu participes, il participe, nous participons, vous participez, ils profitent' [affiche] May 1968.

Source: Bibliothèque nationale de France.

Linguistically, there is a fecund semantic ambivalence built into the idea of participation. To participate evokes the idea of taking (a) part: it may refer to the part that is assigned or given to somebody, separating it from the whole, or the part that is joined with the others in order to reconstitute a whole. The very divisive action of cutting something into parts creates an implicit bond, inasmuch as the parts are still perceived and constructed as belonging to a unity. It means to divide and share at the same time, a semantic richness that is well illustrated by the *partecipanze agrarie* in northern Italy. These are an ancient form of collective property of agricultural land originating in the Middle Ages and still in use in northern Italy (Emilia, Veneto). Powerful abbeys in northern Italy leased as emphyteusis some of their lands to 'participating' peasant families, usually after carrying out major drainage works. Even if the nominal property of the land remained with the abbey, with the exception of the small emphyteutic fee and the commitment to take care of the land improving it, the participants enjoyed full 'possession', such as access to and control of the land and its produce. The participants retained full, collective decision-making powers regarding cultivations, organisation of works, sharing of produce and so on. Crucially, in this case participation refers to taking part in the undivided property of the land. But the part cannot be separated from the whole (Bassanelli, 1979). We have already found a connection between participation and ownership in the literature on new governance. Since the *partecipanze agrarie* literally define participation in terms of social property relations, it provides us with a clearer focus to critically re-examine the former.

With the neoliberal turn from government to governance, from passive social protection to active citizenship, the citizens of contemporary European polities have never enjoyed such a latitude of venues of participation to have their voices heard, their views taken into account (Rhodes, 1996; Shearing and Wood, 2003; Bovaird, 2005; Martens, 2007; Offe, 2009; Sloan and Oliver, 2013). However, the new 'light', regulating-not-owning, service-coordinating-not-providing, governance-open government is still rather expensive and extracts a fair amount of resources from households and companies (Offe, 2013). Part of the state revenues is spent on recruiting an army of new social engineering specialists whose job is to 'activate' the citizenship, creating the spaces and institutional venues where they can participate. After creatively and passionately labouring in start-up factories and offices, the new model citizen will answer to a higher call and moonlight as a city planner when called upon to join participatory urbanism designing new developments. The following month, she will don the wig as a member of a jury or as part of a community of care in an RJ circle. A few days later, he will turn into a public health specialist when scrutinising the local hospital practices to ensure that patients' rights are properly upheld. All this, it goes without saying, as voluntary work happily contributed out of civic duty for the common good, while facilitated by well-remunerated professional 'activators'.

Under the new European social compact, citizens more or less keep paying as many taxes as before, receive fewer social protection (welfare) services, but are now suavely prodded to be entrepreneurial, to be the masters of their own social destiny, to participate more. In sum, the new model active citizen has to work more, and do it in an environment that is both more competitive and highly regulated, so as to prevent anti-systemic alternatives from gaining momentum, surrounded by an army of facilitating specialists who are ultimately answerable to statutory agencies, and for free.

A further example of the characterisation of participation in terms of ownership and decision-making powers can be found in Arnstein's seminal article (1969) on the ladder of active participation. Arnstein defined participation as

> a categorical term for citizen power. [...] It is the strategy by which the have-nots join in determining how information is shared, goals and policies are set, tax resources are allocated, programs are operated, and benefits like contracts and patronage are parcelled out.
>
> (Ibid., p. 217)

This amounts to a sort of checklist for determining the level of participation, looking at the actual decision-making power of the partners on the key passages of public policy making and implementation. These levels are schematically represented in Arnstein's ladder of citizens' participation, going from 'manipulation' and 'therapy' as baseline non-participation, to intermediate forms of 'token' consultation, to partnerships and higher forms of full citizen control.[1]

The experience of the 1960s was mainly concerned with issues of material production and redistribution. When public housing programmes, on the contrary, focused on tenants' values instead of 'important matters', Arnstein saw examples of 'therapy'-level participation. If we fast forward past Inglehart's shift towards post-materialistic concerns when 'values' and 'identities' have taken centre stage (Inglehart, 1997), a similar potential pitfall for restorative practices has been pointed out, for example, by Richards (2011, pp. 99–100), who sees an unwarranted link between 'empowerment' and 'responsibilisation', the moral pressure for an offender (or stakeholder in general) to take responsibility for her actions or those of her children, relatives, neighbours and so on.

If we look at (multi-stakeholder) partnerships as the signature format of new governance implementation, they are higher up in Arnstein's ladder because in a partnership 'power is in fact redistributed through negotiation between citizens and powerholders' (1969, p. 221). Partnership can work most effectively when

> there is an *organised power-base* in the community *to which the citizen leaders are accountable*; [...] when the citizens group has the financial *resources to pay its leaders reasonable honoraria* for their time-consuming efforts; [...] and when *the group has the resources to hire (and fire)* its own technicians, lawyers, and community organisers.
>
> (Ibid., p. 221, emphasis added)

These conditions are hardly met in the average project run by a foreign-funded NGO in developing countries. And they are lacking also in a place like Vienna, with its extensive network of government-related sub-organisations with different but always limited degrees of independence. Anyway, they should be taken into account when designing restorative practices that aim at participation and empowerment.

Within ALTERNATIVE, the overall ambivalence of participation within the new governance discourse was already highlighted by Kremmel and Pelikan (2013). The new governance literature on MSPs that we have briefly surveyed here dovetails with Arnstein's critical approach in stressing the importance of decision-making powers and the resources invested or claimed by participants as defining and qualifying elements of participation itself. Nevertheless, the new liberal project for Europe ultimately seems to envisage a kind of limited participation, more akin to tokenism, where partnerships are diluted because the executive control of agenda-setting, policy making and funding rests firmly, and increasingly so, within the EU's institutional technostructure and organised corporate interests. Leveraging on the insights from the new governance literature itself and its contradictions, we normatively posit that active participation in RJ approaches to conflicts in intercultural settings will have to be a more substantive participation with power and property. Rather than yielding to economic reductionism, we hold that focusing on these hard, infrastructural features of participation is not in contradiction to the thick problematisation of a rich intercultural context, but complements and perhaps demystifies it. We therefore adopt this definition of participation as ownership as radical perspective for the critical appraisal of restorative justice methods, in particular within ALTERNATIVE.

Diachronic accounts from the action research sites: preparing for restorative circles – doing restorative circles

In this section we will ask in which way the paradoxes of active participation materialise. We have been further narrowing down the theme of 'active participation' by focusing on the introduction, preparation and carrying out of restorative circles. According to the definition put forward above, we discuss participation 'with power and property', with community ownership figuring prominently in the case stories presented. Through a comparison of practices and experiences, we attempt to fine-tune the picture of the intricacies and paradoxes of active participation.

And we will attempt a provisional sketch of the state of affairs regarding public–private partnerships, focusing on the role of the agencies of the ALTERNATIVE project. Did they succeed in enhancing a radical understanding and practice of participation of those affected by a conflict? Did they find a place within the maze of political and economic forces that left them with some leeway to exert a kind of influence that could be used for the benefit of the inhabitants of the research sites?

Serbia

The researchers from the ALTERNATIVE team in Serbia had planned and executed a series of seminars in each of its three research sites. They were targeted at representatives of the civil society organisations (including victim support organisations, organisations of victims and war veterans, women organisations, organisations of young people, peace organisations etc.), representatives of the local authorities, representatives of the state agencies and institutions at the local level (police, social welfare service, schools, pre-school institutions, etc.), religious organisations and representatives of the local community.

The ALTERNATIVE team could rely on previous experiences in implementing the 'Joint action for truth and reconciliation network' and the idea of a 'third way' as a 'non-conflict and inclusive way of communication of people with different experiences of war and other conflicts about the past, which implicates dealing with all victims, perpetrators and witnesses regardless of their ethnic or other affiliation or features' (Nikolić-Ristanović *et al.*, 2015, p. 14).

The team in Serbia followed the format presented in the Handbook of Borbala Fellegi and Dora Szegö (2013), using a talking stick and a set of questions that had been prepared by the research team in advance; these questions had been adapted, though. We want to be clear that these were trial circles, based on role play, that served the purpose of making participants acquainted with this instrument. Following the stages of involvement and participation developed by the ALTERNATIVE team from Hungary (Szegö *et al.*, 2015, p. 20), we could categorise this endeavour as aiming at the level of cognition and understanding, including the third level: reflection. The trial circles were to enhance participants' readiness to apply the restorative circle procedure to concrete 'cases' they came across. Transformation of working with conflicts through active participation of those concerned as the highest stage would be the ultimate goal.

On the surface, the *paradox of participation* in Serbia consists of the high willingness of the participants of the seminars provided by ALTERNATIVE despite a history of war and of the deep wounds it has left. But we know that in Serbia the majority of seminar participants belonged to groups that had already been engaged in activities working towards overcoming the new and old boundaries and the injuries and traumas of the past. There, the ideas of RJ fell on fertile ground. Will active participation become realised once the instrument of a restorative circle is tested in social and political reality?

The activities in Serbia were carried out by the Victimology Society, who have both acquired experience and a concomitant excellent reputation in Serbia and its neighbouring countries. They can draw on a remarkable network of individuals and of groups, both governmental and non-governmental, in society. The Victimology Society and the University of Belgrade, albeit remaining detached from the immediate power struggles, are part of a civic movement; they can rely on the movement's indirect influence as a scientifically based 'moral' authority.

Northern Ireland

In Northern Ireland, the team of ALTERNATIVE provided training for about 50 community workers that followed the Practices Manual 'Community Based Restorative Justice for Northern Ireland', containing a section: 'Restorative Community Circles: Addressing Intergroup Conflict'. The training was based on an understanding that RJ requires people to have access to capabilities that enable them to participate actively in justice rather than being passive recipients of the services of institutions and the protection of professionals. This is, indeed, a strong vote for active participation and community ownership. But the introduction to the manual states also: 'Such a community requires a host who enables the parties to communicate, understand each other and make agreements across frontiers and across time through telling and listening to each other's narratives'.

In one case reported, two community workers who had received this kind of training were able to act as facilitators in the case of a neighbourhood dispute between a local resident and a Polish family. It had escalated along ethnic lines, with insults and malicious damage directed against the Polish as well as another family of foreign origin. The social worker, who had been asked by a representative of the Polish community to intervene and who was well acquainted with the local area, started out by listening to both sides of the story, and then he called a meeting inviting the local politician, another community activist (trained by the University), two police officers, neighbourhood wardens, the local resident complaining about the Polish family and her supporters, the Polish family, another Polish family to support, and a Czech family who lived in the same street. During the meeting, everyone had the opportunity to tell their story and question each other. It was agreed that there were faults on both sides, and that although it had an ethnic dimension, it was a dispute between two neighbours, both of whom were prone to conflict. The local people invited the Polish and Czech families to a local celebration and asked them to bring their food to the barbecue to share with the others. People shook hands and committed themselves to be better neighbours in the future.

The researchers concluded that communicative action allowed the full complexity of the stories to emerge and facilitate reconciliation and some steps to integrate the foreign families. Through skilful facilitation, the parties resolved the conflict without the need for advocates or experts. Indeed, the restorative practitioner's role, which was such a valuable catalyst, was almost invisible to the parties. This is what they regarded as good restorative practice. It is interesting to note that the researchers in Northern Ireland use the term 'host' to characterise this role. Extending understanding and, moreover, recognition to both sides is, indeed, contained in the notion of the host.

The *paradox of participation* enacted is the one inherent in the facilitation of a restorative circle. The essence of the 'professional' quality of the facilitator is her/his retreating as much as possible in order to bring the maximum feasible participation of the participants to the fore. The concept of the host is used to 'capture' this highly ambiguous role and position.

Similarly to the situation in Serbia, in Northern Ireland the reputation of the Ulster University comes as a main asset of the ALTERNATIVE team. It can boast a lot of practice-relevant teaching experience in the field of RJ, but is clearly perceived as standing detached from the immediate power struggle of different groups at the research sites. The researchers themselves, though, are not acting as a 'neutral' and 'detached' scientific agent. In fact, 'the University is part of the history of civic life … [i]n Northern Irish society and it is radically engaged in this society' (Chapman *et al.*, 2015, p. 84). Because theirs is indeed a powerful position due to the amount of trust invested in them, abstaining from the direct exertion of power appears convincing. The example thus provided becomes the road towards furthering ownership of conflict resolution.

Vienna, Austria

For many years, the community centre Bassena had tried to find a way, supported both practically and theoretically, that would promote residents' participation, a participation that is neither 'token' nor therapeutic only. Attempts to prepare residents – together with Bassena staff – for a potential application of a restorative circle can be seen as a continuation and expansion of these efforts.

Gerda, the facilitator and trainer for the circle approach, had clarified after the first workshop held at the Bassena that establishing a self-sustaining network/system for handling conflicts does not depend on somebody starting an initiative of recruiting peer mediators, but on people going about reacting to conflicts in a restorative way inside their groups or networks. The workshop could serve as a way of instigating and promoting the readiness to act 'restoratively' in each participant's individual life and regarding conflicts he/she encounters. Gerda also stressed the fact that she was prepared to call off this attempt at any time – it could very well be the case that the residents would not want to continue, and this attitude is essential in order to leave the responsibility for the process with the residents. Community ownership would be attended to in a 'radical' way.

We have to understand this attitude against the backdrop of previous experiences with the establishment of a restorative circle in the Women's Café. There, *wohnpartner*, the other partner organisation of the ALTERNATIVE team of Vienna, had decided at a certain point that they did not want to continue working with Gerda. They had regarded the process as too open and not sufficiently structured, which had resulted at one meeting in some residents voicing fears of the growing influence of a more orthodox brand of Islam in Austria. In the perception of *wohnpartner*, this could set off an avalanche of xenophobia that appeared highly disturbing and disquieting. In addition, the staff of *wohnpartner* wanted to establish a more transparent procedure, a procedure that attended to the situation and to the needs of the women who 'made' and 'used' the *Frauencafé*. They wanted to carefully prepare the ground for these women to help them to fully understand and, on the basis of this understanding, engage with the circle procedure. This procedure, as promoted by Gerda, was intended to follow by and large the steps and especially the sequence of questions recommended by Dominik Barter (who had started to work with and further develop a restorative circles approach in the 1990s in Brazil and has exerted considerable influence in Europe; cf. Barter, 2013). Interestingly, the restorative circle finally set up mirrored these steps. But it introduced both intensive individual preparation of the potential participants and additional coaching for the women whenever it was wanted and needed. *Wohnpartner* staff, as well as a member of the research team, had argued that the more radical understanding of 'ownership' as decision making was rather oriented towards middle-class people, those with some previous experience or understanding of dialogic approaches. The socio-economic background of the Old-Austrian and – mainly – Turkish women in the Women's Café required special consideration, assistance and care. The understanding they achieved in this way served to provide them with the capacity to face confrontation and to make the circle procedure 'their own'.

We now come to contend that in Vienna, the claim to community ownership was abated for the sake of a more caring attitude. In a way, it could be characterised as a return to the time-honoured maternalistic governance model of the 'Red Vienna' taken to a higher level. There remains a delicate balance, though: a tendency towards pacification is always lurking in the background. And opposing the housing agency as an important stakeholder is not in the picture. But the thrust towards more active participation – indeed, community ownership – is there as well. Interestingly, the emphasis on care, *Sorge* in German, was shared as important by the (former) social workers of the Bassena. It has found its way into the guidelines that the Sociology of Law and Criminology (IRKS) researchers, together with Gerda and with the members of *wohnpartner*, have finally set down in a short illustrated booklet.

The Austrian type of *participation paradox* lies with the heritage of the maternalistic policies of the City of Vienna and its sub-organisations. Whereas the social workers of the Bassena had attempted to break free from this heritage and to develop its position as an intermediary agency, the organisation *wohnpartner* has, after a long struggle in the course of the attempt of setting up a restorative circle in the *Frauencafé*, arrived at a higher level of this old new governance model, reconciling the striving for community ownership and conveying transparency and providing care.

In Vienna, the researchers from the IRKS explicitly and deliberately entered a partnership with the most important player in the field of social housing and taking care of conflicts arising there. The organisation *wohnpartner* is part of the powerful administration of the City of Vienna, finding itself in the middle of an intense political struggle around the topic of migration and rising xenophobia. The community centre Bassena had enjoyed a higher degree of independence, albeit also remaining within the orbit of the administration of the City of Vienna. The ALTERNATIVE team intended to influence conflict work in the direction of enhanced participation through and together with these agencies. This afforded understanding of the situation, especially of *wohnpartner*, its political liabilities and its commitments. The trust that had been established with the agency, together with insisting on the larger commitment to the ALTERNATIVE rationale, provided the ground for ALTERNATIVE to contribute to an adaptation of 'community ownership' to the specific situation of women and the conflicts they encountered in the intercultural setting of the *Frauencafé*.

Kisváros, Hungary

In Kisváros, the team of ALTERNATIVE had also used the format of the restorative circle to intervene in conflicts that had occurred in the intercultural setting of the village, although a full restorative circle was performed only twice. Interestingly, it was not – as intended – the adversaries to the conflict that met: in Kisváros, it was the group of those who had won the local elections, on the one hand, and the 'old' mayor and his supporters who had been beaten, on the other hand. Only the supporters, the people caring for the old mayor, were coming together. They got the opportunity to talk honestly about their feelings of disappointment, anger and sadness. 'However, the harms caused by defeat and exclusion were not openly revealed by the mayor and his supporters until today', observed the researchers (Hera *et al.*, 2015, p. 61).

In a way, the circle turned out to be another exemplification of the 'culture of silence' the researchers had diagnosed at the beginning of their activity. To speak out, to criticise, especially in the face of somebody defeated and 'broken', is avoided. It is not just a matter of cowardice; it is an age-old, time-honoured arrangement. Notwithstanding these obstacles, the ALTERNATIVE team had achieved a movement towards a transformation of dealing with conflict, based on a changed awareness of conflicts and the potential of restorative approaches. The key to achieving this transformation and arriving at mutual recognition was 'to move from the level of "grand narratives" to the level of personal stories' (Szegö *et al.*, 2015, p. 30).

The *paradox of participation* in Kisváros was marked by the culture of silence, as explicated above. In their final assessment, the researchers contend:

> The Foresee group interpreted conflicts as a way to understanding and agreement and strived for their resolution, it turned out that this positive orientation towards the dialogue processes was hardly shared by the locals. Some local people (especially formal and informal leaders) were motivated in positioning themselves in the local power space (gaining power, representing their own interests, keeping dominant positions). Closed, hierarchical communication and withholding information often fit more into power plays than partnership-based, open communication.
>
> (Szegö *et al.*, 2015, p. 26)

The ALTERNATIVE research team met with a very difficult situation in Kisváros. There was no call for the group by the villagers. They came there without any official credentials from any powerful official or semi-official agency. They established working relations with the mayor and with the leader of the Roma self-government based on a contract. In what followed, they were perceived as potential supporters of the mayor and his Roma-friendly politics. But in striving for a kind of impartiality, this was bound to result in mutual disappointment. After the defeat of the mayor in the local elections, the ALTERNATIVE team were on the brink of having to terminate their activity altogether. Resorting to their main dialogic approach, they found a new position vis-à-vis the new power elites and the village as a whole. Through both their detachment from power struggles and their commitment to the restorative 'ideal', they achieved a new credibility that enabled them to work towards the promotion of dialogue.

At all four research sites, the respective ALTERNATIVE teams became part of a complex matrix of political forces striving for their specific goals and following an – albeit changing – agenda. In Serbia and in Northern Ireland, the position of ALTERNATIVE within this matrix is marked by its close attachment to, on the one hand, the Victimology Society of Serbia, and, on the other hand, the University of Ulster, and their reputation and recognition as standing outside the day-to-day political struggle but being committed to dialogue and reconciliation. In Vienna, the cooperation with the powerful agencies of the City of Vienna enabled them to strive for a delicate balance between the commitment to the restorative rationale and attending to the needs of the residents but also the liabilities of the agencies, whereas in Hungary, full exposure to local power struggles exemplifies the enormous difficulties in finding a stance and achieving a credibility that rests solely on one's commitment to and one's belief in the power of dialogue.

Conclusion

Action research in the four sites shows that strong leadership and steering by public institutions, combined with effective socio-economic redistributive policies, are associated with lower levels of active participation, on the one hand, and higher perceptions of personal safety – or at least de-securitisation of issues – on the other (Vienna; Hungary in some circumstances). When public actors are effectively hegemonic, the restorative approach experimented with in the project seems to act as a complementary corrective, contributing (through improved communication and dialogue) towards a more effective representation of the interests and identities of stakeholders, including a partial reappropriation of conflicts. Conversely, higher levels of active participation and mobilisation in the presence of weaker social public provision are potentially open to exclusionary practices, are associated with heightened perceptions of insecurity, and are more prone to securitising dynamics. In these more competitive constellations, the restorative methods experimented in the project – in particular, peacemaking circles or 'community mediation' – might contribute towards strengthening social solidarity between stakeholders, building inter-group 'bridging' trust, increasing the sense of fairness in the process, and improving the perceptions of safety.

In the light of the diachronic accounts, let's look once more at the new governance discourse on participation as presented from the outside. The comparison we have attempted traced different manifestations of the paradoxes that are inherent in the concept of active participation. In order to enfold its emancipatory capacity and promote democracy, it has to rest on real voluntary commitment. It is about residents' voices being heard and residents having a say, forging alliances with other stakeholders, probing and challenging the limitations set by existing power structures and power differences. The action research in ALTERNATIVE, following Dworski-Riggs and Langhout's advice (2010, p. 215), has in all of our research sites perceived the action research activities 'as moments of opportunity for the researchers to refine their methods and for the community [...] to challenge existing power structures.'

Moreover, RJ processes – and we have here focused on restorative circles – depend on the willingness of the people to engage in such processes. Participation cannot be enforced – and we do have many instances of resistance to the invitation to participation. We have avoidance, evident as the 'culture of silence', and we have instances of 'usage' that is not in accordance with the principles of RJ. The cautious and careful path we had to follow in ALTERNATIVE was the way the action researcher reacted to these tendencies of resistance and avoidance – this holds especially for Vienna and for Hungary.

Did we find any indication of active participation being used as a device for achieving compliance and subjugation of citizens in a soft and cunning way, as a strategy of the neoliberal state? Did we find instances of an increased demand on individuals according to the new social project Yasemin Soysal has outlined (2012, p. 1): a citizenship model that privileges individuality and its transformative capacity as a collective good? She has stated: 'Thus, while expanding the boundaries and forms of participation in society, this project at the same time burdens the individual, rather than the state, with the obligation of ensuring social cohesion and solidarity.'

We have already asked a similar question in Kremmel and Pelikan (2013) with regard to this thesis, and we have suggested that – at least at the Viennese research site – the empirical evidence did not point in the direction of an increased burden being put on people with a migration background. The 'new governance' agenda of responsibilisation is there, though. But, is this indeed the soft and cunning way of achieving people's subjugation, prodding them to go about 'handling' and resolving their conflicts by engaging in direct confrontation through active participation? We end up with the requirement to closely investigate and analyse in each single case the power play, the effects on the minds of the parties to the conflict, and the long-term effect the interventions had on them.

Based on the finding about participation and its paradoxes from the four sites, we attempt this tentative and mid-level generalisation: notwithstanding the fact that the appearance of these paradoxes is different at the different research sites, their potential resolution follows the same path. It is about offering and establishing dialogic procedures; these procedures all revert to digging up personal stories and evoking the mutual recognition triggered by telling and by listening to these stories. Strategic action becomes transformed into communicative action.

Note

1 The complete Arnstein's ladder of citizen participation: Citizen power (Citizen control, Delegated power, Partnership); Tokenism (Placation, Consultation, Informing); Non-participation (Therapy, Manipulation).

References

ALTERNATIVE project documents: http://alternativeproject.eu (accessed 10 March 2017).

Arnstein, S. R., 1969. A Ladder of Citizen Participation. *Journal of the American Institute of Planners (JAIP)*, 35(4), pp. 216–224.

Barter, Dominik im Gespräch mit Sissi Mazzetti. Restorative Circles. Ein Ansatz aus Brasilien, der Raum für den gemeinschaftlichen Umgang mit schmerzhaften Konflikten schafft. In: TOA – Servicebüro für Täter-Opfer-Ausgleich und Konfliktschlichtung (Hg.) 2013. *Restorative Justice. Der Versuch, das Unübersetzbare in Worte zu fassen.* DBH Materialien nr. 71: Köln, pp. 24–38.

Bassanelli, L., 1979. *Le partecipanze agrarie emiliane*. Milano: Angeli.

Bovaird, T., 2005. Public Governance: Balancing Stakeholder Power in a Network Society. *International Review of Administrative Sciences*, 71(2), pp. 217–228.

Chapman, T., Campbell, H., Wilson, D. and McCready, P., 2015. *Exploring and Crossing the Frontiers of Society: Restorative Approaches to Conflict between Groups*. ALTERNATIVE deliverable 7.6.

Christie, N., 1977. Conflicts as Property. *British Journal of Criminology*, 17, p. 1.

Dworski-Riggs, D. and Langhout, R. D., 2010. Elucidating the Power in Empowerment and the Participation in Participatory Action Research: A Story about Research Team and Elementary School Change. *American Journal of Community Psychology*, 45(3–4), pp. 215–230.

Fellegi, B. and Szegö, D., 2013. *Handbook for Facilitating Peacemaking Circles*. Budapest: Foresee Research Group. Available at: www.foresee.hu/uploads/tx_abdownloads/files/peacemaking_circle_handbook.pdf (accessed 15 June 2017).

Fung, A., 2001. Deepening Democracy: Innovations in Empowered Participatory Governance. *Politics and Society*, 29(1), pp. 4–41.

Hera, G., Benedek, G., Szegö, D. and Balla, L. 2015. *Comprehensive Final Report on RJ in Intercultural Communities*. ALTERNATIVE deliverable 5.5.

Héritier, A. and Rhodes, M., 2011. *New Modes of Governance in Europe: Governing in the Shadow of Hierarchy*. Houndmills: Palgrave Macmillan.

Immerwahr, D., 2015. *Thinking Small: The United States and the Lure of Community Development*. Cambridge, MA: Harvard University Press.

Inglehart, R., 1997. *Modernization and Postmodernization: Cultural, Economic, and Political Change in 43 Societies*. Princeton, NJ: Princeton University Press.

Kremmel, K. and Pelikan, C., 2013. *D4.1 Theoretical Research Report on Activating Civil Society*, ALTERNATIVE project. Available at: www.alternativeproject.eu/assets/upload/Deliverable_4.1_Theoretical_report_on_activating_civil_society.pdf (accessed 4 August 2014).

Martens, J., 2007. *Multistakeholder Partnerships – Future Models of Multilateralism?* Berlin: Friedrich-Ebert-Stiftung.

Nikolić-Ristanović, V., Srna, J. and Copic, S. 2015. *Action Research Report on the Application of RJ in Intercultural Settings*. ALTERNATIVE deliverable 6.3.

Offe, C., 2009. Governance: An 'Empty Signifier'? *Constellations*, 16(4), pp. 550–562.

Offe, C., 2013. Democratic Inequality in the Austerity State. *Juncture*, 20(3), pp. 178–185.

Pelikan, C., 2003. Different Systems, Different Rationales: Restorative Justice and Criminal Justice. In: F. Moyano Marques, ed., *Project DIKÊ: Protection and Promotion of Victim's Rights in Europe*. Lisbon: APAV, pp. 223–227.

Pelikan, C., 2007. The Place of Restorative Justice in Time and Space. In: R. Mackay, M. Bošnjak, J. Declerck, C. Pelikan, B. Van Stokkom and M. Wright, eds, *Images of Restorative Justice Theory*. Frankfurt am Main: Verlag für Polizeiwissenschaft, pp. 35–56.

Pishchikova, K., Mele, V., Croci, C., Greene, O., Lewis, D., Bartolucci, V., Benedek, W., Moore, S., Pedra, A. and Vivona, M., 2010. *Multi-Stakeholder Partnerships in Post-Conflict Reconstruction: The Role of EU: Theoretical and Methodological Framework*, Multipart project. Available at: www.multi-part.eu/images/contenuti/wp_2_3_final_report.pdf (accessed 27 June 2014).

Rhodes, R. A. W., 1996. The New Governance: Governing without Government. *Political Studies*, 44(4), pp. 652–667.

Richards, K., 2011. Restorative Justice and 'Empowerment': Producing and Governing Active Subjects through 'Empowering' Practices. *Critical Criminology*, 19(2), pp. 91–105.

Shearing, C. and Wood, J., 2003. Nodal Governance, Democracy, and the New 'Denizens'. *Journal of Law and Society*, 30(3), pp. 400–419.
Sloan, P. and Oliver, D., 2013. Building Trust in Multi-Stakeholder Partnerships: Critical Emotional Incidents and Practices of Engagement. *Organization Studies*, 34(12), pp. 1835–1868.
Soysal, Y. N., 2012. Citizenship, Immigration, and the European Social Project: Rights and Obligations of Individuality. *The British Journal of Sociology*, 63(1), pp. 1–21.
Szegö, D., Benedek, G. and Györfi, E., 2015. *Lessons Learnt about Implementing Restorative Dialogues in an Intercultural Setting*. ALTERNATIVE deliverable 5.4.
Wood, J., Shearing, C. and Froestad, J., 2011. Restorative Justice and Nodal Governance. *International Journal of Comparative and Applied Criminal Justice*, 35(1), pp. 1–18.

11 Restorative justice in the societies of control

The ambivalence of decentralised state control in participative justice processes

Espen Marius Foss and Brunilda Pali

Introduction

Philosophers and social researchers have described a significant transition from modern nation-states to corporate states, and from *disciplinary societies* to *societies of control* (Foucault and Rabinow, 1997; Agamben, 2005, 2014; Deleuze, 2006; Kapferer, 2010). Due to what has been described as a generalised crisis in traditional forms of state control, and its bureaucratic institutions, a new organisation of state power has emerged and is being constructed through processes that decentralise, distribute and outsource state functions to civil and private actors and agencies. Such processes rely on a neoliberal ideological discourse, whereby agents of authority and control are often presented as partners in common projects with their clients or stakeholders. In developing such partnerships, states take advantage of the logic[1] of non-state sites of governance and direct their operations in a way that enables them to 'govern at a distance' (Rose and Miller, 1992). Thus, despite the rhetoric, critics hold that the form of decentralised corporate state power in reality intensifies the control over citizens, especially due to the blurring of the borders of state and civil society through which the power of the state becomes less visible and thus difficult to counteract.

Emerging as a critique of *disciplinary* punishment, of bureaucratic forms of state control and criminal justice, and of the alienation of citizens from their own conflicts, restorative justice (RJ) emerged during the height of neoliberalism and its attack on the welfare state and state institutions (Walgrave, 2008). RJ attempts to reform the criminal justice system (CJS) by decentralising conflict management from the state to civil parties without the interference of professional state bureaucrats (Christie, 1977). In other words, RJ sets the state in 'brackets'. But despite the bracketing of the state, or maybe because of it, RJ has become in the last decades an increasingly accepted way of dealing with crime and conflict across countries and legislations.

RJ's principles and objectives,[2] although not directly deriving from it, are embedded in and fed by the neoliberal discourse and its techniques of responsibilisation, autonomy and empowerment, active citizenship and democracy, representing thus an approach that is not only acceptable but even attractive to its subjects, and whose goals become closely aligned with those of the corporate state power. In the perspective of the emergence of the societies of control, the relation between corporate state power and decentralised RJ processes remains crucial to understand. In this chapter, we focus on the complex dynamics of this relationship, hoping to shed light on their tight coexistence and co-dependence, and on the consequences the new organisation of state power has for the participants of such processes, and the implications for RJ.

Crisis in the disciplinary societies: changing dynamics of state power

One of the basic pillars of modern nation-states is that certain conflicts between civil parties come to be defined as crime (breaking of a law), 'bracketing' in the process the victim of crime and transforming the conflict into a relation between offender and state, whereby the state has the legitimacy and the monopoly to prosecute and punish (Van Ness, 1986; Weitekamp, 1998; Braithwaite, 2002, pp. 3–8). The state avenges (retributes) on behalf of victim and society, satisfying the public sense of justice so that the public does not take the law into its own hands (Van Ness and Heetderks Strong, 2002).

In this perspective, the CJS is one of the key institutions of the nation-states as they developed and culminated during the nineteenth and twentieth centuries. Foucault described this form of state power as *disciplinary societies*, where the prevailing form of state control was ensured by organising large spaces of enclosure: the family, the schools, the barracks, the factory, the prison and the hospital were enclosed institutions governed by bureaucratic state functions, which also regulated the movement of individuals between these institutions, organised around the main principle of the panopticon.[3] Disciplinary power entered a crisis due to new forces that were gradually instituted but which accelerated significantly after World War II due to the increasing globalisation of the 'free market'.[4] Contrasting disciplinary power with a new form of power Foucault (1991, 2007) called *governmentality*, he argued that its rationale is not to produce a subject that is stopped or prohibited from acting in a certain way, but a subject that respects a code of conduct as a way of life; hence, the coining of governmentality as 'conduct of conduct'. This type of power, Foucault argues, directs the actions of subjects by implicating them in their own governance towards specific ends, without using force, but through structuring their possible fields of action and realigning their goals with the goals of government.

Continuing on the Foucauldian analysis, late Deleuze[5] elaborates further on current trends in neoliberal governmentality and their use in what he calls *societies of control*. While, outside governmental theory, neoliberalism is often understood as the state's retreat from certain policy areas, in terms of governmentality, the state, on the contrary, assumes further tasks, like shifting responsibilities, transforming problems and producing particular subjectivities. According to Deleuze (2006), the *generalised crisis* in the existing state-bureaucratic institutions is related to the acceleration of the liberalisation of the economy, whereby the traditional mechanisms of state control no longer manage to cope with the dynamics of transnational economy. The crisis in the nation-states has led as a result to a new organisation of state power organised in so-called *corporate states*, where the former spaces of enclosure are being opened up to private and civil actors and agents in processes that deregulate, decentralise and privatise state power. The dynamics that threatened the old institutions have been co-opted and used by state actors and agencies in order to serve their interests: control, governing and reproduction of state power. A consequence of this decentralisation and co-option is that state power becomes less visible as the borders between state and private actors wane and as the *conduct of conduct* of population is done through civil society, through modes of 'governing at a distance', 'governing through freedom' or 'governing through community'.

Scholars within criminology have also highlighted (or criticised) such patterns under the name of the new regulatory state, premised upon a neoliberal combination of market competition, privatised institutions and decentred, at-a-distance forms of state regulation, emphasising a new division of labour whereby the control of the state lies in the 'steering' of governance, while encouraging the civil society and citizens to accept responsibility for the 'rowing' (Osborne and Gaebler, 1992; Majone, 1994; Braithwaite, 2000; Moran, 2001; Shearing, 2001; Crawford, 2006). In this nautical analogy, steering means governing by setting the course, monitoring the direction and correcting deviations from the course (Osborne and Gaebler, 1992). The notion of the regulatory state contrasts hierarchical command and control modes of regulation of the bureaucratic welfare state with decentred regulation through non-state networks and hybrid alliances and partnerships (Crawford, 2006).

The implications for RJ

The overall implication of the type of analysis identified above is that less direct government in society does not entail less governing; rather, on the contrary, government is active and interventionist even when seemingly 'minimal'. Given that – in Foucault's words – the efficiency of governmentality can be calculated by its 'ability to hide its own mechanisms' (1976, p. 86), it becomes important to cast a critical look especially at mechanisms, sites and discourses which proliferate under the guise of neutrality, civil society, community, participation and soft power. We consider the RJ discourse to be one such site. Already during the early 1980s, critics of *informal justice* have argued that these forms expand and intensify state control because they occur through 'a process that, on the surface, appears to be a process of retraction' (Santos, 1982, p. 262; see also Abel, 1982; Hofrichter, 1982, 1987; Merry, 1982, 1989; Tomasic, 1982; Delgado, 1985; Harrington, 1985; Selva and Bohm, 1987; Baskin, 1988).

Further scholarship of the so-called 'new informalists' argued that critics should take seriously, rather than simply discard, informal justice (Pavlich, 1996). The work of Michel Foucault in particular was useful for the 'new informalists' in understanding informalism as a form of *governmentality*. Pavlich (1996, p. 712) argued that the 'old' critics of informalism have inappropriately reduced the central question about informal justice to whether it expanded or reduced state control. The new informalists saw it as part of a developing trend towards informal, decentralised modes of exercising power in liberal states, as a site where the disciplinary powers integral to the continued existence of the liberal state and its legality are exercised, hence considering informalism without reducing it to, or declaring it as necessarily independent of, state power.

What sets this type of critique as different from the previous critique is a better understanding of the complex mechanisms of how governance and regulation happen, producing new forms of subjectivities, forms of power and conduct, while at the same time enabling 'practices of freedom'. Thus, the move 'beyond social control' does not, under such a critique, signal a real move beyond social control through informal mechanisms, but signals, rather, an exit beyond posing the question in this form. It invites, instead, new questions to be asked, and new understandings of how power relations operate.

In this chapter, we would like to further contribute to this body of scholarship, mainly through complementing the already existing Foucauldian analysis with a Deleuzean analysis, which has so far not been applied to RJ. Instead of simply asking whether RJ expands state control, we will try to better understand the specific dynamics and forms of power that take place in such processes, making use of the notions of *territorialisation*, *deterritorialisation*, *reterritorialisation*, and *arboreal and rhizomatic power* as articulated by Deleuze. We would also hold, in the same line as the 'new informalists', that it is important to take a look at empirical realities as the main safeguard against theoretical or ideological interpretations that tend to 'dismiss' informal justice on principle (or on *a priori* grounds).

Changing lenses with Deleuze: arboreal and rhizomatic power dynamics

In traditional nation-states, the *arboreal* (i.e. hierarchical) ways of control and governing are exercised by territorialisation[6] through bureaucratic coding and binding of subjectivities (Deleuze and Guattari, 2004; Deleuze, 2006; Kapferer and Bertelsen, 2009; Kapferer, 2010). The *rhizomatic* powers, on the other hand, are a metaphor for lateral power dynamics, which are open and unpredictable compared with the arboreal forms. These powers are difficult to control from an arboreal, hierarchical and territorial standpoint; therefore the arboreal state dynamic needs to control the forces that challenge its power. Deleuze's main point (2006) is that in corporate states, certain rhizomatic dynamics are incorporated by state actors to exercise control and governing tasks formerly handled by the state-bureaucratic institutions. Hence, in corporate states, the two dynamics – the arboreal state power and the rhizomatic anti-forces – are mixed, but not in a dialectical way. The two types of dynamics cannot be reduced to one another, or be synthesised, since the two would then obliterate each other. Hence, the rhizomatic dynamics need to be implemented in certain controlled and particular ways so that the rhizomatic powers do not conflict with the arboreal ones. When the rhizome comes into the centre of the state (the traditional 'arboreal' state dynamic), there will be a reterritorialisation, which – if incorporated successfully from a state control point of view – expands the corporate state power.

How can this analysis be applied to the context of the justice system? RJ, regardless of whether we conceive of it as a full-fledged paradigm or as a complementary approach to the traditional justice system, has aimed consistently at offering an alternative way of thinking about justice. In particular, we can refer here to the characterisation of Christa Pelikan's (2003, 2007) three core elements of RJ as a 'difference that makes a difference', a characterisation which, while on the one hand going beyond a mere enumeration of features, values and taxonomies, on the other hand is sufficiently abstract to allow the whole discourse of RJ to be captured, attending to its polysemic nature and fulfilling the requirement of parsimony. Pelikan articulates the three elements as *lifeworld* (versus system), participation (versus delegation) and reparation (versus punishment). The three elements are inextricably linked and interdependent, as only the perception of an act of wrongdoing as an interaction in the lifeworld provides the ground for the involvement of those concerned and affected to enter a dialogue, an exchange, in turn, which evolves around setting right the wrong that has occurred and the reparation of its consequences (see also Pali and Pelikan, 2014). As such, it is highly rhizomatic, given its reliance on a horizontal approach and the unpredictability of the process. While RJ is based on the principle of direct confrontation and dialogue, the CJS is based on creating distance, both physically and dialogically between the parties, and bureaucratically between the judge/penal authorities and the perpetrator (i.e. blind-folded justice).

We would like to illustrate our argument further through reliance on a concrete application of the more abstract ideas inherent in RJ, by referring here both intrinsically and instrumentally to the case of Norway. We will refer to Norway as a case study intrinsically in the sense of trying to understand the case in itself as much as possible, and instrumentally to illustrate our main arguments about RJ in general.

Mainly, we will argue that in Norway, the implementation of RJ, understood as a potential rhizomatic dynamic, has been controlled in a top-down way through a process of *separation and subordination*. RJ, as a 'different' and 'competing' ideology to the CJS, was from the beginning *subordinated* through the Norwegian Mediation Service (NMS), focusing on petty CJ cases involving mainly young offenders, as an alternative to full CJ processes (prosecution, trial and conviction/punishment). Hasund and Hydle's study (2007, p. 83) of the RJ discourse in Norway indicated how the NMS is regarded as *non-traditional, alternative, new, feminine, soft, goodhearted, easy, young, less serious, under, below* compared with the CJS, which is regarded as *traditional, established, old, masculine, strict/severe, heavy, adult, serious, above, up.* This terminology, apparent among both the CJ and the RJ proponents, exemplifies the reproduction of the notion that the NMS is minor to the superior CJS. Hence, through both the discourse and the organisation of the NMS, the CJS kept its status and hegemony in the more severe and serious criminal cases, and at the same time a pressured CJS got a welcomed removal of load in 'petty cases' through the NMS. The *separation* is apparent, as the NMS was created as a separate institution, first municipal then state based (in 2004), ensuring mediation on a neutral ground for civil parties with lay mediators. Consequently, a clear asymmetry between the two institutions was established, where the 'alternative' competing rhizomatic ideology of RJ was controlled from an 'arboreal' standpoint. From the beginning, it was the proponents from the CJS that decided the premises for the RJ institution (the NMS). Through Deleuzean lenses, the NMS can be understood as an incorporation of the rhizomatic aspects of RJ right into 'the heart of the state', hence creating a reterritorialisation which in practice expands and enforces control/governance.

In the following sections, we will further illustrate the interplay of the arboreal and rhizomatic powers through three empirical cases[7]: the first case is an ordinary and paradigmatic case when mediation works as an alternative to punishment for relatively minor crimes; the second is a 'failed' process where mediation was offered as a supplement in serious violence cases; and the third is a recent development in a piece of legislation where the mediation service assumes a probation function.

Mediation as an alternative to punishment: between civil participation and state control

Four men in their thirties representing an organisation with an immigrant background in Oslo paid a visit to another man from the same country of origin, Irfan, while he was at work, in order to demand payment for a debt to a third person. This organisation belonged to an ethnic minority, and its function was to offer informal social support to its members on various issues of concern. The situation escalated, and Irfan went to the police, accusing the four men of threatening his life. After initial investigations, the police prosecutor raised criminal charges against Ejaz, one of the four men who had threatened Irfan, and issued an interim exclusion order against him. In addition, the prosecutor made use of the Mediation Act, the Criminal Procedure Act §71a (from 1991), which regulates the referral of criminal cases to the NMS.[8]

After individual meetings between the mediator and the parties, they agreed to meet all together at the mediation service. The offender, Ejaz, was accompanied by four other men from the organisation, including two elders who had not been present during the incident at Irfan's workplace but who had earlier tried to negotiate the situation. Initially, Irfan expressed fear of meeting the others at the mediation service, since he had received several additional threats after the incident at his workplace in spite of the interim exclusion order. However, he agreed to meet when the mediator suggested that he could have the police escort him to and from the mediation service, and promised that he would never be left alone in the company of the others. The mediation lasted four intense hours, and was guided by three main questions: *what had happened*; *how were the parties affected*; *and what could be done to meet their needs*? A collective narrative gradually unfolded from the complexity of the situation (including highly different perceptions and points of view), until the parties eventually took responsibility for addressing the two main issues at stake; *the missing money* and *the security of Irfan*. The 'elephant in the room' was the fact that in the event of failure to reach an agreement, Ejaz would risk further criminal charges. After long discussions, they agreed to what can be characterised as a compromise: Irfan got a written guarantee that nobody from the organisation would hurt or threaten him. For his part, he agreed to pay a portion of the initially demanded sum, defined as 'interest'. By defining the demand as 'interest', Irfan managed to stick to his original claim that he had paid back the whole sum, and at the same time to meet the other party halfway by agreeing to pay extra (as he said, because the moneylender was his friend).

Thus, as illustrated by this case, an attempt to resolve a conflict by a civil organisation is taken over by the state the moment the police prosecutor raises charges. According to Christie (1977), the ideological 'father' of the NMS, the state 'steals' the conflict from the parties, whereupon professional legal experts resolve the issue, with the unintended consequence that the parties lose their ability to use their own competences in resolving the conflict. The main aim of most RJ programmes is to give the ownership back to the conflicting parties. Consequently, in the Norwegian setup with mediation as *alternative to punishment*, the state first 'steals' the conflict from the parties through the prosecution process, before 'giving it back' at the mediation service. Nevertheless, this double move of 'taking and returning' the ownership of a conflict has an irreversible effect on the conflict transformation process that not only constrains and controls the participants in certain ways, but also produces certain forms of subjectivity and a specific set of opportunities.

An important principle in RJ, 'ownership' of the conflict is ensured by establishing a neutral and egalitarian space for dialogue between civil participants, where they themselves decide the contents and outcome of the process. In the NMS, the mediators are laypersons with a variety of backgrounds, ideally representing the span of socio-cultural differences in the population. The lay principle is meant to ensure the parties' ownership of the conflict, so that professionals do not take over the process (Christie, 1977, 2004). This guarantees a division of labour between the mediation service and the parties, whereby the parties 'own' the *contents* of the process and its outcome while the mediators ensure the *form*, that is, the facilitation of the process on neutral ground. However, there is an implicit tension between facilitation and participation, form and content, since the two are always mutually constitutive in communicative processes whereby power can be exercised through form over content.

The interaction between the initial CJ process and the RJ process can be said to reproduce the 'morality' defined by the criminal law in the first case, but by other and less expensive means than a full CJ process. The morality defined by the CJ case, that is, *[control over a serious threat, ascribing the roles of prosecuted (presumed guilty) and complainant (victim), by the threat of punishment by law]* is translated into the mediation service as *[control over the same situation by the means of voluntary dialogue at a neutral arena between civil parties defined as offender and offended, as well as support persons].* The initial, half-fulfilled CJ process and its disciplinary effects do not disappear when the case is 'given back' to the parties through the NMS, but lie in the shadow. Hence, the CJS and the NMS cannot be considered as two independent institutions or processes in the Norwegian case, even though the NMS appears in practice, and is promoted, as an independent arena of the CJS (neutral mediation with civil parties and lay mediators). The RJ processes offered in criminal cases (60 per cent of the total number of cases treated in the NMS) reproduce the control and morality of the CJS in a decentralised process with the same controlling effects, but in a less expensive justice process. We could also add that 85 per cent of the total number of cases are referred by the police, in the category of either 'criminal cases' as an alternative (60 per cent) or 'civil cases' (25 per cent) (statistics from 2010); thus, there is a close or, rather, symbiotic collaboration between the NMS and the police/prosecution authorities in Norway.

The main point here is that this process reproduces the same effect as intended by the CJS, namely 'peace, order and governance', and hence arguably state power and control. We could also add that this morality includes the predefined roles of victim and offender, and a normality over the assumed breakage of the law, hence reinforcing the status of that law as just. Also, the 'severity' of the law breaking in this case had an effect on the mediators' way of moralising during the process, by pointing at the lack of trust between the parties when they should, rather, try to trust each other, as they were from the same country of origin and in the same organisation, and reminding the parties about the gravity of the situation ('threats are highly illegal') and what the alternative would be if they did not reach an agreement; namely, further charges against Ejaz. Hence, the mediators took a stand on behalf of one of the parties or, rather, on behalf of the law itself.

We can recall here the well-known argument of George Pavlich (2005), who evoked the *imitor paradox* and the 'impossible structure of restorative justice' to show the incongruity between the purported radical 'alternativeness' of RJ with respect to criminal justice, and the fact that RJ practices are often largely regulated by and shaped within this system, and its identity is constituted by deferring to the very institutions it seeks to replace, reform or counteract. Nevertheless, we also hope to show through a Deleuzean analysis that these concerns are not specific to the RJ field, but apply to all fields that try to create, offer or propose alternatives, and thus, instead of naïve claims of whether something does or does not propose an alternative, more complex forms of analysis which identify forms of power, or conditions of (im)possibility, might offer possibilities to develop both more strategic and normative points of view. Kelly Richards (2005) also argues that RJ is a constitutive part of that same system and its effort for reform rather than a genuine break or departure in the form of an alternative, or a serious attempt at its replacement.

The perception of the NMS as a neutral and civil ground for the parties' ownership in conflict resolution masks the power dynamic at play, making it more difficult to grasp, and hence criticise, for the parties themselves, the lay mediators and employees at the NMS, and the politicians and law-makers. In our view, the problem is not that there is an apparent exercise of state power in the mediation process, but rather, that this sort of power is unarticulated under the guise of neutral mediation between civil parties. The existing setup of the NMS as an 'alternative' to a CJ process is, hence, not an alternative, but rather, a different operation of state power, restoring a sense of *peace, order and good government* where the parties, with the assistance of lay mediators, become their own 'ministers of justice'. Statistics from the NMS saying that more than 90 per cent of the cases lead to written agreements, of which 95 per cent are fulfilled, demonstrate that this arrangement is a highly efficient way of decentralised state control. This process also represents at the same time intensified and unpredictable forms of control: intensified in the sense that the apparently 'voluntary' mediation process produces a higher compliance than an involuntary CJ process, enforcing the participants' compliance within the frames defined by the CJ case, and unpredictable in the sense that it opens up to new forms of subjectivity, where the way 'out of' the criminal case goes through the relationship with the other party, with the mediators as gatekeepers. These relations can lead to what they intend by making the subjects accomplices to the goals of the government through the shadow of coercion, but can also produce unexpected goals and conduct in all possible unforeseeable directions.

The NMS thus results as an extension of the CJS where the double move of 'taking and giving back' the ownership of the conflicts in effect reproduces state control and morality, but in a less costly and more efficient way. We cannot go in depth into the details of this case here, but we intended the considerations made on this quite ordinary case to be an entry point that at the least de-stabilise the narrative of an 'alternative' by showing instead the co-dependence of the two 'systems'. In the following sections, we will dwell on the Deleuzean concepts that we believe further support the understanding of how the two 'systems' interplay, and to what effects.

Mediation as a supplement to punishment: the Agder project

During 2007–2010, a collaboration between three state actors in Agder (the NMS, the police and prosecution authority, and the university) was initiated in order to try out *mediation as a supplement* in serious criminal cases that required public prosecution (Foss 2016). This was based on experiences from other countries (for example Belgium) where RJ has shown significant potential to alleviate the suffering of serious violence, from both a vitcim's and an offender's perspective. Additionally, the project was influenced by recommendations of both the UN and the European Commission, which articulate that RJ should be given as a generalised voluntary supplement during all the phases of a CJ process. Although in Norway there is no law that prohibits civil initiatives of meetings between victims and perpetrators before and after prosecution, the CJS does not facilitate such referrals, and without facilitation such initiatives would be difficult.

The project aimed to understand whether restorative meetings in cases of severe violence could be of support for the parties in question, and whether an RJ process before trial would affect the parallel CJ process, and with what consequences. Although the project lasted almost three years, at the end only three cases went through parallel processing in the two systems. The three restorative meetings showed significant alleviation of the suffering for both the victim and the offender, and had a minimal but positive effect on the following court processes in terms of reduced punishment. The framework and limitations set by the Director General of Public Prosecution (DGPP), as well as by the local police and prosecution authorities, had direct implications for the number of cases that were recruited to parallel treatment in the NMS. When the project report was presented to the DGPP, their response was that they could not recommend any prolongation or expansion of this project or similar projects. The main reason was the limited number of cases that the project had generated. A side-effect of the project, however, was a close collaboration between the two institutions, the local NMS and the police/prosecution authorities, which, according to the two institutions, had generated useful experience on how to handle referrals to RJ in criminal cases generally. The project also generated many referrals to the NMS outside the limited focal point of the project itself. This was also described in the project report to the DGPP, in which the police acknowledged an increased interest in and knowledge about use of RJ in criminal cases, both as supplement and as alternative to CJ processes.

The project can be described as a Catch-22 situation: the restrictions and conditions set by DGPP for the project had a direct limiting effect on the low number of cases that were referred to the project, which subsequently 'failed' from the DGPP's point of view. As a consequence, the DGPP rejected 'parallel treatment' as a viable way of implementing RJ in Norway, as this would, according to our argument, have challenged the status quo of the dynamics of *separation and subordination* of RJ that we described above. This sort of 'parallel treatment' represents a threat to the existing CJS, since the rhizomatic aspects of RJ would be put on a symmetrical level with the arboreal dynamics of the CJS, potentially then undermining it. In one of the cases, the parties (two 15-year-old boys who had been in a serious fight in public space) agreed during the RJ process that they were 'equally guilty'. At the end of the meeting, they shook hands and agreed to put the case behind them. The complainant withdrew his report to the police concerning the guilt of the other. However, at this stage the public prosecutor had already taken over, and in respect to *public prevention*, one person had 'to pay' for the criminal offence. One of the boys was sentenced to a conditional punishment. Both of the boys and their significant others, as well as the defence lawyer, found the court case unjust and therefore questioned its legitimacy. The rationales of the two processes (CJ and RJ) serve conflicting needs: the CJS basically assists public prevention as well as *mental hygiene* (as stated in governmental documents), whereas RJ, on the contrary, seeks to empower the conflicting parties themselves to take ownership of the conflict and during the meeting take care of their mutual needs.

The example illuminates how the present incorporation of the NMS within the CJS through *subordination and separation* (as an alternative to punishment in petty crime cases) is a functional control technology, where the state proliferates on the rhizomatic aspect of RJ in reproducing state power through control and governing. Hence, the arboreal dynamics control and utilise the rhizomatic dynamics of RJ, and not the other way around. This is a clear indication of how corporate state control makes use of the rhizomatic aspects of RJ by separation and subordination. In what follows, we will describe new developments in Norway, which make the trend towards control even clearer.

Back to (corporate) state control? The Youth Punishment Act

The Youth Punishment Act, presented in June 2014, was supported by a unanimous vote in the Norwegian parliament. Its aim is to hinder the imprisonment of minor offenders by diverting their case to the NMS as an alternative to unconditional prison. The young offender will have a compulsory (involuntary) *youth conference* ('*ungdomsstormøte*'), based on restorative principles, together with the victim of the crime (voluntary for the victim) and parents, guardians, probation officers, the child welfare service, the police and other representatives from the CJS. The conference will result in an individual plan of action for the offender in order to avoid future criminal offences. The act gives the NMS extended control functions, following up and controlling the implementation of the action plan.

Following the act, all mediation services in Norway have employed a so-called *youth coordinator* who will lead the follow-up of the young offender, including unannounced home visitations for illegal use of substances and other prohibitions made in the follow-up plan. If the offender does not comply with the restrictions and commandments in the action plan, the case will be sent back to the prosecution authorities, with possible punitive responses such as jail. A follow-up team will have responsibility to implement the individual action plans at local level. During the supervision time, up to three years, there will be several youth conferences with all the stakeholders (the young offender, the youth coordinator, the police and the follow-up team) as a sort of *social panopticon*.

The criminologist Nils Christie – acknowledged originally as 'the father' of the NMS – has criticised the new act with a 'Farewell to the NMS', claiming that 'mediation services with power are powerless' (Christie, 2014). According to Christie, the NMS now assumes a veiled form of social control, but without the type of legal protection built into the CJS. In the former setup of the NMS, lawyers and prosecution officers are not allowed in the mediation meetings, but with the new act, representatives from the CJS will be present. Christie claims that this poses a problem, because it raises no question about the *control of the controllers*, which are now invading the NMS; hence, critical issues related to legal protection are being veiled by the good intentions of keeping youth out of jail. Christie also worries that the civil arena for conflict management will be undermined when the professionals join. Laypeople – civil parties and lay mediators – have a tendency to keep quiet, he says, when professionals are present. Overall, Christie argues that the new arrangement represents a new control institution.

The new act and its effects must arguably be evaluated by research, and it is too early to argue about its benefits and dangers on an empirical basis. Nevertheless, looking at it through Deleuzean lenses, we can argue that the new act represents another (or an increased) type of incorporation of the rhizomatic aspects of RJ in the arboreal CJS. The offender is sentenced to youth conferences based on the restorative principles of dialogue, ownership and responsibility, without knowing the contents of the outcome of that conference, which can have many possible unintended consequences. This can be read as a *reterritorialisation* and expansion of state control in decentralised justice processes; however, again with the rhizomatic aspects being co-opted by the arboreal forces, and not the other way around.

Similarly, Christie argues that it would have been better if the control function had stayed at the CJS and that the civil solutions had inspired the punitive institutions, rather than the opposite, as in the case of the Youth Act. However, in the perspective of Deleuze and Guattari (2004), such an assemblage would imply a decrease of state power and control, and hence, it would not be a realistic political option. On the one hand, putting a typical probation scheme under the scheme of RJ will make it difficult to criticise the power operations, given its voluntary and participatory rhetoric (justice as something done by you). On the other hand, maybe the clear challenge to the voluntary principle, the inclusion of professionals in what has typically been defended as a lay principle protecting 'civil society', the *social panopticon* infusion, and the openly watchdog function that the mediation service is suddenly assuming might enable researchers and participants to name the control at last, and thus enable them to openly challenge it.

Conclusions

In this chapter, we argued that a significant transition has taken place from modern nation-states to corporate states, from *disciplinary societies* to *societies of control*, where a new organisation of state power has emerged. In light of such changes, we think the relation between corporate state power and decentralised RJ processes remains crucial to understand, and we hoped to illustrate their tight coexistence and co-dependence. In the same line as some of the 'new informalists', we also aimed to demonstrate that empirical research shows that analysis should move beyond the question of whether RJ expands or reduces state control. Making use of the notions of territorialisation/deterritorialisation/reterritorialisation and rhizomatic/arboreal power by Deleuze, we argued, will help us to better understand the specific dynamics and forms of power that take place in such processes. Deleuze's main point is that in corporate states certain *rhizomatic dynamics are incorporated by institutions in their governing tasks, but in ways that do not conflict with the arboreal state dynamics*. As was clear from the case of Norway, this merging of powers in the mediation service was done through *separation and subordination*, creating a reterritorialisation which in practice expands and enforces governance.

The problem, we argued, is not that there is an apparent exercise of state power in the mediation process, but rather, that this sort of power is unarticulated under the guise of neutral mediation between civil parties, and potentially more prone to higher governance, due to the higher compliance the restorative process can lead to, given its voluntary rhetoric. Through various examples, we also showed how projects in which the two types of power tend to conflict and challenge the *separation and subordination* model are prone to fail, as it is often the arboreal dynamics which controls and utilises the rhizomatic dynamics of RJ, and not the other way around, through a reterritorialisation and expansion of state control in decentralised justice processes.

Nevertheless, although briefly, we argued that such processes also offer specific opportunities for the parties, as governance leads always towards unexpected and unpredictable outcomes. In our empirical work (Foss, 2016; Pali, 2016), we elaborate such opportunities in more depth, both within the heart of the mediation processes and at a distance from them. Thus, although the tone in this chapter has been more critical, we think this is the first necessary step in articulating alternative ideas and processes, the understanding of existing forms of power and dynamics. Only on the basis of this knowledge can further normative steps follow towards an elaboration of what is possible and necessary. We would like to conclude our chapter by arguing strongly for the need for more extended empirical studies of both the intended and unintended *controlling* and *liberating* effects of various RJ implementations, not only state-financed evaluations but independent research.

Notes

1 Similarly, around 1968, when the social critique of exploitation and the artistic critique of alienation converged and challenged the mid-century bureaucratised capitalism, they conjointly produced a critique of the parties and trade unions of the old labour movements, aiding the neoliberal capitalism that emerged during the 1970s to recuperate into its own project the libertarian values and demands of 1968: fluidity, autonomy, creativity, hostility to bureaucracy and the like.

2 RJ has been articulated – especially in its beginnings – as a new paradigm of justice which challenges criminal justice mainly on three grounds: (a) by considering crime as, first of all, harmful for the people concerned rather than simply a breaking of the law and an abstract assault on society; (b) by insisting that those affected by crime must be given the power to participate, engage in a dialogue, and deliberate about and handle their own conflicts; (c) by asking that the harm caused must be repaired, through mending broken relations, offering reparations to the victims, and restoring a sense of security and justice, rather than applying punishment for the sake of inflicting pain.

3 The concept of the Panopticon – a type of institutional building designed by Jeremy Bentham in the late eighteenth century – is to allow a single watchman to observe all inmates of an institution without the inmates being able to tell whether or not they are

being watched. Although it is physically impossible for the watchman to observe all cells at once, the fact that the inmates cannot know when they are being watched means that they must act as though they are watched at all times, effectively controlling their own behaviour constantly. Foucault's analysis in *Discipline and punish* (1975) viewed the panopticon as a vast experiment and described how the subject was made to internalise particular forms of conduct, and how it conditioned subjects to be 'free'.

4 In *The great transformation*, Karl Polanyi ([1944] 2001) discusses the development of the idea of the free self-regulating market, arguing that the nation-state is not a consequence of or a reaction to the 'free market' but, rather, its key instrument. According to Polanyi's analysis, the economy and the market, and the state, are fundamentally intertwined, so that state forces fetishise the market at the same time as engaging in a restructuring of social orders so that the market can expand. According to Kapferer (2010), this dynamic sowed the seeds of a further transformation that accelerated after the Second World War up to the present *societies of control*.

5 While Foucault never thought of a clear chronological replacement of powers (sovereignty, discipline, government), he did make an analytical differentiation between the three rationalities trying to understand and characterise the changes taking place. Foucault warned that the new forms of powers should not be seen as the replacement of forms of societies but as coexisting (Foucault, 2007). Deleuze is less cautious of this 'warning' by characterising the displacement as 'societies of control', but nevertheless, the diagnosis he makes of the new mode of power is the same as identified by Foucault under his analysis of governmentality. If Foucault had coined a term that characterises a type of society, this would have been *societies of security* rather than societies of control. Thus, we have to understand the term 'societies of control' proposed by Deleuze as fitting the analysis that Foucault makes of the apparatus of security as the main technology of governmentality, targeting the population under the rationale of political economy. The gist of Foucault's argument is that freedom, naturalness and circulation are the core governmentalities of such societies, instead of confinement, or prohibition, and this must also be understood under the notion of Deleuzean control, which presents itself as a kind of freedom, but where everything is determined in reference to a certain code. According to Deleuze, we can move endlessly and still be perfectly controlled (Deleuze, 1987).

6 The notion of territory in Deleuze's work must be thought not only in terms of space, but in terms of signs. It corresponds closely to the problem of subjectivity or identity, which is constituted, assembled by a multiplicity of partial objects mainly through habit, and thus never stable. Likewise, deterritorialisation involves detaching a sign from its context of signification or a separation from a given purpose, and reterritorialisation then usually follows as a resignification or repurposing in another domain. Thinking in terms of capitalism, Deleuze and Guattari contend that deterritorialisation is at the heart of its logic: it disrupts forms of meaning, uproots people, desubstantialises work and reterritorialises it by reinscribing it in terms of money. This is also the main point about the notion of the societies of control, whereby rules have become fluid, but rather than freeing us from the structures of the territory of the state, the diffusion of power places us all the more under the control of the forces of capitalism. (For descriptions of similar dynamics related to consequences of the 'new capitalism', see Beck, 1992; Bauman, 1997; Sennett, 1998.)

7 The data analysed here were gathered by Espen Marius Foss (2016) during his PhD dissertation.

8 If both the offender and the offended in a criminal case agree to meet at the NMS, facilitated by a mediator, and reach a written agreement, which they manage to fulfil, the criminal charges are dropped. The police prosecutor (in Norway there is a prosecutor at local police level and a prosecutor at trial level) assesses whether a criminal case is suitable for alternative treatment in the NMS on the basis of the Mediation Act as well as circular letters from the Director of Public Prosecution. There is a large

variation in the cases referred to the NMS, in terms of both types and degrees of criminal offences. Normally, criminal cases will not be referred to the NMS as an *alternative to punishment* if the offence would lead to an unconditional prison sentence. An agreement will be in writing, and is signed by the parties and a legal guardian if one of the parties is under 18 years. If the agreement involves a settlement, there is a week's cancellation period in which the parties may change their minds after the agreement has been entered into. The mediator has the right and duty to refuse to approve an agreement which favours one of the parties to an unreasonable degree – or is unfavourable for other significant reasons. The mediation service's administration will send a copy of the agreement to the prosecution authority. If the agreement includes a deadline, the complainant shall inform the mediation service whether it has been met or broken, and the prosecuting authorities will be notified of the result. If the agreement is broken, the police can take up the case again and evaluate taking other penal actions. If the agreement is complied with, the case is over and done with. Criminal cases solved at the mediation service are not noted in the extracts from police records, but will be included in the police certificate of good conduct for two years. The note in the record is deleted after two years on condition that no new punishable offences are committed (available at www.konfliktraadet.no/other-languages.315050.no.html, accessed June 2016).

References

Abel, R. L., 1982. The contradictions of informal justice. In: R. Abel (ed.), *The politics of informal justice, volume 1, the American experience*, 267–320. New York: Academic.

Agamben, G., 2005. *State of exception*. Chicago: University of Chicago Press.

Agamben, G., 2014. From the state of control to a praxis of destituent power. Public lecture in Athens on 16 November 2013.

Baskin, D. R., 1988. Community mediation and the public/private problem. *Social Justice*, 15(1), pp. 98–115.

Bauman, Z., 1997. *Postmodernity and its discontents*. Cambridge: Polity.

Beck, U., 1992. *Risk society: Towards a new modernity*. London: Sage.

Braithwaite, J., 2000. The new regulatory state and the transformation of criminology. *British Journal of Criminology*, 4, pp. 222–238.

Braithwaite, J., 2002. *Restorative justice & responsive regulation*. New York: Oxford University Press.

Christie, N., 1977. *Konflikt som eiendom*. Oslo.

Christie, N., 2004. *A suitable amount of crime*. London: Routledge.

Christie, N., 2014. Farvel til konfliktrådene [Goodbye to the Norwegian Mediation Service]. In *Klassekampen* (newspaper), June 17. Also at: www.jus.uio.no/ikrs/tjenester/kunnskap/kriminalpolitikk/meninger/2014/farvel-til-konfliktradene.html (accessed 16 June 2017).

Crawford, A., 2006. Networked governance and the post-regulatory state? Steering, rowing and anchoring the provision of policing and security. *Theoretical Criminology*, 10(4), pp. 449–479.

Deleuze, G., 1987. What is the creative act? Lecture available at https://discordion.wordpress.com/2015/02/01/what-is-the-creative-act-gilles-deleuze-1987/ (accessed June 2016).

Deleuze, G., 2006. Postscript on the societies of control. In: D. Wilson and C. Norris (eds), *Surveillance, crime and social control*, 35–39. Aldershot: Ashgate.

Deleuze, G. and Guattari, F., 1987. *A thousand plateaus. Capitalism and schizophrenia*. Minneapolis: The University of Minnesota Press.

Deleuze, G. and Guattari F., 2004. *A thousand plateaus: Capitalism and schizophrenia*. London: Continuum.

Delgado, R., 1985. Fairness and formality: Minimizing the risk of prejudice in alternative dispute resolution. *Wisconsin Law Review*, 1359–1404.

Foss, E. M., 2016. *Dialogens paradoks. Framveksten av gjenopprettende prosesser i Norge*. [The dialogical paradox of the emergence of restorative justice in Norway]. PhD Dissertation, monograph. Oslo: University of Oslo.

Foucault, M., 1975 (original date, French edition, trans. A. Sheridan, 1995, 2nd edition). *Discipline and punish*. New York: Vintage.

Foucault, M., 1976. *The history of sexuality. Volume I. An introduction*. New York: Pantheon Books.

Foucault, M., 1991. Governmentality. In: G. Burchell, C. Gordon, and P. Miller (eds), *The Foucault effect: Studies in governmentality*, 87–104. Chicago: University of Chicago Press.

Foucault, M., 2007. *Security, territory, population. Lectures at the Collège de France, 1977–1978*. London: Palgrave Macmillan.

Foucault, M. and Rabinow, P., 1997. *The essential works of Michel Foucault, 1954–1984*. London: Allen Lane.

Harrington, C. B., 1985. *Shadow justice: The ideology and institutionalization of alternatives to court*. Westport, CT: Greenwood.

Hasund, I. K. and Hydle, I. (2007). *Ansikt til ansikt: konfliktrådsmegling mellom gjerningsperson og offer i voldssaker. [Face to face: Conflict mediation between perpetrator and victim in cases of violence]*. Oslo: Cappelen.

Hofrichter, R., 1982. Neighborhood justice and the social control problems of American capitalism: A perspective. In: A. Richard (ed.), *The politics of informal justice, volume 1, the American experience*, 207–243. New York: Academic.

Hofrichter, R., 1987. *Neighborhood justice in capitalist society: The expansion of the informal state*. New York: Greenwood.

Kapferer, B., 2010. The aporia of power: Crisis and the emergence of the corporate state. *Social Analysis* 54(1), pp. 125–151.

Kapferer, B. and Bertelsen, B. E., 2009. *Crisis of the state: War and social upheaval*. New York: Berghahn.

Majone, G., 1994. The rise of the regulatory state in Europe. *West European Politics*, 17, pp. 77–101.

Merry, S. E., 1982. Defining 'success' in the neighborhood justice movement. In: R. Tomasic and M. M. Feeley (eds), *Neighborhood justice: Assessment of an emerging idea*, 172–192. New York: Longman.

Moran, M., 2001. Not steering but drowning: Policy catastrophes and the regulatory state. *Political Quarterly*, 72, pp. 414–427.

Osborne, D. and Gaebler, T., 1992. *Reinventing government: How the entrepreneurial spirit is transforming the public sector*. New York: Addison-Wesley.

Pali, B., 2016. Doing restorative justice in intercultural contexts: An alternative discourse of justice and security. PhD Thesis. KU Leuven.

Pali, B. and Pelikan, C., 2014. Con-texting restorative justice and abolitionism: Exploring the potential and limits of restorative justice as an alternative discourse to criminal justice. *Restorative Justice: An International Journal*, 2(2), pp. 142–164.

Pavlich, G., 1996. *Justice fragmented: Mediating community disputes under postmodern conditions*. London: Routledge.

Pavlich, G., 2005. *Governing paradoxes of restorative justice*. London: Glasshouse.

Pelikan, C., 2003. Different systems different rationales: Restorative justice and criminal justice. In: F. M. Marques (ed.), *Apoio à Vitima, Project DIKÈ, Seminar: Protection and promotion of victim's rights in Europe*, 223–229. Lisbon: APAV.

Pelikan, C., 2007. The place of restorative justice in society: Making sense of developments in time and space. In: R. Mackay, M. Bosnjak, J. Deklerck, C. Pelikan, B. van Stokkom, and M. Wright (eds), *Images of restorative justice theory*, 35–56. Frankfurt/Main: Verlag für Polizeiwissenschaft.

Polanyi, K., [1944] 2001. *The great transformation: The political and economic origins of our time*. Boston: Beacon.

Richards, K., 2005. Unlikely friends? Oprah Winfrey and restorative justice. *Australian and New Zealand Journal of Criminology*, 38(3), pp. 381–399.

Rose, N. and Miller, P., 1992. Political power beyond the state: Problematics of government. *British Journal of Sociology*, 43, pp. 173–205.

Santos, B. d. S., 1982. Law and community: The changing nature of state power in late capitalism. In R. Abel (ed.), *The politics of informal justice*, 249–266. New York: Academic.

Selva, L. H. and Bohm, R. M., 1987. A critical examination of the in-formalism experiment in the administration of justice. *Crime and Social Justice*, 29, pp. 43–56.

Sennett, R., 1998. *The corrosion of character: The personal consequences of work in the new capitalism*. New York: W.W. Norton.

Shearing, C. D., 2001. Punishment and the changing face of the governance. *Punishment and Society*, 3(2), pp. 203–220.

Tomasic, R., 1982. Mediation as an alternative to adjudication: Rhetoric and reality in the neighborhood justice movement. In: R. Tomasic and M. Feeley (eds), *Neighborhood justice: Assessment of an emerging idea*, 251–248. New York: Longman.

Van Ness, D. W., 1986. *Crime and its victims*. Downers Grove, IL: Intervarsity Press.

Van Ness, D. and Heetderks-Strong, K., 2002. *Restoring justice*. 2nd edition. Cincinnati, OH: Anderson.

Walgrave, L., 2008. *Restorative justice, self-interest and responsible citizenship*. Cullompton: Willan.

12 Looking at the European policy level

The place of restorative justice in intercultural environments

Edit Törzs, Katrien Lauwaert and Ivo Aertsen

Introduction

Dealing with Europe's increasing cultural diversity in a democratic manner has become a pressing need. Cultural diversity is rooted in the history of the European continent, but has increased significantly in the context of globalisation. People are moving in and out of Europe, but also relocating within Europe. People move for job opportunities or family-related reasons. Newcomers try to escape wars, persecution, or difficult economic and political situations in their home countries or regions.

At the European political level, and specifically with regard to incoming refugees, EU officials call for a united and integrated response, but at the same time, Member States have great difficulties in coming up with a common and coherent plan. The language used, including in official statements, regularly betrays an implicit – and sometimes explicit – perception of refugees as a threat.

Political reactions by Member States diverge, ranging from a '*wir schaffen das*' attitude, through 'we will accept some of them but they will have to make do with an inferior social status', to building walls and enforcing borders to keep refugees out. Political discourse regularly mixes references to immigration and crime, and immigration and terrorism, thus spreading a stigma of danger and undesirability over whole groups of newcomers. Right-wing politicians make use of terrorist attacks to proliferate an alarmist language by speaking of their country as being in 'a war of cultures' and a 'war of religions', thus polarising society and even inciting hatred among culturally diverse communities.

Reactions within the population are equally divided. Volunteer citizens get organised in impressive ways, but at the same time also organise protest marches against refugees and, even worse, violent attacks on centres for asylum seekers. Opinion polls show that the coming of immigrants and refugees induces fear and anxiety in a significant part of the European populations: fear that crime will rise, that the newcomers will take their jobs, fear of their culture being threatened by foreign cultures. The Brexit campaign in the UK (2016) has shown horrible examples of how these fears can be politically (mis)used. It is clear that Europe is still far from being a land of immigration (Melossi, 2013), in which the movement of incoming and outgoing groups becomes natural and the blending of diverse cultural groups does not provoke anxiety, but can be seen as an enrichment.

Recent policy developments are mainly the product of looking at the issues involved through a securitisation lens. The illegal aspects of immigration and the role of human trafficking are emphasised, not the human conditions and the social, economic and political causes of migration. Therefore, the reaction is predominantly focused on containment, keeping the problem or threat under control. This approach risks contributing to an atmosphere of distrust and anxiety and further polarisation within our societies.

The ALTERNATIVE project[1] opted for a different approach and feeds in to movements working bottom up, at the grass-roots level, to deal with these situations with a focus on inclusion, participation and dialogue between the people directly concerned at the local level. Restorative justice approaches try to do just that: creating spaces for equal and safe participation with a view to building or restoring trust and using dialogue to resolve conflicts which have arisen.[2] The baseline assumption is that through contact and dialogue, fear among people will decrease and trust will increase. That will lead to less (feelings of) insecurity for individuals and local communities. In the ALTERNATIVE project, this approach has been tried out through action research at the micro, macro and meso levels. It has become clear that this is a promising strategy, but involves processes which are organic and slow.

One of the most important lessons learned from ALTERNATIVE, and also from the introduction of restorative justice in other contexts, such as schools or prisons, concerns the necessity of creating a receptive context for such an approach. One cannot just introduce dialogue, mediation and so on as standalone methods. These methods can only be implemented fruitfully if a context of mutual respect is in place. Key to the further development of the ALTERNATIVE approach is, therefore, the development of a policy context which is supportive of this approach.

In this chapter, we explore existing references to European policies and actions which are supportive of this alternative lens for looking at current developments and of alternative approaches based on restorative justice values. Supportive policies might be crucial for these approaches to take root in society and become sustainable. Speaking about 'European policies', we will refer to EU policies as well as Council of Europe (CoE) policies. This chapter is, nevertheless, neither an evaluation of EU and CoE policies, nor an exhaustive list of supportive policies. The different fields our theme relates to are far too complex and broad to achieve that. Indeed, if we try to answer the question of which European policies support this approach, we need to address different fields of policy. It is a transversal topic at the crossroads of different policy areas of the EU and the CoE. The chapter touches upon the areas of security, crime prevention, restorative justice, migration, inclusion and integration, and intercultural cities. We will deal with strictly legislative policies, but also with more informal, civil society-oriented ones. Some of the policies are shown to be pillars of support, while others appear, rather, as obstacles. Some policies address methods one can use (such as dialogue, mediation …), while others are important because they influence the climate necessary for introducing new approaches.

EU policies on security, migration and integration

The EU (more precisely, the former Communities) focused initially on economic integration and on the creation of a common market. Over time, the basic principles that served this goal, namely the free movement of persons, products, services and capital, were improved. However, it is often claimed that the free movement and, in addition, the elimination of internal EU border controls opened up new opportunities for crime and for the easy movement of criminals. In turn, this called for enhanced cooperation at the EU level (Joutsen, 2006, p. 7), which led to the development of the EU's competence and policy development in the so-called 'Area of Freedom, Security and Justice' (AFSJ). Even though it is today one of the most prominent policy fields of the EU, there is no definition of the concepts of 'freedom', 'security' and 'justice' within the AFSJ (Kaczorowska, 2013, p. 937). As Kaczorowska argues, the concepts of freedom as well as justice are linked to the concept of security, the latter being dominant in this policy area.

Security

As a fundamental part of the AFSJ, the EU's Internal Security Strategy (ISS) – adopted in March 2010 – constituted a shared agenda for tackling common security challenges.[3] The Commission's Communication of November 2010, 'The EU Internal Security Strategy in Action: Five steps towards a more secure Europe',[4] translates the strategy's principles and guidelines into concrete actions.

It is interesting to note that the strategy reflects on the fundamental rights aspects of the security strategy, highlighting, among other things, dialogue as means of resolving differences in accordance with the principles of tolerance, respect and freedom of expression, as well as integration, social inclusion and the fight against discrimination, as key elements for EU internal security (ISS, p. 20). However, in the text of the action plan itself, only a short paragraph refers to the need to respect the EU Charter of Fundamental Rights. The text fails to mention dialogue, respect, tolerance, social inclusion or discrimination. Moreover, while the action plan clearly states the need for a solid EU security industry, the strategy does not reflect on this aspect of security in the EU. Furthermore, in 2012, the European Commission (EC) adopted a Security Industrial Policy and Action Plan. These observations might well illustrate the twofold picture of security policies in Europe. While in the strategy there is a high emphasis on fundamental rights, in reality, when operationalised, security policies are highly influenced by the logic of the security industry and technology. However, the fact that the strategy calls for dialogue and mentions integration and social inclusion as key elements for internal security can be seen as an acknowledgement of the importance of approaches beyond technology, and supports the approach followed in the ALTERNATIVE project.

Concerning radicalisation, the ISS proposes to address radicalisation because it can lead to acts of terrorism. A new element of the approach to terrorism is the consideration of social processes and reasons behind radicalisation. The Commission proposes interventions that aim to prevent the process of radicalisation and highlight the importance of ongoing support for local community-based approaches and prevention policies.[5]

While the operationalisation of the ISS showed the dominance of the security lens, a change in the language used concerning migration was noticeable in the following years. However, the recent migratory movement (more than one million people arrived at the EU seeking asylum in 2015[6]) and the terrorist attacks (e.g. November 2015 in Paris, March 2016 in Brussels and July 2016 in Nice) have again been strongly linked to security in the political discourse in Europe.

The Fundamental Rights Agency (FRA) of the EU – to counterbalance this strong security-focused approach – suggested in 2015 that a fundamental rights-based approach should be taken when developing a new European Agenda on Security (adopted in April 2015)[7] and noted that 'Poorly designed security policies that are perceived as targeting an entire community rather than individual suspects can further exacerbate the problem.'[8] Related to the topic of prevention of radicalisation, the FRA called for a comprehensive approach to combatting terrorist threats, which 'needs to look beyond law enforcement measures to the prevention of radicalisation by measures that support social inclusion and participation.'[9]

This line of thinking was shared by the Justice and Home Affairs ministers in their Joint Statement from Riga (January 2015), in which they emphasised the importance of promoting a culture of social inclusion and tolerance as a means of addressing the underlying factors of radicalisation.[10]

In the same vein, an EC communication entitled 'Preventing Radicalisation to Terrorism and Violent Extremism: Strengthening the EU's Response' – published on 15 January 2014 together with a collection of approaches compiled by RAN (Radicalisation Awareness Network)[11] – had already explicitly mentioned intercultural dialogue and personal exchanges as potential ways to develop resilience to extremist propaganda. The RAN publication lists and explains several useful methods and strategies as well as best practices to break down and tackle violent extremism. The document lists among the key strategies 'bridging gaps through dialogue' as well as 'community engagement and empowerment'.[12]

The 2015 European Agenda on Security states that 'education, youth participation, interfaith and intercultural dialogue, as well as employment and social inclusion, have a key role to play in preventing radicalisation by promoting common European values, fostering social inclusion, enhancing mutual understanding and tolerance'.[13]

Migration

When looking at EU policy development in the field of migration and integration, a move from a strong security-based approach to a more balanced approach can be traced.

The Maastricht Treaty (1992) created the 'Justice and Home Affairs' pillar, in which it put together migration with other law enforcement issues, such as terrorism and organised crime (Babayan, 2010, p. 20). The Vienna Action Plan in 1998 explicitly linked migration policies to security, especially to the security of European citizens, with a hidden assumption that non-Europeans pose a security threat: 'to ensure increased security for all European citizens, achieving this objective requires accompanying measures to be drawn up, particularly in the areas of external border controls and the combating of illegal immigration'.[14] Babayan (2010, p. 7) notes that since the Seville European Council in 2002 – probably under the influence of the 2001 terror attacks – the 'securitisation' of migration has intensified. The phrase 'migration flow' became commonly used in the EU discourse on migration, associating migration with a flux, which needs management and control. In Seville, the idea of urgency entered the discourse, and 'together with terrorism illegal immigration became represented as an issue that needs to be "combated"' (Babayan, 2010, p. 21). Melossi (2013, p. 125), referring to the fact that migrants are overrepresented in the EU countries' criminal justice systems, argues that immigration policies oriented towards exclusion, and the irregular legal status of immigrants, are the most important reason for their criminalisation.

A couple of years later, however, we can trace changes in the EU policy development, towards a more balanced approach. The Communication from the Commission on Policy Priorities in the fight against illegal immigration of third-country nationals (2006)[15] draws attention to the fact that linking immigration to societal problems might have undesirable consequences in society, leading to racism and xenophobia. In 2005 a new policy framework, the Global Approach to Migration and Mobility, was launched, which can be defined as the new external dimension of the EU's migration policy. The Communication of the Commission[16] in 2008 explains its essence, while explicitly mentioning the security-oriented approach of its previous policies.

In 2010, the new lines of communication about migration could be explicitly seen. According to the action plan implementing the Stockholm Programme (2010),[17]

> immigration has a valuable role to play in addressing the Union's demographic challenge and in securing the EU's strong economic performance over the longer term. It has great potential to contribute to the Europe 2020 strategy, by providing an additional source of dynamic growth.

Also, while in 2006 'fight against illegal immigration' was the terminology used, the term 'irregular(ly staying) immigrant' came to the fore later, and the strategies of 'fight' were replaced by those with more sophisticated terminology.

The previous wording also added to the misinterpretation that the EU is at war with immigrants, whereas the policy is clearly aimed at the phenomenon of irregular immigration and not against the immigrant persons themselves. However, this previous rhetoric might have contributed to the growing negative attitudes towards immigrants in general across Europe. The fact that the concept of 'migrant' is linked to criminality is proven by the Qualitative Eurobarometer on Migrant Integration published in 2011,[18] which found that 'for many general public participants there is a strong association with migrants and criminal activities (such as acquiring visas illegally, evading tax, involvement in corrupt business activities and so on)' (p. 6).

Now, it seems that the EU aims to tackle these consequences with measures adopted against racism, as well as by more intensively communicating the added economic and cultural value immigrants bring to Europe.[19] What could further improve the situation is, as Melossi (2013, p. 133) suggests, the *regulation* of migration as the focus of policy making in Europe. However, in the external dimension of this policy area, the double rhetoric of the opposing logics of inclusion and exclusion remains.

To summarise, although new developments seem to be more supportive towards immigration, migration policies are still intertwined with concepts of security, protection, threat, risk and control. The new EU agencies, such as Frontex and the European Asylum Support Office (EASO), put a strong emphasis on technological development of efficient control. Referring to Bigo and Carrera (2004), Babayan (2010, p. 22) notes that '[t]echnology became to be presented at the EU official level as the "solution to every security threat, as an ultra-solution to the permanent state of fear"'. The setting up of the Eurosur, a pan-European border surveillance system, in December 2013, with the aim of preventing illegal migration and cross-border crime, might well demonstrate this emphasis. Although the EU stresses the importance of fundamental rights of migrants and asylum seekers, the national implementation of these measures is often insufficient (Melossi, 2013, p. 135). As Melossi (2013, p. 140) phrases his view on Europe, 'If we consider the reality of today's *European* policies of migration and border control, we seem to be quite far away from the ideal of Europe, and the EU, as a "land of immigration" ' (italics in original).

Even if recent EU documents emphasise the importance of intercultural dialogue and other inclusive and participatory, bottom-up approaches, the picture is still twofold. On 14 June 2016, the EC presented further steps to build on the security agenda to better tackle violent radicalisation leading to terrorism, which, again, calls for a focus on the security dimension and suggests more repressive measures.[20]

EU policies to support integration

Although the multi-annual programmes of the ASFJ had set out aims concerning the integration of migrants since 1999, it was not until the Lisbon Treaty in 2009 that this matter got a clear legal reference at the treaty level. The Common Basic Principles for Immigrant Integration Policy in the EU[21] (2004) forms the foundations of EU initiatives in the field of integration. Principle 7 states that

> Frequent interaction between immigrants and Member State citizens is a fundamental mechanism for integration. Shared forums, intercultural dialogue, education about immigrants and immigrant cultures, and stimulating

> living conditions in urban environments enhance the interactions between immigrants and Member State citizens

and Principle 8 that 'The practice of diverse cultures and religions is guaranteed under the Charter of Fundamental Rights and must be safeguarded, unless practices conflict with other inviolable European rights or with national law.'

The Basic Principles 'underline that integration is a dynamic, two-way process of mutual accommodation by migrants and by the societies that receive them'.[22] As Agustín (2012) notes, '[a]lthough it is defined as a two-way process, integration consists mainly of immigrants learning the norms and culture of host societies'. The two concepts of integration and inclusion, even if often used as synonyms, do not have the same meaning. While integration means that a person or a group labelled as different can participate in and adapt to a 'normal' setting and be helped to achieve this, inclusion accepts diversity as the normal situation and as a rich source for all, while accommodating different cultures, needs and styles and acting for the benefit of all (not targeting explicitly those with a significant difference). To put it more concretely, while integration helps the 'different' to adapt to the mainstream, inclusion requires adaptation on all sides for a successful coexistence. Integration is often seen as the first step to inclusion (for a detailed explanation of the two concepts, see Vislie, 2003). In this respect, the concept of inclusion instead of integration could be more useful to lead the EU project and agenda.

To support the implementation of the Basic Principles, the Commission presented a Common Agenda for Integration[23] in 2005, which proposed measures to be taken both at the national and at the EU level, including facilitating interaction between immigrants and the host society, developing constructive intercultural dialogue and thoughtful public discourse, and promoting inter- and intra-faith dialogue platforms between religious communities and/or between communities and policy-making authorities. Although intercultural dialogue is an important element in the texts, its actual realisation and the way it should be promoted and practised remained unclear.

The integration policy has been further framed by the Stockholm Programme and received a significant boost in 2011, when the Commission proposed a new European Agenda for the Integration of Third-Country Nationals[24] accompanied by the aforementioned working document, entitled 'EU initiatives supporting the integration of third-country nationals'.[25] The new European Agenda focuses on three main policy priorities highlighting that integration is a shared responsibility: participation, actions at the local level, and involvement of countries of origin. The European Agenda states that the actions set out in 2005 have been completed; however, not all the measures have been successful in meeting their objectives. In this respect, it underlines the importance of the will and commitment of migrants to be part of the society that receives them. If we do not see this latter statement as a blaming of migrants for not being cooperative enough, at least we can deduce that measures that engage migrant persons more actively should be further developed.

While the European Agenda stresses the importance of a genuine 'bottom-up' approach, close to the local level, most of the measures proposed need a 'top-down' approach from the Member States when it comes to implementation. When the Commission calls for more action at the local level, it does not mention local non-governmental organisations (NGOs) or other local non-profit organisations whose role, besides that of the local authorities, might be crucial. In this respect, the local action research in four countries in the ALTERNATIVE project brought useful insights about the key actors at a local level, as well as best practices on how to engage them when dealing with conflicts in intercultural settings. The accompanying document to the European Agenda on different EU initiatives provides information about the understanding of intercultural dialogue which, according to the document, needs to accompany and support economic and social integration. This is the only source that mentions intercultural conflicts and that these, when dealt with by dialogue, can be sources of further common understanding.

The possible use of restorative approaches is underlined by the European Integration Modules[26] too. Designed to help local policy making, these Modules serve as flexible reference frameworks that can be adapted to the different contexts of Member States in order to contribute to successful integration policies and practices across Europe. The Modules contain some important references to initiatives where restorative approaches could contribute, such as the improvement of the public perception of migrants, or intercultural dialogue. They also refer to intercultural mediation, which can be described as a special form of social work. The intercultural mediator's aim is to mediate between members of specific groups in fields such as education or health. An example is a situation between migrants and public service providers, in which the mediator both facilitates the migrants' increased access to services and facilitates the service providers in accommodating the migrants. Having the trust of both sides is, therefore, crucial. As for the process, the document states:

> The mediation process is based on the principle that people with different backgrounds may have different needs, exhibit cultural differences and see things differently. Such a principle provides scope for clearly identifying problematic issues, breaking down communication barriers, exploring possible solutions and, should the parties decide on such a course of action, arriving at a solution satisfactory to both parties.
>
> (European modules on migrant integration, European Commission DG HOME, 2014, p. 68)

This is in line with the aim and approach of restorative practices. In the ALTERNATIVE project, mediation or other restorative processes mainly involved fellow citizens, and the dialogues were centred around conflicts in which all the participants had a stake. In this way, restorative approaches may contribute to widening the scope of interventions and offer restorative services for individuals, such as neighbours, or for local communities, who perceive their conflict as having an intercultural element.

The most recent policy document regarding integration is the 'Action Plan on the Integration of Third-Country Nationals' issued on 7 June 2016.[27] It raises attention to the fact that well-integrated migrants contribute to economic development, even if their proper integration requires resources and time. The main focus of the new action plan is on housing, education and labour market (similar to the fields of action regarding Roma inclusion), but it also aims at active participation and social inclusion. The concrete actions proposed in this latter topic, are, however disappointing, limiting intercultural dialogue to culture and arts, and social inclusion mostly to sports and to programmes for the young. Actions aimed at the host societies are limited, and they only concern preventing discrimination and hate crime. One of the main focuses of the European Agenda for the Integration of Third-Country Nationals (2011) was to support more actions on the local level, while this is completely missing from the new Action Plan (2016). Inclusive ways of dealing with issues and conflicts, especially on the local level, are also not tackled; this, we believe, would be an important element for creating tolerant and inclusive societies.

One final remark concerning integration policies is that while they focus on the integration of non-EU country nationals, intra-EU mobility of EU citizens might also raise questions of integration or inclusion. Although perceived cultural differences might seem less large, some challenges are the same: lack of language competences, employment under their skills level, differences in lifestyles and, sometimes, inhospitable attitudes from the host country citizens. Therefore, the extension of the availability of integration practices to all non-national persons should be striven for within the EU.

European policies related to restorative justice in intercultural settings

In order for restorative justice to develop into a mainstream approach to prevent and deal with conflict in intercultural settings, the sector still has to grow considerably. Restorative justice in Europe started as a grass-roots movement in the 1980s. Its implementation at the national level was most successful in those countries that allowed a consistent bottom-up development, supported by legislation at the right moment. Regulation at the supranational level (UN, CoE and EU) reinforced the movement, influencing but not taking over the process in most countries (Aertsen, 2007; Dünkel *et al.*, 2015). There is no doubt that to a certain extent – in Europe – CoE and EU policies have been supportive of this approach. However, the potential of restorative justice in general, in a quantitative way, is underused, notwithstanding the legal basis that mediation and other restorative justice practices have acquired in most European countries (Dünkel *et al.*, 2015; Miers and Aertsen, 2012). Therefore, the possibly decisive role of European institutions 'to make a difference' has to be investigated (Willemsens, 2008).

In what follows, we will first summarise the currently applicable CoE and EU policies on restorative justice in general, and we will point out strengths and weaknesses of their regulations. Then, we will focus on some – less formalised – CoE and EU initiatives in the area of conflict in intercultural environments, whereby we try to understand what meaningful contribution restorative justice could offer in these contexts.

European policies on restorative justice: from Council of Europe to European Union

First, the CoE has supported the restorative justice movement in Europe since the 1980s, but has become somewhat more cautious in the recent past. The most important achievement is without doubt the adoption of Recommendation No R (99) 19 on 'Mediation in Penal Matters' by the Committee of Ministers in September 1999 (Aertsen *et al.*, 2004).[28] At a European level, this remains the most elaborated set of guidelines, although legally not binding. It sets out guidelines concerning the voluntariness of the process and its outcome, the principle of confidentiality, the role of the criminal justice actors, the legal basis and procedural safeguards, the need for taking into account the outcome of the process in the criminal justice procedure, the role of minimum standards and codes of conduct for mediators, the importance of training, and the general rules concerning the operation of mediation services. The content of this almost 20 years old, non-binding instrument still stands the test of time (Lauwaert, 2013, p. 416). Consecutive evaluations confirm the strong influence the recommendation had on practice and implementation of mediation in criminal matters in Europe, but also reveal large differences between countries (Lhuillier, 2007; Pelikan, 2003). Based on the study by Lhuillier, the CoE Commission for the Efficiency of Justice (CEPEJ) formally adopted guidelines for a better implementation of the existing recommendation concerning mediation in penal matters in 2007, in which, among other things, cooperation in certain topics with the EU was suggested.[29] After this work, the CoE unfortunately became less active in the area of mediation/restorative justice in criminal cases.

On the side of the EU, policy on restorative justice was developed in line with victim support initiatives. As early as 1999, in its Communication on Crime Victims in the European Union: Reflections on Standards and Action,[30] the Commission proposed the use of mediation, especially in property crime cases, and called for more research and pilot projects on mediation and its possible effects on the interests of the crime victims. The first EU legislative act on restorative justice was adopted in 2001, namely the 2001/220/JHA Council Framework Decision of 15 March 2001 on the standing of victims in criminal proceedings. Its Article 10 stipulated that Member States shall seek to promote mediation in criminal cases for offences which they consider appropriate for this sort of measure, and they shall ensure that any agreement between the victim and the offender reached in the course of such mediation in criminal cases can be taken into account. Soon after the Framework Decision, an initiative of Belgium aimed at the adoption of a Council Decision setting up a European network of national contact points for restorative justice.[31] The European Parliament approved this initiative; however, after it was sent over to the Council, it was not further discussed (Willemsens, 2008, p. 92).

While new legislative steps have been taken at the EU level in the field of criminal justice, for more than a decade no new legislation was adopted at the EU level concerning restorative justice. However, the EU's supportive role towards restorative justice can be traced in other measures during this period as part of the Criminal Justice Support Programme between 2007 and 2013, such as supporting networking and the development of guidelines and training for practitioners, and funding of a large number of projects around specific topics.[32]

The weak implementation of the 2001 Framework Decision and the new legislative tools provided by the Lisbon Treaty were among the main reasons why the EU pursued a new legislative act concerning the rights of crime victims, which resulted in the Directive 2012/29/EU of the European Parliament and of the Council of 25 October 2012 establishing minimum standards on the rights, support and protection of victims of crime (Directive), replacing the Framework Decision 2001/220/JHA. It is important to highlight the change of the terminology, as in the Directive restorative justice is mentioned instead of mediation. This is in line with the generally accepted understanding of the concept of restorative justice, namely as representing a certain approach and vision, rather than just standing for a specific method. The broadening of the concept is also an acknowledgement of the development of the practice of restorative justice in Europe beyond mediation, including different models such as conferencing and circles. Nevertheless, within Europe, victim–offender mediation is by far the most important expression of restorative justice (Dünkel *et al.*, 2015).

The Directive's provisions concerning restorative justice were analysed critically by Lauwaert (2013), pointing to the fact that the Directive falls short in promoting restorative justice and in establishing a *right to access* of restorative justice services. Looking at the concrete provisions concerning restorative justice, the Directive ensures the right of victims to receive information on restorative justice services from the first contact with a competent authority. Concerning the safeguards in the context of restorative justice, the Directive highlights two basic principles of restorative justice: voluntariness and confidentiality. A new, but important, rule of the Directive – following the example and formulation of the CoE 1999 Recommendation – is that restorative justice will only be possible if the offender acknowledges the basic facts of the case (Article 12.1 (c)). The connection between restorative justice processes and the criminal justice procedure – a link which was already made in the Framework Decision – is ensured by a relatively weak regulation in the Directive, formulated as that agreements reached in restorative processes 'may be taken into account in any further criminal proceedings'. Besides these important aspects of restorative justice being regulated in a binding EU legislation, the Directive implies that safeguards and protection of victims are the most important aspects to be regulated in restorative justice (Pali, 2016).

To summarise, first, it can be noted that restorative justice within the EU is clearly linked to and approached from the perspective of victim policies. While the Directive states that restorative justice can be beneficial for victims of crime

(Recital 46), the possible benefits of restorative justice for the offenders and for communities are not reflected in this EU legislation. Restorative justice is an approach that aims to find balance between the victim and the offender of a crime. In spite of this, the EU legal instruments concerning the rights of the accused do not focus on restorative justice at all. For example, the Directive 2012/13/EU on the right to information in criminal proceedings establishes minimum rules concerning the information suspects or accused persons have the right to receive, without mentioning information concerning available restorative justice processes.

A second observation is that restorative justice in the EU policies is clearly limited to the field of criminal justice (notwithstanding the EU initiative on mediation in civil matters), while – as we argue in the ALTERNATIVE project (see Foss *et al.*, 2012; Campbell *et al.*, 2013) – the use of restorative approaches should be broadened, as they prove beneficial in conflicts and tensions which are outside the criminal justice sphere, especially in involving affected persons who do not have a clearly defined role as an offender or a victim (or supporter) according to criminal law.

We may also notice that even if the EU aims to broaden the field of mutual recognition and harmonisation of national criminal law, the way restorative justice processes are accessible and how their outcomes are taken into consideration in the criminal procedure have not yet been subject to these harmonising regulations. Therefore, cross-border restorative justice cases still might be difficult to deal with at the level of the Member States.

Finally, despite the limited attention given to restorative justice approaches in formal EU policy documents so far, it is to be expected that the topic will not disappear from the EU agenda in the near future. A discussion paper presented at the 'Assises de la justice', a forum on the future of EU justice policies held in November 2013 in Brussels, presented a clearly supportive stance concerning the future of restorative justice.'[33]

European initiatives in intercultural environments

Intercultural dialogue

The idea of intercultural dialogue emerged within the context of CoE policies in the mid-1990s (Agustín, 2012). Of particular interest is the CoE White Paper on Intercultural Dialogue (2008), which stimulates cross-cultural exchange and debate and emphasises the importance of work done at the local level.[34] According to the White Paper, 'Intercultural dialogue is critical to the construction of a new social and cultural model for a fast-changing Europe, allowing everyone living within our culturally diverse societies to enjoy human rights and fundamental freedoms' (White Paper, p. 51). The White Paper (p. 17) provides a clear definition of intercultural dialogue and its objectives:

> For the purpose of this White Paper, intercultural dialogue is understood as a process that comprises an open and respectful exchange of views between

> individuals and groups with different ethnic, cultural, religious and linguistic backgrounds and heritage, on the basis of mutual understanding and respect. It requires the freedom and ability to express oneself, as well as the willingness and capacity to listen to the views of others. Intercultural dialogue contributes to political, social, cultural and economic integration and the cohesion of culturally diverse societies. It fosters equality, human dignity and a sense of common purpose. It aims to develop a deeper understanding of diverse world views and practices, to increase co-operation and participation (or the freedom to make choices), to allow personal growth and transformation, and to promote tolerance and respect for the other.

The White Paper continues (p. 17) stressing the complicated and challenging nature of intercultural dialogue:

> There is no question of easy solutions. Intercultural dialogue is not a cure for all evils and an answer to all questions, and one has to recognise that its scope can be limited. It is often pointed out, rightly, that dialogue with those who refuse dialogue is impossible, although this does not relieve open and democratic societies of their obligation to constantly offer opportunities for dialogue. On the other hand, dialogue with those who are ready to take part in dialogue but do not – or do not fully – share 'our' values may be the starting point of a longer process of interaction, at the end of which an agreement on the significance and practical implementation of the values of human rights, democracy and the rule of law may very well be reached.

The White Paper formulates five policy approaches to the promotion of intercultural dialogue, structured along the following axes: democratic governance of cultural diversity; democratic citizenship and participation; learning and teaching intercultural competences; spaces for intercultural dialogue; and intercultural dialogue in international relations. Each of these domains results in a list of recommendations and policy orientations for future action. To create spaces for intercultural dialogue, for example, 'civil-society organisations in particular, including religious communities, are invited to provide the organisational framework for intercultural and interreligious encounters' (p. 46).

Agustín (2012) interprets the policy of the CoE related to intercultural dialogue as having a focus on conflict prevention and being indirectly linked with security:

> The CoE interprets the challenge of dealing with cultural diversity in terms of the opposition between the universal and the particular, and it is seeking a way to reconcile the need for social cohesion with the value of diversity. Assuming that globalisation has increased both diversity and insecurity, the CoE aims to manage cultural diversity, which means being able to predict and solve cultural conflicts.

In our view, restorative justice approaches fit in this framework, as they offer the possibility to engage stakeholders voluntarily in a respectful dialogue on conflicts led by a neutral mediator. Restorative encounters can empower participants, lead to common understanding, enable participants to make their choices, restore relationships and prevent future conflicts.

Intercultural cities

The intercultural dialogue approach is confirmed in the CoE and EU joint initiative on Intercultural Cities.[35] This initiative promotes intercultural mediation for conflict resolution among its proposed strategies (Wood, 2009, p. 63). The Commission's working document on EU initiatives supporting the integration of third-country nationals[36] refers to the Intercultural Cities initiative concerning the issue of conflicts: 'Management of intercultural conflict, which is often inevitable, is also at the centre of such strategies. Handled well, it can lead to mutual learning and growth for all participants, including city authorities' (p. 24). According to the CoE Opatija Declaration on Intercultural Dialogue and Conflict Prevention (2003, point 2.4),[37] creating a public space for dialogue and allowing the expression of disagreement is not only part of the democratic process but also its guarantee. Indeed, not only disagreements or conflicts, but also not providing space for safe and open dialogue, can lead to negative consequences. In the CoE White Paper on Intercultural Dialogue (2008, p. 16), this is explained clearly:

> The risks of non-dialogue need to be fully appreciated. Not to engage in dialogue makes it easy to develop a stereotypical perception of the other, build up a climate of mutual suspicion, tension and anxiety, use minorities as scapegoats, and generally foster intolerance and discrimination. The breakdown of dialogue within and between societies can provide, in certain cases, a climate conducive to the emergence, and the exploitation by some, of extremism and indeed terrorism. Intercultural dialogue, including on the international plane, is indispensable between neighbours.

More recently, one of the ten themes in the portfolio of the EC Directorate-General Migration and Home Affairs is the 'Europe for citizens programme'. The programme facilitates activities supporting democratic engagement and civic participation, 'getting citizens involved'. For 2016, one of the priorities under this strand of supported activities was 'combatting stigmatisation of "immigrants" and building counter narratives to foster intercultural dialogue and mutual understanding'.[38] The activities are channelled through town twinning, networks of towns and civil society projects.[39] In 2016, for example, funds were awarded for a civil society project called 'Restorative Circles for Citizens in Europe'.[40]

Conclusions

This chapter provided an overview of European policies in the field of security, migration, integration, restorative justice and dealing with intercultural environments, with particular attention to policies supporting or impeding constructive approaches for dealing with conflicts in intercultural settings, based on restorative justice principles.

It has become clear that the EU policies provide few direct 'keys' of support for restorative justice approaches to dealing with conflict in intercultural contexts specifically, and that they reflect ambivalent positions in the fields we scanned. The CoE's policies are – because of its history and aims – more experienced and seem more coherent in this respect, although we have to note that the continent's leading human rights organisation's focus, role, and political and legal influence are different from those of the EU.

The most striking thing is undoubtedly the difficulty to European policy makers of developing coherent policies in the fields addressed here. There is a yawning gap and strong tension between the hostile attitude underlying the dominating security lens, which colours migration policies, and the constructive views reflected in promising initiatives concerning intercultural dialogue and intercultural cities, for example. This creates, one may contend in a friendly analysis, confusion in citizens' minds, with policy makers blowing hot and cold. Through a more critical lens, we see European policy makers operating in an ambivalent and perhaps hypocritical spirit, asking their citizens' support for being tough on immigration – or, at best, allowing it when it benefits our European demography and economy – and, on the other hand, receiving newcomers and working with existing cultural minorities through constructive intercultural dialogue.

It should be clear that a securitisation attitude towards immigration – connecting immigration to security threats, illegality and crime – influences citizens' perception of newcomers and minorities. Little importance is given to discourses of positive safety, rather than security in terms of protection against threats. References to fundamental rights in European policy documents, and actions aimed at the prevention of discrimination and hate crime, are important, but not enough to counterbalance the effects described above. A strictly fundamental rights-based approach may influence the expected changes to become reality only in the long run.

In the field of conflicts within intercultural settings, preventing discrimination and providing better access to justice tackle only the tip of the iceberg, as they only apply to situations in which conflicts have already escalated. National and EU-level policies should support the development of mechanisms to identify low-level conflicts in intercultural settings and to create channels to bring these to the attention of restorative justice professionals, who can then intervene. This is only possible if cooperation is stimulated between local civil society and restorative facilitators.

It is crucial that the EU adopts a different mindset on intercultural issues, and shows the courage to conceive and implement constructive policies in a systematic way, on the basis of the in-depth expertise that is clearly available. Those policies should target not only migrants but also the host societies. Offering restorative justice approaches for conflicts in intercultural settings clearly could be part of these constructive policies. Moreover, for the restorative interventions to be fruitful, they have to land on fertile ground. Creating receptive communities implies a firm and sustained support for restorative justice principles and values at policy level, and training in non-violent communication for community and educational workers.

Additionally, restorative justice facilitators should be up to meeting high quality standards in their work. Working in intercultural contexts brings additional complexity, and therefore support to the restorative justice field is needed in terms of providing resources, including funding and training for practitioners. Such policy development is best done bottom-up, with the active participation of practitioners, using their first-hand knowledge and experience. Moreover, such processes should be guided by the outcomes of monitoring and evaluation on existing practices and further research in the field of restorative justice processes in intercultural contexts.

Restorative justice approaches as a security solution for conflicts within intercultural settings fit within the EU Internal Security Strategy framework. Further, they offer tools to develop more concrete steps to meet the need for reflecting dialogue, tolerance and inclusion related to security matters in the EU. Restorative justice approaches can have an added value when it comes to changing perceptions and attitudes, and to increasing citizens' feelings of justice and safety while ensuring their freedom. So far, almost no links appear in European regulations and policy documents between the field of restorative justice and contexts of interculturality. The CoE White Paper on Intercultural Dialogue and the joint EU and CoE initiative on Intercultural Cities are stepping stones for introducing this link more clearly at the European level.

Notes

1 www.alternativeproject.eu (accessed 26 June 2017).
2 For a thorough analysis of the role of trust, its development and social determinants in a European intercultural context, the impact of public policies and civil society, and the function of restorative justice as shown in empirical findings from the ALTERNATIVE action sites, we refer to one of the deliverables of the ALTERNATIVE project by Ragazzi (2016, pp. 107–135).
3 European Council, 2010. Internal security strategy for the European Union. Towards a European security model (www.consilium.europa.eu/uedocs/cms_data/librairie/PDF/QC3010313ENC.pdf, accessed 26 June 2017).
4 European Commission, 2010. Communication from the Commission to the European Parliament and the Council. The EU Internal Security in Action: Five steps towards a more secure Europe, COM(2010) 673 final.
5 COM(2010) 673 final, p. 7.
6 FRA – European Union Agency for Fundamental Rights, 2016. Asylum and migration into the EU in 2015. Vienna: FRA (http://fra.europa.eu/sites/default/files/fra_uploads/fra-2016-fundamental-rights-report-2016-focus-0_en.pdf, accessed 26 June 2017).

7 European Commission, 2015. Communication from the Commission to the European Parliament, the Council, the European Economic and Social Committee and the Committee of the Regions. The European Agenda on Security, COM(2015) 185 final.
8 FRA – European Union Agency for Fundamental Rights, 2015. Embedding fundamental rights in the security agenda. FRA Focus 01/2015, p. 4 (http://fra.europa.eu/en/publication/2015/embedding-fundamental-rights-security-agenda, accessed 16 June 2017).
9 FRA – European Union Agency for Fundamental Rights, 2015. Embedding fundamental rights in the security agenda. FRA Focus 01/2015, p. 3 (http://fra.europa.eu/en/publication/2015/embedding-fundamental-rights-security-agenda, accessed 16 June 2017).
10 European Council, 2015. RIGA Joint Statement following the informal meeting of Justice and Home Affairs Ministers in Riga on 29 and 30 January (https://eu2015.lv/images/Kalendars/IeM/2015_01_29_jointstatement_JHA.pdf, accessed 26 June 2017).
11 Preventing radicalisation to terrorism and violent extremism: Strengthening the EU's response, RAN Collection, Approaches, lessons learned and practices. 2014 (https://ec.europa.eu/home-affairs/sites/homeaffairs/files/what-we-do/networks/radicalisation_awareness_network/ran-best-practices/docs/collection_of_approaches_lessons_learned_and_practices_en.pdf, accessed 26 June 2017).
12 It's worth mentioning that the EU also supports a new, independent European Network of Deradicalisation, which was officially inaugurated on 1 November 2013. This is a network of European NGOs to research and disseminate promising practices aiming at deradicalisation (www.european-network-of-deradicalisation.eu/, accessed 26 June 2017).
13 COM(2015) 185 final, p. 15.
14 Article 32 of the Vienna Action Plan (Council and Commission Action Plan of 3 December 1998 on how best to implement the provisions of the Treaty of Amsterdam on the creation of an area of freedom, security and justice, OJ C 19/1, 23.1.1999).
15 European Commission, 2006. Communication from the Commission on policy priorities in the fight against illegal immigration of third-country nationals, COM(2006) 402 final.
16 European Commission, 2008. Communication from the Commission to the European Parliament, the Council, the European Economic and Social Committee and the Committee of the Regions. Strengthening the global approach to migration: Increasing coordination, coherence and synergies, COM/2008/ 611 final.
17 European Commission, 2010. Communication from the Commission to the European Parliament, the Council, the European Economic and Social Committee and the Committee of the Regions. Delivering an area of freedom, security and justice for Europe's citizens. Action Plan Implementing the Stockholm Programme, COM(2010) 171 final, p. 7.
18 European Commission, 2011. Migration Integration. Qualitative Eurobarometer. Brussels: Directorate General Communication (http://ec.europa.eu/public_opinion/archives/quali/ql_5969_migrant_en.pdf, accessed 26 June 2017).
19 According to an EC Working Paper, while the proportion of migrants living in EU countries has reached only 4 per cent, in the period of 2000–2005 they accounted for 21 per cent of the average GDP growth in the EU-15 (European Commission, 2011. Commission Staff Working Paper. EU initiatives supporting the integration of third-country nationals European, SEC(2011) 957 final, p. 12).
20 European Commission – Press release. Stronger EU action to better tackle violent radicalisation leading to terrorism, Brussels, 14 June 2016 (http://europa.eu/rapid/press-release_IP-16-2177_en.htm, accessed 16 June 2017).
21 European Council, 2004. Common basic principles for immigrant integration policy in the EU, Council document 14615/04, 19.11.2004.
22 SEC(2011) 957 final, p. 3.

23 European Commission, 2005. Communication from the Commission to the European Parliament, the Council, the European Economic and Social Committee and the Committee of the Regions. A common agenda for integration framework for the integration of third-country nationals in the European Union, COM/2005/389 final.
24 European Commission, 2011. Communication from the Commission to the European Parliament, the Council, the European Economic and Social Committee and the Committee of the Regions. European agenda for the integration of third-country nationals, COM(2011) 455 final.
25 SEC(2011) 957 final.
26 European Commission, 2014. European modules on migrant integration. Brussels: DG HOME (https://ec.europa.eu/migrant-integration/librarydoc/european-modules-on-migrant-integration---final-report, accessed 16 June 2017).
27 European Commission, 2016. Communication from the Commission to the European Parliament, the Council, the European Economic and Social Committee and the Committee of the Regions. Action Plan on the integration of third country nationals, COM(2016) 377 Final.
28 In parallel, the UN also worked on the topic, leading to the UN basic principles on the use of restorative justice programmes in criminal matters (ECOSOC Res 2000/14 and Res 2002/12). There is a strong similarity in content between these CoE and UN instruments.
29 CEPEJ (2007)13.
30 European Commission, 1999. Communication of the Commission to the European Parliament, the Council and the Economic and Social Committee on Crime Victims in the European Union: Reflections on standards and actions of 14 July 1999, COM(1999)349 final.
31 European Council, 2002. Initiative of the Kingdom of Belgium with a view to the adoption of a Council Decision setting up a European network of national contact points for restorative justice, OJ C 242/09, 8.10.2002.
32 http://ec.europa.eu/justice/grants1/programmes-2007-2013/criminal/index_en.htm (accessed 16 June 2017).
33 European Commission, 2013. Assises de la justice: Discussion paper 2: EU criminal law, p. 3 (http://ec.europa.eu/justice/events/assises-justice-2013/files/criminal_law_en.pdf, accessed 26 June 2017).
34 Council of Europe, 2008. White Paper on Intercultural Dialogue. Living together as equals in dignity (www.coe.int/t/dg4/intercultural/Source/Pub_White_Paper/White%20Paper_final_revised_EN.pdf, accessed 26 June 2017).
35 Council of Europe, European Intercultural Cities Programme (www.coe.int/t/dg4/cultureheritage/culture/Cities/Default_en.asp). See also *The intercultural city step by step. Practical guide for applying the urban model of intercultural integration.* Strasbourg: Council of Europe Publishing (2013). Moreover, see also Council of Europe Recommendation CM (2015)/1 on intercultural integration (www.coe.int/en/web/culture-and-heritage/-recommendation-on-intercultural-integration, accessed 26 June 2017).
36 SEC(2011) 957 final.
37 European Ministers of Culture conference, 2003. Declaration on intercultural dialogue and conflict prevention (www.coe.int/t/e/com/files/ministerial-conferences/2003-culture/declaration.asp, accessed 26 June 2017).
38 Priority 2.3 for 2016, p. 5 (https://eacea.ec.europa.eu/sites/eacea-site/files/priorities_2016_en_full_text_en.pdf, accessed 26 June 2017).
39 European Commission, Europe for Citizens Programme (http://ec.europa.eu/dgs/home-affairs/what-we-do/policies/citizenship-programme/index_en.htm, accessed 26 June 2017).
40 Kreisau-Initiative Ev. Restorative Circles for Citizens in Europe (www.kreisau.de/aktuell/seminar-restorative-circles-for-citizens-in-europe/, accessed 26 June 2017).

References

Aertsen, I., 2007. Restorative justice through networking: A report from Europe. In: E. van de Spuy, S. Parmentier and A. Dissel, eds, *Restorative Justice: Politics, Policies and Prospects*. Cape Town: Juta and Co., pp. 91–112.

Aertsen, I., Mackay, R., Pelikan, C., Willemsens, J. and Wright, M., 2004. *Rebuilding Community Connections – Mediation and Restorative Justice in Europe*. Strasbourg: Council of Europe Publishing.

Agustín, Ó. G., 2012. Intercultural dialogue – visions of the Council of Europe and the European Commission for a post-multiculturalist era. *Journal of Intercultural Communication*, 29 (online: www.immi.se/intercultural/nr29/garcia.html, accessed 26 June 2017).

Babayan, D., 2010. *Balancing Security and Development in Migration Policy – EU Mobility Partnerships*. Natolin: College of Europe.

Bigo, D. and Carrera, S., 2004. *From New York to Madrid: Technology as the Ultra-solution to the Permanent State of Fear and Emergency in the EU. CEPS Commentary*. Brussels: CEPS.

Campbell, H., Chapman, T. and Wilson, D., 2013. *Report on the Contribution of Restorative Justice to Peace Building. Working across Frontiers: Restorative Justice with Conflicts in Intercultural Settings. Deliverable 7.2 of the ALTERNATIVE project*. Belfast: University of Ulster. Available at: www.alternativeproject.eu/assets/upload/Deliverable_7.2_Report_on_the_contribution_of_RJ_to_peace_building.pdf (accessed 26 June 2017).

Dünkel, F., Grzywa-Holten, J. and Horsfield, P., eds, 2015. *Restorative Justice and Mediation in Penal Matters. A Stock-Taking of Legal Issues, Implementation Strategies and Outcomes in 36 European Countries* (Vol. 1+2). Mönchengladbach: Forum Verlag Godesberg.

European modules on migrant integration, European Commission DG HOME, 2014.

Foss, E. M., Hassan, S. C., Hydle, I., Seeberg, M. L. and Uhrig, B., 2012. *Report on Conflicts in Intercultural Settings. Deliverable 2.1 of the ALTERNATIVE Project*. Oslo: NOVA. Available at: www.alternativeproject.eu/assets/upload/Deliverable_2.1_Report_on_conlicts_in_intercultural_settings.pdf (accessed 26 June 2017).

Joutsen, M., 2006. The European Union and cooperation in criminal matters: The search for balance. *HEUNI Paper*, No. 25. Helsinki: HEUNI.

Kaczorowska, A., 2013. *European Union Law*. Third edition. Abingdon: Routledge.

Lauwaert, K., 2013. Restorative justice in the 2012 EU Victims Directive. *Restorative Justice: An International Journal*, 1(3), pp. 414–425.

Lauwaert, K. and Aertsen, I., 2002. Restorative justice: Activities and expectations at European level. *ERA Forum*, 3(1), pp. 27–32.

Lhuillier, J., 2007. *The Quality of Penal Mediation in Europe*. Strasbourg: European Commission for the Efficiency of Justice (CEPEJ).

Melossi, D., 2013. The processes of criminalisation of migrants and the question of the European Union as a 'land of immigration'. In: T. Daems, D. van Zyl Smit and S. Snacken, eds, *European Penology?* London: Hart, pp. 125–144.

Miers, D. and Aertsen, I., eds, 2012. *Regulating Restorative Justice. A Comparative Study of Legislative Provision in European Countries*. Frankfurt am Main: Verlag für Polizeiwissenschaft.

Näss, H. E., 2010. The ambiguities of intercultural dialogue: Critical perspectives on the European Union's new agenda for culture. *Journal of Intercultural Communication*, 23 (online: www.immi.se/intercultural/nr23/nass.htm (accessed 26 June 2017)).

Pali, B., 2016. *Briefing Paper about the Regulation of Restorative Justice in the Directive 2012/29/EU.* Leuven: European Forum for Restorative Justice. Available at: www.euforumrj.org/wp-content/uploads/2017/03/EFRJ-Briefing-Paper-RJ-in-the-Victims-Directive.pdf (accessed 26 June 2017).

Pelikan, C., 2003. Follow-up study of Recommendation No R(99)19 of the Council of Europe. *Newsletter of the European Forum for Victim-Offender Mediation and Restorative Justice*, 4(2), pp. 6–7.

Ragazzi, M. 2016. *Report on Comparative Analysis in the Action Research Sites. Deliverable 8.5 of the ALTERNATIVE Project.* Leuven: KU Leuven. Available at: www.alternative-project.eu/wp-content/uploads/2014/12/Deliverable-8.5-Report-on-comparative-analysis.pdf (accessed 26 June 2017).

Vislie, L., 2003. From integration to inclusion: Focusing global trends and changes in the western European societies. *European Journal of Special Needs Education*, 18(1), pp. 17–35.

Willemsens, J., 2008. *Restorative Justice: An Agenda for Europe – The Role of the European Union in the Further Development of Restorative Justice.* Leuven: European Forum for Restorative Justice. Available at: www.euforumrj.org/assets/upload/AGIS-Report_The_role_of_the_EU.pdf (accessed 26 June 2017).

Wood, P., ed., 2009. *Intercultural Cities – Towards a Model for Intercultural Integration.* Strasbourg: Council of Europe Publishing.

Conclusion

Restorative justice – a tool for conviviality

Brunilda Pali

This book is the result of a four-year-long action research project which explored the potential and limits of restorative approaches to tackle conflicts in intercultural contexts. The intercultural contexts included villages with minority populations where heavy right-wing politics prevail; social housing estates in traditionally welfare societies; multi-ethnic environments caught in transition democracies; urban neighbourhoods and streets where society is organised around sharp borders; and European capitals where immigration is now an unquestionable reality.

Applying restorative justice principles and methods to such contexts required an exploration of the restorative field far beyond criminal justice, and raised a whole set of conceptual, as well as practical, challenges. This book is, therefore, an extremely original addition to the existing restorative justice literature, revitalising a field that has almost exhausted its creative potential.

At the same time, it repositions restorative justice as a fresh solution to the repressive security responses to intercultural contexts, responses which are characterised by four tendencies: an excessive focus on technology and surveillance as a way to achieve security; the heightened and obsessive concern with security, which has put at risk other principles and concerns; the merging of the security discourse with intercultural settings in general; and reliance on exclusionary and immunitary mechanisms for social groups to coexist.

Restorative justice, as applied through action research in the project, relied on an idea of deep, thick, relational and sustainable security, a security that is built on and sustained through human relations by means of proliferating participatory practices, encounters and dialogue, elaborating norms, restoring relations, building trust and promoting cooperation. The project's empirical and theoretical findings will substantially contribute towards the development of similar alternative discourses within the fields of criminology and security studies that propose alternative approaches to security, such as everyday security, emancipatory strands of security, sustainable security and positive security.

Given the current obsessive concern with security, the book proposed an overall balance between justice and security. Under the given socio-political constellations and dynamics, any search and agenda for security must be realigned with an emancipatory approach, whereby security and social justice are part of the same agenda. Bringing back justice considerations to counter the primacy of security is important also in the light of recent trends in crime control and management that indicate a move towards *a security society* even at the heart of the criminal justice system, whereby crime is being redefined from an action that breaks the law to the notion of pre-crime, becoming one of the other threats and risks in society that lead to insecurity, a risk that must be forestalled. Justice under these conceptions dissolves into the pursuit of security and becomes preventative instead of transformative. As we argued throughout the book, the proliferation of restorative justice as a governmentality of conflicts must therefore be promoted, based on the goal of participation as a social activity which leads to endless *norm-clarification* (transformation, reconfiguration, social justice), rather than speedy crime prevention and management.

Reading the trends towards the *culturalisation of politics* together with the notions of biopower, racism, the apparatus of security and the paradigm of immunity helped to understand the current trends towards the merging of security with migration, the unification of external and internal security, the persistence of fear and insecurity politics, the constant creation and maintenance of hierarchies and divisions in societies, and as a consequence the endangerment of justice, community life and collective actions. The implications of this analysis were that both the security apparatus and racism as a biopolitical technology are constitutive elements of our democracies instead of exceptional features, and reading security as a technology of immunity indicated that a certain level of immunity is vital to a community; it is only a high level of immunity that endangers a community. Thus, in intercultural communities, boundary-making and boundary maintenance were not deemed in themselves to be the problem, as long as these processes go along with simultaneous processes of boundary-unmaking. Only rigid and hermetic boundaries which can feed homogenisation, essentialisation and therefore demonisation of the other are the problem. We argued that notions that run counter not to the idea of difference but to the idea of constant and perpetual division and hierarchisation in societies, such as *communitas*, conviviality and precarity, must be developed and nourished.

Our research shows that despite all the talk to the contrary, neither conflict nor insecurity is necessarily linked to intercultural communities. Challenging the idea of 'cultural difference' as insecurity, restorative justice seems able to contribute to the unveiling of relations of power in communities and especially to focus on the differences which are conditioned by political inequality or economic exploitation, thus moving beyond a 'culturalised politics' while at the same time recognising that intercultural sites involve uncertainty (linguistic or otherwise) of sharing of norms, expectations and interests. Even the most usual conflicts are increasingly being framed in Europe in cultural terms, and these framings are creating further divisions and proliferating sentiments of resentment, fear and anxiety in our societies. Identity-affirming policies seem to feed rather than subdue resentment; therefore, either transformatory types of policies or more universal approaches have to be designed and enacted. Policies have to be developed at multiple levels – redistribution, recognition and representation –

and there should be a proliferation of projects and social actors working simultaneously on affects, frames, norms, trust-building, relations, welfare and citizenship rights, and cooperation and solidarity forms of action. Despite the fact that we did not find a link between conflict and insecurity, we did find ample space for working around uncertainties in intercultural communities. People have increasingly more uncertainty with regard to shared norms, values, feelings and languages, and it is these uncertainties that – if not worked with – can lead to anxiety and withdrawal. Public venues, forums and projects which contribute to deliberation about these norms and values must therefore be proliferated.

Our research points to an increasing fear of conflict throughout Europe and shortcuts being taken in the name of security and prevention in that regard. On the contrary, the importance of conflict for social life, for gluing communities together, for democracy, and for further societal development of norms and values should be rehabilitated. Conflict does not necessarily lead to violence, but too quick a subduing of conflict, without creating creative forums where it can be released, will most likely lead to the proliferation of violent reactions. Furthermore, our research points to an increasing withdrawal of people from social life as a result of rapid diversity combined with social insecurity (poverty) due to both the fast-changing demography of Europe and increasing neoliberal policies. This is leading to immunitary forms of coexistence that result in the perversion of ideas of communities. Public spaces are being cut down, collective forms of actions are being discouraged, and cooperative actions reduced. This, while seemingly a natural way of coexistence, is leading to autoimmunitary forms which will end up destroying the glue that holds societies together, especially relevant for the EU.

As groups withdraw into themselves, more room is left for the radicalising of boundaries among them and the proliferation of dangerous elements which move further into radicalised forms of thought and action, be this on political or religious fronts, as can be seen from the recent terror attacks and the reactions to the refugee crisis. Our research clearly shows that courage and reaching for deeper understanding and moving towards the other is the only real immunising form of security. Therefore, the role of restorative approaches as a counteracting force for these tendencies, towards becoming a *revitaliser of communities*, is extremely important. The multiplication and transformation of common spaces, and the role of women as key agents of such endeavours, become important especially in the light of the role of public space in the proliferation of conflict and the role of women as key markers of certain 'cultures'. The 'community' that is to be revitalised (or created) must nevertheless be different from the close, bounded community usually understood as a 'common being', moving towards a *convivial 'being together', or 'being in common'*. Restorative justice can become *a tool for conviviality*, which requires constant labour as well as technical and semi-formal organisation, and this is where restorative justice, and action research, can provide a valuable contribution towards social craftsmanship.

The most important implication that European policy makers have to draw from this type of project is that more resources and more faith have to be put into human and social elements, rather than technical elements, as ways of tackling security, insecurity and conflict. In the long run, the techno focus will proliferate insecurity, increase boundaries and produce very thin forms of security. Muslim communities in particular have to become partners in further research and action (especially on radicalisation) rather than simply being studied, marginalised or further excluded. The same goes for refugees. Clearly, long-term plans and projects that support their inclusion in the communities must be developed so that resentment does not take the lead. Currently, no importance at all seems to be granted to forms of social mediation or large peacemaking circles, with the focus being strictly on legal rights or humanitarian forms of coexistence. But human, especially collective, sentiments cannot be ignored for long, because despite the fact that we don't see them, they are the driving force either for creating forms of solidarity or for leading to violence. Security feeds on the affect of fear, so *other affects* like trust and solidarity need to be promoted to counteract fear. Securitisation also feeds on dualistic (hierarchical and divisionary) frames of responsibility (good and evil, self and other); thus, *counteracting those frames* through dialogic processes that nurture complexity and shifting of subject positions becomes paramount. Everyday security can become more *deep* and *sustainable* if it relies on encounters, dialogue and participatory actions, and only meeting real others makes a difference by counteracting images and ideologies that promote fear.

The research also pointed overall to the need for *changing the register for the evaluation of restorative practices* from the outcome (agreement, reparation of harm, reconciliation, pacification) and efficiency, towards the restorative process and its potential (staging of different values, identifying and communicating contradictions, clarifying different social norms among social actors, unblocking dialogue and challenging the monologising forces and voices, uncovering inequities which might have generated the conflict, nurturing the conflict, and creating collective actions that aim to challenge the status quo). Restorative justice can contribute overall towards countering and crafting alternative affects, frames, communication patterns, trust, norms, forms of conviviality notions of community, collective actions and cooperation.

Index